The Religious Quest of India (Series-08)

HINDU ETHICS

A Historical and Critical Essay

THE RELIGIOUS QUEST OF INDIA (SERIES-08)

HINDU ETHICS

A Historical and Critical Essay

By

JOHN McKENZIE, M.A

GYAN

Published by

GYAN

Gyan Publishing House
5, Ansari Road
Daryaganj, New Delhi-110002
Phone: 011-47034999, 9811692060
E-mail: books@gyanbooks.com

Distribution Network
gyanbooks.com
India, USA, Canada, UK, Australia, France

ISBN : 978-81-212-6781-6 (HB)
First Published, 1922

2nd Impression 2023

Printed at: Gyan Press, Delhi.

THE RELIGIOUS QUEST OF INDIA (SERIES-08)
Hindu Ethics
A Historical and Critical Essay
Author: JOHN McKENZIE

THE RELIGIOUS QUEST OF INDIA

EDITED BY

J. N. FARQUHAR, M.A., D.Litt. (Oxon)

LITERARY SECRETARY, NATIONAL COUNCIL OF YOUNG MEN'S CHRISTIAN ASSOCIATIONS, INDIA AND CEYLON

AND

H. D. GRISWOLD, M.A., Ph.D.

SECRETARY OF THE COUNCIL OF THE AMERICAN PRESBYTERIAN MISSIONS IN INDIA

EDITORIAL PREFACE

THE writers of this series of volumes on the variant forms of religious life in India are governed in their work by two impelling motives.

I. They endeavour to work in the sincere and sympathetic spirit of science. They desire to understand the perplexingly involved developments of thought and life in India and dispassionately to estimate their value. They recognize the futility of any such attempt to understand and evaluate, unless it is grounded in a thorough historical study of the phenomena investigated. In recognizing this fact they do no more than share what is common ground among all modern students of religion of any repute. But they also believe that it is necessary to set the practical side of each system in living relation to the beliefs and the literature, and that, in this regard, the close and direct contact which they have each had with Indian religious life ought to prove a source of valuable light. For, until a clear understanding has been gained of the practical influence exerted by the habits of worship, by the practice of the ascetic, devotional, or occult discipline, by the social organization and by the family system, the real impact of the faith upon the life of the individual and the community cannot be estimated; and, without the advantage of extended personal intercourse, a trustworthy account of the religious experience of a community can scarcely be achieved by even the most careful student.

II. They seek to set each form of Indian religion by the side of Christianity in such a way that the relationship may stand out clear. Jesus Christ has become to them the light of all their seeing, and they believe Him destined to be the light of the world. They are persuaded that sooner or later the age-long quest of the Indian spirit for religious truth and power will find in Him at once its goal and a new starting-point, and they will be content if the preparation of this series contributes in the smallest degree to hasten this consummation. If there be readers to whom this motive is unwelcome, they may be reminded that no man approaches the study of a religion without religious convictions, either positive or negative: for both reader and writer, therefore, it is better that these should be explicitly stated at the outset. Moreover, even a complete lack of sympathy with the motive here acknowledged need not diminish a reader's interest in following an honest and careful attempt to bring the religions of India into comparison with the religion which to-day is their only possible rival, and to which they largely owe their present noticeable and significant revival.

It is possible that to some minds there may seem to be a measure of incompatibility between these two motives. The writers, however, feel otherwise. For them the second motive reinforces the first: for they have found that he who would lead others into a new faith must first of all understand the faith that is theirs already—understand it, moreover, sympathetically, with a mind quick to note not its weaknesses alone but that in it which has enabled it to survive and has given it its power over the hearts of those who profess it.

The duty of the Editors of the series is limited to seeing that the volumes are in general harmony with the principles here described. Each writer is alone responsible for the opinions expressed in his volume, whether in regard to Indian religions or to Christianity.

THE RELIGIOUS QUEST OF INDIA

REDEMPTION

HINDU AND CHRISTIAN

BY

SYDNEY CAVE, D.D.

Per omnia fides ad Christum penetrat

1919

To my Teachers

THE REV. P. T. FORSYTH, D.D.

AND

THE REV. A. E. GARVIE, D.D.

IN

Gratitude and Honour

PREFACE

THIS Essay is an attempt to relate to the Christian Gospel the living forces of Hinduism. Of the inadequacy of my understanding both of Hinduism and of Christianity I am deeply conscious, but at least I have striven to deal with Hinduism as a living faith, and to speak of it with the fairness and sympathy with which we discuss the convictions of honoured friends. It is hard to express another's faith. I have sought to make the Sacred Books speak for themselves, and in the first half of the Essay have tried to illustrate the three great doctrines of Hinduism, *karma*, *bhakti*, and redemption, in a way that shall at least be textual and to that extent authoritative. The second half of the Essay is an endeavour to relate Christianity to these Hindu doctrines. Though Christ indeed is adequate, our Christianity often is not. To answer the aspirations of Hinduism an enlarged interpretation is required. We need to affirm that, for the Christian, eternal life is a present and indubitable possession. Christianity must be proclaimed as a religion of redemption, not from sin only, but from the world.

Some sections of the Essay have already appeared in tentative form. Thus much of Chapter VII was given in the first instance as a lecture to educated Hindus at Palamcottah and afterwards appeared in the *Young Men of India*, and in Chapters I, V, X and XI I have utilized some articles I wrote when in India for the *Madras Christian College Magazine*; whilst parts of Chapters I and XI formed the basis of an article which appeared in the *Expository Times* in March and April of this year.

I have to express my thanks to the Rev. G. E. Phillips, M.A., of the United Theological College, Bangalore, for his suggestive criticisms, and to Hindu friends who helped me in my understanding of Hinduism by their confidence and candour. It is a great pleasure to inscribe to Principals Forsyth and Garvie, the teachers of my student days, a book which would probably not have been written but for their teaching and encouragement.

HENLEAZE,
BRISTOL.
June, 1919.

CONTENTS

INTRODUCTION

CHAPTER PAGE

I. Religions and Religion 1

PART I.

THE PRESUPPOSITIONS OF ESSENTIAL HINDUISM

II. The Religion of the *Ṛigveda* and the Beginnings of Brāhmanic Speculation 23

ESSENTIAL HINDUISM

III. A Study in the *Upanishads* 52

THE WAY OF KNOWLEDGE

IV. The Vedānta Doctrine 76

THE WAY OF LOVE

V. The *Bhagavadgītā* 98

VI. The Lovers of God 116

PART II.

VII. Jesus Christ and His Gospel 141

VIII. Classic Christianity, or the Apostolic Experience of Christ and His Gospel 159

IX. Christianity and the Doctrine of Cyclic Recompense 179

X. Christianity and the Way of Devotion . . . 206

XI. Redemption: Hindu and Christian 223

INDEX 257

Quotations from the Sacred Books are from the following translations:

The Hymns of the Ṛigveda, translated by R. T. H. Griffith. 2nd edit. 2 vols. Benares, 1896 and 1897.

The Hymns of the Atharvaveda, translated by R. T. H. Griffith. 2 vols. Benares, 1897.

The Bhagavadgītā, translated by L. D. Barnett. London, 1905.

The Poems of Tukārām, translated by J. Nelson Fraser. Madras. From 1909.

The Rāmāyaṇa of Tulsī Dās, translated by F. S. Growse. 4 vol. edit. Allahabad. Various dates.

The Tiruvāśagam, translated by G. U. Pope. Oxford, 1900.

In the Sacred Books of the East Series, the following volumes:

The Śatapatha Brāhmaṇa, translated by J. Eggeling. Vols. xii, xxvi, xli, xliii, xliv.

The *Upanishads*, translated by F. Max Müller. Vols. i and xv.

The *Laws of Manu*, translated by G. Bühler. Vol. xxv.

The *Vedāntasūtras*, with the commentary of Śaṅkarāchārya, translated by G. Thibaut. Vols. xxxiv and xxxviii.

The *Vedāntasūtras*, with the commentary of Rāmānuja, translated by G. Thibaut. Vol. xlviii.

Abbreviations Used

Ait. Br.	*Aitareya Brāhmaṇa.*
A. V.	*Atharvaveda.*
B. G.	*Bhagavadgītā.*
Br.	*Brāhmaṇa.*
Bṛih. Up.	*Bṛihadāraṇyka Upanishad.*
Chhānd. Up.	*Chhāndogya Upanishad.*
E. R. E.	*Encyclopaedia of Religion and Ethics.*
Kāṭh. Up.	*Kāṭhaka Upanishad.*
Kaush. Up.	*Kaushītaki Upanishad.*
Mait. Up.	*Maitrāyaṇa Upanishad.*
Muṇḍ. Up.	*Muṇḍaka Upanishad.*
R. V.	*Ṛigveda.*
S. B. E.	*Sacred Books of the East.*
Śat. Br.	*Śatapatha Brāhmaṇa.*
Śvet. Up.	*Śvetāśvatara Upanishad.*
Taitt. Up	*Taittirīya Upanishad.*
Up.	*Upanishad.*

INTRODUCTION

CHAPTER I

RELIGIONS AND RELIGION

IT has become a commonplace to say that no great event or movement can be any longer of merely local importance. The world seems smaller now than it did to our forefathers. Humanity is like one great family whose members, in spite of estrangements and aversions, live their life in common, each influenced by each. Not even the most ignorant can identify civilization with Christendom. The great powers of the world include not only America and those that once made up the 'Concert of Europe', but also the non-Christian empire of Japan. East and West, if they have not 'met', are yet far nearer to each other than before. Indian students will often know their Shakespeare and their Tennyson better than those in English colleges. An Indian poet like Rabindranath Tagore receives from the West the homage of all those who can appreciate noble emotion and exquisite expression. Science also is international. It is clear to-day that whatever is ultimately true must be universally valid.

It is not easy in this modern world for any one religion to claim for itself finality. Nowhere is such a claim more resented than in India. The culture of the East and of the West has here mingled as nowhere else, and the problems of religion are being discussed with an interest, not academic, but vital. Any one familiar to some extent with the writings of the early fathers of the Church will feel, if he lives in India, that he is living in a world surprisingly like theirs. Such books as Harnack's *Expansion of Christianity*, or Glover's

Conflict of Religions in the Early Roman Empire, would, *mutatis mutandis*, serve, far better than any missionary reports, to describe the religious situation in India to-day. It was in its strife with Greek and Oriental religion and philosophy that Christian theology was chiefly formed. It is in its contact with Indian thought that Christianity has, as nowhere else in the non-Christian world, to face the most incisive criticism and is driven to answer the hardest questions. And of these questions none is so much discussed as that of the relative value and validity of religions, or, to put it in its more concrete form, 'What right has Christianity to claim to be the absolute religion? Why is it not content to be one religion among many?'

I

Such a question would have had little meaning to the pioneers of Protestant missionary enterprise. They had felt for themselves God's infinite grace in Jesus Christ, and were assured that Christ was the world's only Saviour. Without this faith, missionary work would not have been begun; nor can it continue. But such men were of necessity little qualified to look for the best in the non-Christian world to which they went. Their theology was that of their time, deep but not broad. Very literally they believed that the world lay in the evil one. So in India they saw only gross idolatry and superstition. For this they cannot well be blamed. Missionaries reflect always the theology of the Church which sends them. It is unreasonable to expect them to be other than men of their own time and Church. And if we could suppose that the most tolerant and refined of modern students had been a pioneer missionary, it is not certain that he would have been more successful in discovering the best in Hindu religion. Its Sacred Books were closed to the stranger and little known to the mass of the people. Just as Christianity at the first had its hardest fight not with gross idolatry but with a paganism which Christian influences had refined, so we to-day are confronted with a Hinduism very different in its emphasis from that of a century or so ago. So competent an observer as Abbé Dubois bears witness to the religious degradation of the people. Then as now men spoke much of Kṛishṇa; but the Kṛishṇa men spoke of then was not the ideal Kṛishṇa of the *Bhagavadgītā*, but the gross and foolish Kṛishṇa of the *Bhāgavata Purāṇa*.[1] In such a Hinduism it was hard to see anything but an idolatry degrading and often obscene.[2] It was impossible for foreigners to discern the higher elements of Hinduism when these were unknown to the immense majority of the Hindus of that time. Even to-day in India it is the lower forms of religion that are most in evidence, and 'Higher Hinduism' is still far more limited in its influence than would be supposed by Europeans whose knowledge of Hinduism is derived from Max Müller's lectures and a few choice anthologies.

It is with this 'Higher Hinduism' that we are chiefly concerned. Idolatry is doomed. True, the excuses provided for it by Theosophy may be utilized by educated men who find it convenient to have the superstitions of their women-folk defended by a pseudo-science. But such men will speak as little of idolatry as possible, and seem to know that their defence of it is clever but not convincing. One great modern

[1] I can find no reference to the *Gītā* in Dubois's text. The word occurs once in the index of the third edition, but it refers there to a note by the modern editor (Abbé J. A. Dubois, *Hindu Manners, Customs, and Ceremonies*).

[2] Compare the following sentence of the prayer uttered by Schwartz at the dedication of his church in Trichinopoly in 1766—a prayer now inscribed on a marble tablet there. 'When strangers who do not know Thy name hear of all Thy glorious doctrines and methods of worshipping Thee preached in this house, incline, oh mercifully incline, their hearts to renounce their abominable idolatry and worship Thee, O God, in the name of Christ.' We would not so describe idolatry to-day, yet any one who knows the obscene carving at the neighbouring Vaishṇavite temple of Śrīraṅgam or has been to Tanjore, the other sphere of Schwartz's labours, and seen on the *gopuram* at the entrance of the Śaivite temple there, the powerful sculpture of Kṛishṇa with the (very) naked Gopis, and seen too in the cloister the 108 *liṅgas* conjoined with *yonis* before which worship is made, will understand Schwartz's adjective, however much he may deplore it.

movement, the Ārya-Samāj, denounces the worship of idols uncompromisingly, and denies that it ever formed part of true and primitive Hinduism. Yet this does not mean that there is a greater responsiveness to Christianity. On the contrary, the opposition offered to Christianity is more determined and articulate than it was a generation ago, and no section of Hinduism is more hostile to Christianity than the monotheistic Ārya-Samāj. Men are not so content as once they were merely to claim that Hinduism is best for India although Christianity may be intrinsically superior.[1] The rediscovery of the Sacred Books and their enthusiastic praise by Western scholars, have brought a new confidence and pride to men who had become bankrupt of hope. Why should the East despise what the West seemed so highly to value? Many educated Indians are as convinced as any Hegelian that religion is only a symbol of the truth that philosophy alone can teach. Christianity is an admirable religion. Its moral code is beautiful, if impracticable, but philosophy is the supreme thing, and Hinduism has in the *Vedānta* the one philosophy finally true and adequate for the interpretation of the eternal. Even the moral supremacy of Christianity can no longer be spoken of as a truism. Men are aware that not all in England are Sāhibs. The 'slums' there, the social vice and misery, are familiar facts. The victory of Japan did much to rehabilitate Oriental self-respect. Now, on the gigantic scale of a world war, Indians have seen not only the failure of Christianity to preserve Christendom from war, but its failure to keep war free from needless cruelty and lust. And Indians can point with pride to the equal comradeship of their troops with British on the field of battle and their proved discipline and valour.[2]

[1] Dr. Farquhar, that most competent of observers, dates from 1870 what he calls 'the full defence of the old religions', and from 1895 the reinforcement of this defence by 'religious nationalism'. *Modern Religious Movements in India*, chapters 4 and 5.

[2] Before it was announced that Indian troops would go to the main theatre of war, I found my Hindu friends loyal but not enthusiastic. Afterwards they were proud and eager.

Even the influence of Christ's teaching has in many cases militated against the belief in the supremacy of any one religion. Men, who themselves observe caste, and approve of the outcaste being kept in his degradation, often understand enough of Christianity to appreciate its doctrines of man's essential equality and God's universal Fatherhood. Such men realize how unchristian is any feeling of racial superiority, and on this account also object to the assumption that the religion of the Westerners must be the best.

To a people thus sensitive and self-conscious, the claim that Christianity is the absolute religion seems often simply a piece of Western arrogance. And such resentment is largely justified. The missionary enterprise has used too much the language of warfare. There is a war we are called to fight with relentless zeal, but that is the war between good and evil, between truth and falsehood. We may not equate our empirical Christianity with goodness and truth. Still less can we identify Hinduism with evil and falsehood. And in using the terminology of warfare we may easily adopt war's ethics. It is well-nigh impossible for a nation at war to appreciate the virtues of its enemy. It looks for the worst and discovers it. If a missionary is a soldier in this sense, he will see only the darker aspects of Hinduism, and he will make the Christianity for which he strives appear as an alien and hostile faith, and such a man will be regarded, not as the bearer of good tidings, but as the enemy of all that men prize, of things good, as well as evil.

In South India the very success of missions has increased the estrangement. The great mass movements have been chiefly among the outcastes. For such, religion meant devil-worship, and Hinduism the system which sanctioned their degradation, and denied to them the elementary rights of manhood. A locomotive is an admirable thing, but the man pinioned beneath its wheels will not be thinking of the beauty of its mechanism. It is not surprising if those whom Hinduism has thus treated should regard the very phrase 'Higher

Hinduism' as an oxymoron. With no tradition from the East, they have grasped eagerly at the culture of the West. Prevented often by caste from becoming artisans, many have found in English education the effective means of social advancement. It is scarcely to be wondered at if many such outwestern any Westerners. There are Christian teachers whose illustrations are nearly all from English life, and who can scarcely preach a sermon without introducing English words. Christians themselves are often as incredulous as Hindus that Christianity will ever supersede Hinduism.[1] And in our great Christian communities even men of university education are often almost incredibly ignorant and indifferent in their attitude to Hinduism.

It is just here that there seems to be the great contrast between the Church in India and the Church in the times of the Roman Empire. It is true that Tertullian in his fierce exuberant way denounces all philosophy. 'What has Athens to do with Jerusalem or the Academy with the Church? What have heretics to do with Christians? . . . Away with all who attempt to introduce a mottled Christianity of Stoicism and Platonism and dialectic. . . . To be ignorant of everything outside the rule of faith, is to possess all knowledge.'[2] Yet Tertullian was not himself thus ignorant. The very invective of his words derives its power from the training he had received in pagan rhetoric. Our Christian theology owes most to the great Greek fathers, and these were men who knew and utilized the philosophy and literature of Greece. Thus, in his *Address to the Greeks*, Clement of Alexandria denounces, indeed with needed severity, the immorality of many of the tales told of the gods, yet he appeals with admiration to the poets of antiquity, and summons Hesiod, Aeschylus, and

[1] I have heard Christians of high character and incontestable Christian experience speak as if no man became a convert unless there was persecution to evade, or education to gain. On the other hand, there are in the Indian Church many men whose conversion was as costly as St. Paul's and whose zeal is as wholehearted.

[2] *De praescr.* vii.

Sophocles, as witnesses to the One God.[1] In discussing the benefits conferred on men by Christ he can quote as freely from Homer and Aratus as from the Psalms.[2] And in another book, he declares that the philosophy of the Greeks was a covenant given to them as a stepping-stone to the philosophy which is according to Christ.[3] And in this the Greek fathers were only doing as Paul had done. In writing to Greek Churches, Paul uses freely the categories of Greek thought. He is courteous when addressing Pagans. Even at Ephesus, where idolatry was so rife and so degraded, the 'Town Clerk' can claim that neither in action nor in language has Paul failed in respect towards the many-breasted Artemis, the guardian goddess of the city.[4] Such a testimony could increasingly be given to the Christian preacher in India. Yet it is possible, while refraining from all discourtesy to other religions, still to fail to recognize in them any good. Even to-day there are too many who forget God's universal Fatherhood and speak as if, outside Christendom, men were completely orphaned of the Father's care. Truer to the spirit of Christ is this legend of Him. Outside the gate of a city lay rotting the carcass of a dead dog. And as men passed by they turned away in disgust from the loathesomeness of the decaying flesh. But when Jesus saw it, He said, 'Pearls are not whiter than its teeth.' Even in the corruption He saw the one thing beautiful. To those that have learnt from Him, the humblest record of religion may become sacred as a transcript of human experience, pathetic often in its failure, yet sublime in its prescience of a higher truth. And in the case of a religion so rich as Hinduism is with the devotion and the speculations of the past, blind indeed must that man be who can see in it only the record of perversity and folly.

[1] *To the Greeks*, vii. [2] *Op. cit.* xi. [3] *Stromata*, vi. 8.

[4] As showing the practice of a later age, it is interesting to note Chrysostom's comment that this was a false statement made to calm the riot. But the Clerk was clearly appealing to well-known facts. See Ramsay, *St. Paul the Traveller and Roman Citizen*, pp. 146–57.

II

The intolerance which refuses to recognize in other religions any truth is a folly commoner among Christians than Hindus. The question 'Is any religion final?' which, as we have seen, has offended many Christians because it assumes that there is more than one genuine religion, offends many Hindus because it appears to presuppose that one religion can claim supremacy over others. Very common among Hindus is the attitude: all religions are alike true; let each man abide in the religious community in which he was born. The popularity of this position is sometimes due to its very great convenience. In the West, men indifferent to religion speak little of it. In India, even a College Debating Society will find in religion its most exciting theme. But in the East, as in the West, there are but few who are willing to seek truth at all costs and obey it. If all religions are true, there is clearly no certainty in religious truth. We may continue to exercise our wits upon it, but the one reality is this present life and its prosperity. We can well be content to live

> 'With ghastly smooth life dead at heart,
> Tame in earth's paddock as our prize'.[1]

If the position is thus held by men whose genial tolerance is only a cloak for their intellectual indolence or moral superficiality, it is also the position of men to whom religion is life's chief concern.

Rāmakṛishṇa declares that a truly religious man should think that other religions also are paths leading to the truth. Every man, therefore, should follow his own religion. A

[1] Dr. Glover's description of Plutarch applies to many in India to-day: 'He will never take a firm stand; there are always possibilities, explanations, parallels, suggestions, symbolisms, by which he can escape from facing definitely the demand for a decisive reform of religion.' There is 'a radiant mist of amiability' in which 'the old myths seem capable of every conceivable interpretation and everything is a symbol of everything else and all is beautiful and holy'.—*The Conflict of Religions in the early Roman Empire*, p. 110.

Christian should follow Christianity, a Muḥammadan should follow Muḥammadanism, and so forth. For the Hindus the ancient path, the path of the Āryan Ṛishis, is the best. In Dr. Farquhar's recent book there is reproduced a picture, painted at the order of one of Rāmakṛishṇa's disciples, to represent his master's veiws. In the background are a Christian church, a Muḥammadan mosque, and a Hindu temple. Before the church is seen Rāmakṛishṇa, pointing out to Keshab Chandra Sen, the religious leaders in front of the mosque and temple. In the centre of the picture is depicted Christ and Chaitanya,[1] engaged in a religious dance. Round about stand a Confucian, a Muḥammadan, a Sikh, a Parsee, an Anglican clergyman, and various Hindus, each carrying some symbol of his faith.[2]

Doubtless God is one, and doubtless He receives all honest worship to whomsoever it is addressed. But is such catholicity as Rāmakṛishṇa's true to fact? Can religion be thus independent of its objects? Thus Rāmakṛishṇa himself worshipped an image of Kālī as the Mother of the Universe, and believed in his enthusiasm that it took food from his hand. When later he desired to experience the ecstasy of Kṛishṇa's love, he put on woman's clothes, lived in the women's part of the house, spoke in a woman's voice, until at last, as Rādhā, Kṛishṇa's paramour, in a trance he saw standing before him the Kṛishṇa he so passionately loved. Surely we cannot say that it makes no difference whether men see God in the dreaded Kālī or in the holy Christ. A devotion to Kṛishṇa which is the ecstasy of human passion in its moment of breathless abandonment, is not the same as that quiet constant faith in Christ which means repentance, forgiveness, and a new moral ideal and power. The truly religious man will recognize and appreciate in other religions, sincerity and zeal, but, when we remember how diverse religions are, to say that all religions are alike true is impossible, unless we hold that all religions are alike false, or regard God as so unknown that it simply does not matter how

[1] A Bengali religious leader of the sixteenth century.
[2] *Modern Religious Movements in India*, pp. 198 and 199.

we think of Him.[1] Truth after all is not a mere question of geography. Humanity is one. In religion *svadeshiism* is out of place. We may try to ignore religion, but its problems will not be evaded. Sooner or later, when religions meet, we are forced back yet once again to the question, Is any religion of final value? Is Christianity, for example, the absolute religion, and if so, in what sense?

III

As we turn to the books of the New Testament, this much at least seems clear. From its inception Christianity was proclaimed as a religion of universal significance. The Gospel is essentially a missionary message, and 'missions are a brutality unless undertaken with the consciousness that Christianity transcends other religions, and with the knowledge in what respects it does so'.[2] The Apostolic Church saw in its crucified and risen Lord not a local and temporary teacher, but the Saviour of the world. Even those who, like Harnack, for reasons which to many of us seem arbitrary and inconclusive, deny that Christ bade His disciples preach the Gospel

[1] Here again Christianity is facing in India to-day the same situation as it faced in the Roman Empire in the third and fourth centuries. Thus Dr. Lindsay's description of Neo-Platonism would apply almost without change to the attitude of many educated Hindus. 'If the universe of things seen and unseen be an emanation from Absolute Being, the Primal Cause of all things, the fountain from which all existence flows, and the haven to which everything that has reality in it will return when its cycle is complete, then every heathen deity has its place in this flow of existence. Its cult, however crude, is an obscure witness to the presence of the intuition of the supernatural. The legends which have gathered round its name, if only rightly understood, are mystic revelations of the divine which permeates all things.' ... 'The "common man" was not asked to forsake the deities he was wont to reverence.' ... 'The very conjurer was encouraged to cultivate his magic. Pantheism, that wonder child of thought and of the phantasy, included all within the wide sweep of its sheltering arms and made them feel the claim of a common kinship.' ... Porphyry 'was too noble a man not to sympathize with much in Christianity,' but 'its claim to be the *one* religion, its exclusiveness, was hateful to him.'—*The Cambridge Mediaeval History*, vol. i, p. 94.

[2] M. Reischle, in his suggestive book on *Theologie und Religionsgeschichte*, p. 78.

to the Gentiles, admit 'that by His universal religion, which at the same time was the religion of the Son',[1] Christ bids men come unto Him as unto one who has a perfect and certain knowledge of the Father. He presents Himself to men, and has from the first been preached by His disciples as the sole sufficient Saviour.

How can such a claim be substantiated? Fortunately Christian scholars have by now abandoned the attempt to give 'proofs' of Christianity which shall be convincing to the intellect.[2] The sciences of which mathematics is the supreme example may be studied objectively. The solutions of their problems depend not on character but on intellect. But our answers to the perennial questions of philosophy and religion depend less on our mental alertness than our moral choice. Our judgements become inevitably judgements of 'value': indications of what we regard as good. And it is in this way that in recent years the truth of Christianity has been very suggestively indicated. The moral self—the practical reason of Kant's philosophy—demands for its highest good a faith in God, and an ideal for life at once personal and social. But this 'highest good' we cannot find in the world-life around us. From it we cannot gather inner peace nor power. By 'the inner dialectic of faith'[3] we are led to look for this good in history, and we find just what we need in the kingdom of God—that spiritual realm into which Christ calls men, where men know God as Father, and strive to do His will in the world with the obedience of subjects and the glad freedom of children.

[1] *Expansion of Christianity*, i. 48.

[2] The old 'proof' from miracle would be almost ludicrously inappropriate in India. In the West the 'proof' has been abandoned because, through the influence of science, miracles for many do not support faith but require it. In many-fabled India the 'proof' must always have been useless because to believe in miracles is so easy. College students assure me they have seen them. Even to ask the meaning of the name of a village or hill, will often be to hear of a miracle so portentous that the Gospel miracles seem ordinary events.

[3] J. Kaftan, *Die Wahrheit der Religion* (p. 550), the classic statement of this proof.

Such an apologetic is full of suggestiveness. It is certainly right in its abandonment of any attempt to 'prove' Christianity intellectually, but is it right in assuming that by the moral reason a common idea may be realized? Does this 'highest good' appeal to all men as the highest? Thus in India ethics has always been less esteemed than metaphysics, and the highest good has been conceived not as moral activity, but as absorption into the infinite. Only if its moral ideal is recreated will India see in Christ's proclamation of the kingdom its highest good. Yet the apologetic is so far true and useful. If Christianity be the final religion, then it must be able not only to reveal new moral needs, but to satisfy all worthy aspiration in itself. History, if it cannot prove, can disprove. Though the claim of Christianity to be the final religion cannot be proved by the history of religion, yet, if true, it will be congruous with its data.

To bring to the test of history the claim of Christianity to be the absolute religion may well seem a counsel of despair. Christianity claims to be religion—the full and perfect satisfaction of the religious needs of man. The history of religions shows at once that, whether Christianity be thus religion or not, it is, at any rate in the first place, *a* religion, one among the many religions of the world. Nor has it lived its life solitary and unaffected. It is not only on the periphery of interest that ethnic words and conceptions have entered into Christianity. Even to express its central doctrines the Church has utilized, from the first, categories of an alien philosophy. It has long been a complaint among Protestants that, after a few centuries of progress, Christianity absorbed from the Roman world pagan thoughts and customs, and that Catholicism, as we know it, is an amalgam of Christian and pagan ideas. The complaint is true, but it can be brought against Protestantism also. As soon as it began its Gentile mission, Christianity came to be influenced in its form by Greek philosophy and religion, Roman conceptions of law and legislature, and, possibly even, pagan cults and mysteries. This was inevitable. The definition of biology applies also to religion. Life means response to environment. It is mere foolishness for modern missionaries to imagine that the Christianity they bring with them from highly industrial nations like Great Britain and America, or from a military state like Germany, is a Christianity pure, and uninfluenced by its surroundings. Mr. Temple's words are applicable to every one of us: 'I am, as I hope, a Christian Englishman, but then I am only an English Christian, and my character is moulded not only by the spirit of Christ but also by the spirit of contemporary England, which are not the same.'[1] The Church not only influences, it is influenced by, the society in which it lives. It is only prejudice or ignorance which can claim for any extant form of polity or doctrine a final and universal value.

The scientific study of the history of religions has thus made it impossible to suppose that Christianity is absolute in any of its concrete forms. Does that mean, then, that we must abandon our belief in the finality of the Gospel and, with it, the missionary enterprise? It does not follow. Missions have been hindered much and helped little by the schemings of ecclesiastics. Their impulse has come from the desire to share a gift, not to propagate a system. However it may be with other men, religion means for the Christian, communion with God. God has shown us Himself in Jesus Christ. We know that He is the holy Father; we know that we are called to lives of trust and service. And we are sure that this knowledge of God is a true knowledge and a certain possession. Our communion with Him depends on what we know Him to be. Doubtless all men may draw near to God and come into intercourse with Him, but intercourse is not communion.[2] Communion is only possible with those we really know, the few whose lives we are permitted to share. Such a communion we may have with God in Jesus Christ. Our certainty of the finality of Christianity—which is

[1] *Foundations*, pp. 355, 356.

[2] Cf. L. Ihmels, *Centralfragen der Dogmatik in der Gegenwart*, p. 46.

only another way of saying, our recognition of its missionary nature—depends on the experience of our Christian faith. It is a conviction not based on proof nor capable of it. It is unreasoned, but it need not be irrational. It cannot be proved, but it can be tested. Christianity, as the religion of true communion with God, claims to be religion. If so, it must be adequate to the religious needs of the race as expressed in the great religions. If true, the history of religions, though it cannot prove, should support its claim.

IV

It must be admitted that to attempt to make any deductions from the history of religions is a perilous task. 'The science of comparative religion', as M. Loisy says, 'is not yet very old. It gives the impression of still looking for its sphere and of not yet possessing its method.' Yet, as he adds, 'the chaos is more in appearance than reality. History is history, the knowledge of what has been, and the history of religion is the history of religion, the knowledge of that great human fact, the religions of the world.'[1] Nor are the diversities of religion so illimitable as to make impossible a rapid glance at their characteristics. Their seemingly innumerable forms resolve themselves into a few classic types. 'It is indeed surprising on how few ideas humanity has had to live.'[2] Thus the lower forms of religion, apparently so multitudinous, are found to be essentially one in their conception. That very common form of religion—the animism which peoples the world with spirits good and bad, ignores the good, and worships the evil spirits with abject fear—is the same in principle wherever it occurs. And, in any case, a phase of religion so low is irrelevant to the discussion of whether any religion is of final value. Nor do even the higher polytheisms help. However suitable he may regard the worship of the gods for the common people, every educated man knows that really to believe in a multiplicity of gods would

[1] A. Loisy, *A propos d'histoire des religions*, p, 101.

[2] E. Troeltsch, *Die Absolutheit des Christentums und die Religionsgeschichte*, p. 56—a book to which in the next few pages I owe much.

involve the confusion of his thought and the negation of his culture. Polytheisms are inextricably bound up with the countries of their origin. In the nature of the case they can contribute nothing to the quest for the absolute. Historical religions which transcend in thought the place of their origin are but few, and these we find fall into two distinct types. We have Judaism and Islām, religions of law, and Brāhmanism and Buddhism, religions of redemption.[1] And it is of interest to note that these two divisions correspond to the two great world-families of religious genius, the Semitic and the Āryan, and in all cases these religions represent the successful quest after unity of peoples who originally worshipped many gods.

Of the religions of law, Judaism may provide a convenient illustration.

At first the higher religion of the Hebrews is one long conflict with the idolatry native to the people. The spiritual genius of Moses had proclaimed that, for the Jews, Jehovah was the only God. Other gods there might be, but in these the Jews had no concern. Gradually the prophets saw and preached a vaster truth. Not for the Jews only, but for all men, this God is the only true God; all other gods are vanity; the God of Israel is the Maker of heaven and earth, the Ruler of the universe. The spiritual freshness of the prophets passes away and we have Judaism, the religion of law. The one God becomes remote from His people. His will is revealed in the infallible Book of Law. To do that will thus externally revealed is the sole duty of religion. The law is explained in increasing detail and complexity. The perfect religious man is the Pharisee, who alone has time and opportunity to fulfil all the behests of God.

The moral advantage of such a rigorous monotheism is obvious. From Jew and Muḥammadan alike comes the strong and unfaltering assertion that God is one and is almighty. The will of the distant God is revealed in a sacred writing, in

[1] In a fuller sketch Zoroastrianism would be added to the first division, and Neo-Platonism to the second.

the law (*Torāh*) of Judaism, and the *Qu'rān* of Islām. In rites and pilgrimages, in regularity of prayer, in the giving of tithes, in obedience to all the revealed laws of God, religion consists. History shows the power and force of such religions. The worship of one almighty God gives unity and strength to the worshippers, and endows them often with a splendid tenacity of faith. These 'law religions' give life a meaning and a moral content. The law has been revealed. It is man's duty to obey. God, as the supreme Law-giver, will reward men according to that obedience—a heaven of happiness for the good, a hell of torment for the evil.

Experience shows that the emphasis on obedience to a revealed and detailed law tends to externality. Men think more of conduct than of character. The attention is directed to good works and the good things in this life and the next, which good deeds ensure. An ideal is held before men, but not the power to realize it. Men are still left helpless amid the turmoils and uncertainties of life. There is little answer to man's cry to be redeemed from himself and from this world of change and sorrow. There is no adequate recognition of that homesickness in the world which no happiness can remove; no response to that deep mystic craving not for goods but for God.[1] Such religions do not speak with power to the heart saddened by the 'burthen and the mystery', 'the heavy and the dreary weight of all this unintelligible world'.

It is otherwise with the great religions of redemption, of which Brāhmanism may well serve as a type.

As early as the later hymns of the *Ṛigveda* we get the quest for unity, the search for the unknown but only real God; and in the *Upanishads* the question takes a deeper, and more sombre, form. Amid the multiplicity of deities, where is reality? Amid the sorrow and the futility of life, where is life's meaning? And if life circles on in wearisome *saṁsāra*,[2] when at

[1] The fact that, within these law-religions, mystic sects have arisen, does not contradict, but supports, the argument.

[2] *Saṁsāra* literally, 'wandering' (i.e. of souls).

length can peace be reached? And the *Upanishads* gave to this question their great answer. Brahman alone is real, and with Brahman the cosmic and the individual soul are one. He who thus knows himself identical with Brahman, is freed from the illusion of the seen, and thus the soul, harassed by the flux and distress of life, may attain to peace through its sense of oneness with God, the sole reality.

As we look, even in this most inadequate and scanty way, at these two classic and characteristic forms of religion, the Semitic and the Āryan, we are struck by their difference. It is not so much that one consciously excludes or forbids the other. It is rather that each religion revolves round a different focus. Their reference is to different parts of man's spiritual need. Does not this suggest in each type some limitation, some imperfection?

The legal religions proclaim a God of distinct moral content but remote from His worshippers. In a religion of redemption like Brāhmanism the reverse is the case. The worshipper is identified with Deity, but at a heavy cost. For this unity of the soul with God is only possible by the elimination from each of all distinction. God becomes the ultimate universal of being, ineffable and unknowable. Because God is thought of as attributeless without definite moral content, life has no moral meaning. The struggle for the good, the remorse of conscience, lose their reality. For ethics, we have an ontology. Because the sense of unity with God is realized not in the 'trivial round, the common task' of life, but through philosophy or asceticism, religion at its highest becomes the prerogative of the few. The perfect Buddhist is the monk. The perfect Platonist is the philosopher free from human ties; and in Brāhmanism is it not the meditative recluse who best reaches that shore where is eternal peace?

The one type of religion, the Semitic, is interested and influential in the conduct of this life, but fails to meet man's mystic yearnings. The other type, the Āryan, seeks to meet man's mystic yearnings, but fails to give to life in the world a moral content and meaning. To which type does Christianity belong?

That Christianity is an ethical religion will be universally conceded. It demands of its followers obedience to the law of Christ. It proclaims as its 'good tidings', forgiveness and deliverance from the power of sin. But can we claim that Christianity is also a religion of redemption, redeeming not from sin only but from the world? In view of Christendom the claim may seem hard to prove. The most prominent Christian nations today are the rich and aggressive nations of the West. It is little wonder that many in India, who appreciate the practical value of Christianity, yet assert that it cannot meet their deepest needs. Christianity, they say, is absorbed in the present. It cannot redeem from the seen and transient.

That Christianity is a religion of deliverance and, as such, meets the aspiration of Hinduism, it is the main purpose of this essay to show. Very summarily may we anticipate its results?[1] The presentation of Christianity as ethics and not redemption is one-sided, and, as such, false to the Christian Gospel. Christ came to deliver men not from guilt only, but from bondage to the temporal. Our homesickness for the infinite He meets. Not as orphans are we meant to live in this world of change and darkness. We are God's children. As such we may make the eternal our present, and find in God life's meaning and reality. Born on the Semitic soil of Jewish legalism, Christianity went out into the Āryan world of Greek culture, where the craving for redemption was so intense, and found there a congenial home. It redeems from the world, yet gives moral content to life in the world. As we have seen, to speak of any form of Christianity as absolute is to ignore the teaching of history. But can we claim for the Christian Gospel an absolute and final value? To that, history can give no conclusive answer. But even from the standpoint of the history of religions, this much may be said. If there be a universal religion, we may expect it to be adequate to the spiritual

[1] See especially Chapter VII, pages 147-9, and Chapter XI.

necessities revealed by the two great types of world-religions. We may look for it in a reconciliation of the two types in the higher synthesis of an ethical religion of redemption—a religion which redeems from the world, and yet enables us to find in the world a sphere for moral activity and progress. Just such a religion is the Gospel of Jesus Christ. So the claim of Christian faith that the Christian Gospel is of absolute and universal value is not irrational. Though unprovable by history, it is congruous with its data.

V

It is with Hinduism alone that Christianity will in this essay be related. And the task is one of extraordinary difficulty. In the case of Christianity, though definitions may vary, it is possible for any one to form from the New Testament a tolerably accurate conception of the Christian message and the classic Christian experience.[1] But who shall say what Hinduism is? In view of proportionate representation, the question 'What is a Hindu?' is of political as well as of religious importance.[2] And on this account a great Indian paper[3] invited leaders of Hinduism to answer this question. The answers are for the most part strangely vague. In many, the recognition of the Vedas is regarded as a sufficient sign of Hinduism. In others, even this is regarded as superfluous. Thus Mr. Śrīnivāsa Iyeṅgar regards the question, 'What are the beliefs and practices indispensable in one professing the Hindu faith?' 'as a good illustration of what the logicians call the fallacy of many questions.' Really while 'the Muḥammadans

[1] See Chapters VII and VIII. Professor Paterson well remarks, 'In spite of the ecclesiastical and theological divisions of Christendom, there is a groundwork of the Christian religion which is traceable in the divergent forms and which invests all with an unmistakable family likeness' (*The Rule of Faith*, p. 389).

[2] Politically the point at issue is: Are the millions of outcastes to be classed as Hindus even although they are excluded from Hindu worship?

[3] *The Leader* of Allahabad. Twenty-five of these articles have been reprinted under the title *Essentials of Hinduism* (Natesan & Co., Madras).

are one because they have a common religion and a common law, and the Christians are one because at least one point of faith is common, the Hindus have neither faith, nor practice, nor law to distinguish them from others.'[1] So Mr. Babu Bhagavān Dās writes, 'We must content ourselves with saying that any and every one is a Hindu (1) who does not insist that he is a non-Hindu or, more positively, believes and says he is a Hindu, and (2) accepts *any* of the *many* beliefs, and follows *any* of the *many* practices, that are anywhere regarded as Hinduism.'[2] It is probably impossible to make the definition any more precise. Empirically Hinduism means the observance of caste rules and has no authoritative and universal standards either of belief or conduct. Although this be so, it would not retain its hold over a great and gifted people unless it had some meaning and some value.

If it is impossible to give any comprehensive definition of Hinduism, it does not seem impossible to indicate its great and distinctive doctrines. Are they not these—the doctrine of *karma*,[3] the doctrine of devotion to a God or Gods, and the doctrine of redemption? As the logical *prius* of Hindu thought and practice is the doctrine of *karma*. Men feel themselves bound and seek release; some by the way of love, others by the way of knowledge. The power of a religion lies not in its falsehood but in its truth. Christianity can only supersede Hinduism as it perfectly fulfils the aspiration these great doctrines seek to answer.

Hinduism is not a book-religion, yet in its sacred books its doctrines find their classic presentation. Hindus themselves

[1] *Op. cit.*, p. 8.
[2] *Op. cit.*, pp. 33, 34.
[3] So Mr. V. Kṛishṇasvāmī Iyer writes, 'I cannot conceive of a follower of Hinduism who repudiates *karma* and Reincarnation' (*Essentials of Hinduism*, p. 39). It has to be said that members of the Brāhma and Prārthanā Samājes ignore the belief in *karma*. The contrast here between the Brāhma and the Ārya Samāj is suggestive. Dayānanda Sarasvatī retained the doctrine of *karma*, and the Ārya Samāj, in spite of its monotheism, is wholeheartedly Hindu, Rām Mohan Rai rejected the doctrine, and the Brāhma Samāj, with its devoted belief in the fatherhood of God and the brotherhood of man, is in many ways less Hindu than Christian in its outlook.

recognize for the most part a triple canon[1]—the *Upanishads*, the *Vedānta-sūtras* of Bādarāyaṇa, and the *Bhagavadgītā*—and it is in these that we may partly find a norm of Hinduism. As this essay is concerned only with the vital forces of Hinduism, in one respect it may seem to exceed its task. Essential Hinduism is based on the belief in *karma* and has its first literary expression in the *Upanishads*; but without reference to the earlier literature the *Upanishads* themselves can scarcely be understood; so, even at some loss of symmetry, it seemed necessary to give a brief description of the religion of the *Ṛigveda* and the Beginnings of Brāhmanic Speculation. In chapter three we reach essential Hinduism in the Philosophy of the *Upanishads*. The most influential school of Indian thought finds in Śaṅkarāchārya's commentary on Bādarāyaṇa's *Sūtras* its normative expression, and in expounding these *Sūtras* in chapter four this commentary has been followed.[2]

The *Gītā* speaks of the way of devotion, but it seemed well to illustrate also from vernacular literature that *bhakti* which forms so beautiful and characteristic a part of Hinduism. So in chapter six the love of Kṛishṇa is shown in the poems of Tukārām and the love of Rāma in the famous epic by Tulsī Dās; then, at somewhat greater length, the love of Śiva is described in the poems of Māṇikka Vāśagar, the Tamil saint. It is a perilous task to attempt to describe the religion of others.[3] The endeavour has been made to let the sacred books tell their own story that thus the peril may be less.

In the second half of the book the attempt is made to supply

[1] *Prasthānatraya.*

[2] In a comprehensive exposition of Hinduism, however brief, it would be necessary to deal more adequately with Rāmānuja's interesting and significant interpretation of these *Sūtras*. But no attempt at such an exposition is here made. The aim of the chapters is to illustrate the great Hindu doctrines from a few classic instances, and it seemed better to illustrate the more theistic aspects of Hinduism from the *bhakti* literature.

[3] How dangerous, the misinterpretations of Christianity show. Thus a writer in the *Brahmavādin* sees in Matt. viii. 20 'the idea of unlimitedness of spirit', whilst a Muḥammadan writer will assert that in Luke xviii. 29 there is a conception of heaven as sensuous as that of Islām in that a 'hundredfold' of wives is promised.

an answer to the long quest of Hinduism. Christ's Gospel and the Apostolic experience of it are described in chapters seven and eight, and in the three concluding chapters this Gospel is brought into relation with the great Hindu doctrines of *karma*, *bhakti*, and redemption. Our empirical Christianity does not suffice to meet the demands thus made upon it by the ancient religion of a people so richly endowed with emotional fervour and intellectual acumen, so deeply conscious of the transiency of the present and the reality of the eternal. But though Christianity, as we know it, is insufficient, it is the faith of the writer that Christ is adequate. In meeting new needs, new resources are revealed. We do not increase our inheritance but we learn to possess it.

PART I

CHAPTER II

THE PRESUPPOSITIONS OF ESSENTIAL HINDUISM

THE RELIGION OF THE *ṚIGVEDA* AND THE BEGINNING OF BRĀHMANIC SPECULATION

IT has often been asserted that nowhere can the phenomena of religion be so clearly studied as in India. And for that study the vast collection of literature known as the *Vēda* is the chief source. *Veda* means simply knowledge. The *Veda* is knowledge, absolute and perfect. In extent the *Veda* is more than six times as long as the Bible.[1] Its heterogeneous contents represent more than ten centuries of religious culture. Its oldest part, the mantra or songs, exists in four collections:

The *Ṛigveda*, the *Veda* of Praises.

The *Sāmaveda*, the *Veda* of Sacrificial Chants.

The *Yajurveda*, the *Veda* of Sacrificial Formulae.

The *Atharvaveda*, the *Veda* of Magic Incantations.

Appended to these four collections are the *Brāhmaṇas* and the *Sūtras*. The *Brāhmaṇas* are chiefly concerned with the connexion of the Vedic hymns with the sacrifices. The explanation of the ritual is combined with theosophic discussions, myths, and etymologies, often of the most tedious and fantastic kind. Appended to them are the distinctively theosophic *Forest Books* (*Āraṇyakas*), books so profound that only in the solitude of the forest could they be studied. At the end of

[1] So P. Deussen, *Allgemeine Geschichte der Philosophie*, I. i.; *Einleitung und Philosophie des Veda bis auf die Upanishads*, p. 65.

these we have the *Upanishads*. These are regarded as Vedānta, i. e. they are the end and aim of the *Vedas*. In them, in unarticulated form are the rich philosophic speculations which are India's greatest glory. To them go back the classic philosophic systems of India, and they are still the cherished study of Indian thinkers. The *Sūtras*, which depend very closely on the *Veda*, consist of compendious aphorisms giving, in language compressed to the extent of greatest obscurity, rules for the exact observance of rites and practices. With these it will be unnecessary to deal.

To give a general account of the *Veda* is beyond the scope of this essay. It is our intention to deal with the *Ṛigveda* with great brevity, but with just sufficient adequacy to indicate the general character of the *Ṛigvedic* religion. The philosophic hymns of the *Ṛigveda* will then be discussed at greater length, and the attempt made to trace in them, and in the *Atharvaveda* and the *Brāhmaṇas*, the decadence of the *Ṛigvedic* religion, and the rise of the conceptions afterwards classic in Indian thought. So we shall reach the *Upanishads*, that rich storehouse of materials, to which all subsequent Indian philosophy has been so greatly indebted.

We may give as approximate dates:

I.	The period of the *Ṛigveda* . .	1500–1000 B.C.
II.	The period of the *Atharvaveda* and the *Brāhmaṇas*	1000–600 "
III.	The period of the *Upanishads* . .	600– "

A

THE RELIGION OF THE *ṚIGVEDA*

The interpretation of the *Ṛigveda* is still one of the unsettled questions of historical criticism. The early Vedic scholars spoke with enthusiasm, and sometimes even with rapture, of the fresh simplicity 'of these primaeval hymns'. 'They are the naïve songs of simple herdsmen extolling the mighty works of the nature around them.'[1] Such a view appears to-day impossible. Unlike Max Müller, who asserted that 'the collection of hymns was made for its own sake, and not for the sake of any sacrificial performance', many scholars to-day would connect every hymn with the sacrifice. Some go so far as to call the *Ṛigveda* a kind of 'technical magic', and to regard the hymns throughout as incantations used in the service of a theurgy.[2] Probably the truth lies between the two extremes. The *Ṛigveda* is not homogeneous. It professes to be a *saṁhitā*, a collection, and includes strata of very different ages. The earlier hymns seem to be genuine prayers made without reference to the sacrificial cult. But the bulk of them, and especially those connected with the fire and the sacred liquor (Agni and Soma), are clearly connected with the rubric.

Most popular of all the gods is INDRA, the Vedic god *par excellence*. His greatest work is the slaying of the dragon. The account of his great victory is one that those who have lived in India will understand. The monsoons are for many the chief interests of the year. Before the monsoon comes, the clouds are banked up, heavy and rain-laden. Day after day there is the lightning, but still no rain. At last the clouds break and the rain comes in tropical abundance. Vṛitra it is who keeps the waters locked up in the clouds. Indra with his deadly thunder smites him. The rain falls, and, after the storm, sky and sun again are visible. In every conflict, Indra is the great and always victorious warrior. And in his case the personification goes far beyond the physical substratum. He is the friend of the Āryans, slaying their dark-skinned foes. He is the genial hero, fond of liquor, sometimes drunken. Thus into his mouth is put a half-tipsy, boastful song with this refrain:

'Have I not drunk the Soma juice?'[3]

[1] So Max Müller, *India, what can it teach us?* pp. 108, 109.

[2] La religion des Vedas, mieux connue, nous apparaît aujourd'hui comme une sorte de magie très savante.' M. S. Lévi, quoted in Louis de la Vallée Poussin's *Le Védisme*, p. 41.

[3] *R. V.* x. 119.

At his birth the heaven and earth trembled. Because of his mighty deeds men call him creator and sustainer of the world. He is kind to those who give him the Soma drink he loves, but to the miserly he is stern in vengeance.

Next in popularity is AGNI. Agni is the domestic friend. To him men pray for the bride that she may have happiness in her new home and abundant offspring. He is the messenger between gods and men. He it is who summons the gods to the sacrificial feast. At the sacrificial fire he burns up sin's contamination. As friend of man and as the sacrificial fire he is the mediator between sinners and the wrath of the sublime Ādityas. The case of Agni illustrates well the fact that in the *Ṛigveda*, though there are gods many, there is no regularly ordered pantheon in which each god performs only his peculiar work. Thus Agni in Indra's company became a Soma-drinker; he kills the dragon and wields the thunderbolt. To him are assigned even the attributes of the Ādityas:

> 'Thou at thy birth art Varuṇa, O Agni,
> When thou are kindled thou becomest Mitra,
> In thee, O Son of strength, all gods are centred;
> Indra thou art to man who brings oblation.'[1]

Varuṇa and the Ādityas. Above all the other gods tower the Ādityas, of whom Varuṇa, grandest of all Vedic conceptions, is chief. It is in these hymns to Varuṇa that the thought of India approximates, as rarely elsewhere, to the moral sublimity of Hebraism. Here is proclaimed a holy God, omniscient, the punisher of sin. We quote some stanzas from one of the best known of these hymns. To the Christian reader its words inevitably suggest verses from the Psalms and Job:[2]

> 1. 'Whatever law of thine, O God, O Varuṇa, as we are men,
> Day after day we violate,

[1] *R.V.* v. 3. 1. So too in *R.V.* ii. 1, Agni is identified with a crowd of greater and lesser deities.

[2] For numerous parallels between these hymns to Varuṇa and the Psalms and Job, see Kaegi, *The Ṛigveda*, translated by Arrowsmith, pp. 62–4.

2. Give us not a prey to death, to be destroyed by thee in wrath,
To thy fierce anger when displeased.

10. Varuṇa, true to holy law, sits down among his people, he,
Most wise, sits there to govern all,

11. From thence perceiving, he beholds all wondrous things, both what hath been,
And what hereafter will be done.

20. Thou, O wise God, art Lord of all; thou art the king of earth and heaven:
Hear, as thou goest on thy way.

21. Release us from the upper bond, untie the bond between and loose
The bonds below, that I may live.'[1]

A later hymn speaks of sin with much insight and recognizes its solidarity:

3. 'Fain to know this my sin, I question others: I seek the wise, O Varuṇa, and ask them.
This one same answer even the sages give me, Surely this Varuṇa is angry with thee.

4. What, O Varuṇa, hath been my chief transgression, that thou shouldst slay the friend who sings thy praises?
Tell me, unconquerable Lord, and quickly, sinless, will I approach thee with mine homage.

5. Free us from sins committed by our fathers, from those wherein we have ourselves offended.
O King, loose, like a thief who feeds the cattle, as from a cord the calf, set free Vasishṭha.

6. Not our own will betrayed us, but seduction, thoughtlessness, Varuṇa, wine, dice or anger.
The old is near to lead astray the younger; even slumber leadeth men to evildoing.'[2]

It is the supreme tragedy of India's religious history that this sublime conception of a holy God was so uninfluential. Even in the *Ṛigveda* the worship of the Ādityas is already in the background. Of the thousand and more hymns of the

[1] *R. V.* i. 25, stanzas 1, 2, 10, 11, 20, and 21.
[2] *R. V.* vii. 86. 3-6.

Ṛigveda, nearly one-half are devoted to Indra and Agni. To Varuṇa only twelve hymns are addressed. In one of the later hymns there seems a clear reference to the power of Varuṇa passing into Indra's hands [1] and in Brāhmanic times Varuṇa becomes an unimportant god of the waters. So the noblest intuition of Vedic religion faded into obscurity, and, as we shall see, religious speculation became more concerned with the immense than the holy.

The Character of the Ṛigvedic Religion. In the *Ṛigveda* the gods are for the most part kindly. True there is Rudra whom men call auspicious (Śiva), but whose destructiveness they dread; but, as a rule, the worshipper thinks of his deity not with fear but with cheerful expectation.

The sublime Ādityas, Varuṇa and Mitra, are indeed held in awe as the august protectors of the moral order, the punishers of sin, but, as has been noted, the worship of the Ādityas stands in the background only of the Ṛigvedic hymns. Indra was the popular and much-praised god, and Indra is the warrior's god and warrior's ideal—always brave, always victorious, kindly, and loving much the Soma juice. But in the worship of Indra and the other favourite gods it is not so much justice that is looked for as partiality. In return for the sacrifice they will bestow favours upon their worshippers, and niggardliness in offering is the offence they most abhor.

That the sorcery and magic of the *Atharvaveda* existed in Ṛigvedic times is very probable, but the compilers of the *Ṛigveda* have for the most part ignored these darker aspects of religion.[2] True, occasionally there are charms, sometimes harmless but sometimes malicious. For robbers is provided an incantation to lull the inhabitants of a house to sleep.[3] There are spells to prevent evil spirits causing women to miscarry,[4] and charms to expel diseases.[5]

[1] *R. V.* x. 124.
[2] See especially Rhys Davids's *Buddhist India*, p. 214.
[3] *R. V.* vii. 55. [4] *R. V.* x. 162. [5] *R. V.* x. 163.

In a well-known hymn to Indra-Soma, fierce imprecations are called down upon malicious evil spirits who spoil the sacrifice, ensnare the pious, and bring about their destruction.[1] But, as a whole, the compilation represents a bright and cheerful worship. If optimism means a belief that life is good and its continuance a blessing, then the religion of the *Ṛigveda* is optimistic. Men are content with their genial prosperous life on earth.

Thus the opening stanzas of a funeral hymn pray that death may be far distant from those assembled there and that they 'may survive a hundred lengthened autumns'.[2] So, if death must come, they desire in the next world a life like that of this world, only richer. Yama, the first man who died, is the leader and ruler of the fathers who live in happiness. The wicked go down indeed to the dark pit, but the *Ṛigveda*, unlike the later *Brāhmaṇas*, makes little mention of their punishment. In a hymn to Soma Pavamāna occurs a happy description of the heavenly life :

7. 'O Pavamāna, place me in that deathless, undecaying world,
Wherein the light of heaven is set and everlasting lustre shines.
Flow Indu,[3] flow for Indra's sake.

8. Make me immortal in that realm where dwells the king Vivasvat's son.[4]
Where is the secret shrine of heaven, where are those waters young and fresh. Flow Indu, flow for Indra's sake.

9. Make me immortal in that realm where they move even as they list.
In the third sphere of inmost heaven, where lucid worlds are full of light. Flow Indu, flow for Indra's sake.

10. Make me immortal in that realm of eager wish and strong desire,
The region of the radiant moon, where food and full delight are found. Flow Indu, flow for Indra's sake.

11. Make me immortal in that land where happiness and transports, where
Joys and felicities combine, and longing wishes are fulfilled.
Flow Indu, flow for Indra's sake.'[5]

[1] *R. V.* vii. 104. [2] *R. V.* x. 18. [3] The drops of Soma.
[4] i.e. Yama. [5] *R. V.* ix. 113. 7–11.

The joys of heaven are thus not spiritual: they are the joys of earth perfected. How different is this estimate of life, and this desire for its continuance, from the pessimism of later Indian thought, with its profound sense of the futility and illusion of the seen.

Monotheism or Polytheism? Even in so brief a sketch as this there is one question which claims an answer. It is often asserted by modern Indians that the *Ṛigveda*, rightly understood, teaches monotheism. It is hard to avoid the conclusion that this is a discovery which could only have been made by men who, through Western influences, recognized the crudity of polytheism, and were unwilling to admit that their most sacred book could be in this respect so mistaken. If there was only one God, why should there be the worship of so many? It is no answer to say, as is so often said, that the many gods bring out the variety of the great god behind them. Such clearly was not the view of the composers of the large majority of the Vedic hymns. The conception of Varuṇa as the holy God, the punisher and forgiver of sins, marks the nearest approach of ancient India to a monotheistic faith.

But that path was not pursued. Even Varuṇa, however exalted, was only one God among many, and the worship of Varuṇa recedes behind that of the deities more congenial but less august. Max Müller, admitting the absence of monotheism, sought to distinguish the Ṛigvedic religion from polytheism. If the ordered pantheon of Greece be the test and model of polytheism, then the Ṛigvedic religion cannot be so called. In the *Ṛigveda* there is no Olympus on which the gods dwell in well-ordered state and function. The particular deity praised is extolled above all others. To the gods 'one at a time' are ascribed the highest attributes. This Max Müller called 'henotheism' or 'kathenotheism'.[1] The former term is commonly employed now in another sense.[2]

[1] See *India, what can it teach us?* p. 147.

[2] A religion is said to be 'henotheistic' when it teaches that although the gods of other nations may exist yet for its followers there is one God

The later term may be used, but this 'kathenotheism' has little relation to monotheism. There is indeed little fixity of definition, and to god after god is assigned even the creation of the world. Some hymns are ascribed to all the gods (*Viśvedevās*). Thus one begins:

1. 'Not one of you, ye gods, is small. None of you is a feeble child.
   All of you verily are great.

2. Thus be ye lauded, ye destroyers of the foe,
   Ye three and thirty deities.
   The gods of men, the holy ones.

3. As such defend and succour us; with benedictions speak to us.'[1]

And the fact that the attributes of many gods were ascribed to one blurred the conceptions of the gods, and, by elevating every god, depressed them each. Yet the gods are rarely thought of as mere manifestations. Usually they are held to be absolute, and powerful enough in their own right to be able to succour their worshippers.

The Ṛigvedic religion is, then, a polytheism, but a polytheism unstable and in decay. If the exigencies of the rubric demanded that to so many gods in turn the highest honours should be ascribed, the sacrifice itself was a contract by which the gods gained as well as their worshippers.

In one verse the singer who has won by his song the service of Indra offers to sell him for ten milch-kine.[2] Whether, as Deussen thinks, this is a piece of flippant mockery, or whether, as seems more probable, it is a proof of an irreligious theurgy, in either case, it shows the decay of simple piety. In an age of faith, as Deussen shrewdly says, men do not pray for faith, yet in one of the later hymns of the Ṛigveda we have a prayer for faith.

Faith in the early morning, Faith at noonday will we invocate:
Faith at the setting of the sun, O Faith, endow us with belief.[3]

alone who may be worshipped, e. g. the Hebrew religion at the time of Moses. [1] *R. V.* viii. 30. [2] *R. V.* iv. 24. 10.

[3] *R. V.* x. 151. 5; Deussen, *Allgemeine Geschichte der Philosophie*, I. i, p. 95.

But the decay of polytheism did not lead to the worship of one God, but to the quest of a unitary principle which finds expression in the familiar cosmogonic hymns of the last book of the *Ṛigveda.* Even apart from them we can see at work in the *Ṛigveda* the two tendencies which are at once the product and the cause of the dissolution of its religion—the quest for the one behind the many, and the theurgic view of sacrifice which in the end was to make Brahman, the magic word or prayer, the master of the gods, until at length the two tendencies converge and Brahman becomes the metaphysical principle of the universe.

So the Ṛigvedic thought leads to monism, not monotheism. The moral sublimity of Varuṇa is forgotten. The quest for unity is not the quest for the one holy God. It is the search for the immense, the infinite, the substrate of all being.

B

The Beginnings of Brāhmanic Speculation

The Philosophic Hymns of the Ṛigveda. In Greece, where there was an ordered pantheon, philosophers developed their search for unity in conscious opposition to the popular worship. In India, where the polytheism was ill-defined and unstable, such a strife was needless. Philosophy could have its one god without in any way conflicting with the worship of the many. Already the attributes of the gods were interchanged and confused. It was not so great a step from this to assert that behind all the gods there was one great unifying principle. The first book of the *Ṛigveda*, like the last, is clearly later than the other eight. In it occurs a famous hymn in which the one is thus sought behind the many.[1] The poem is probably the earliest of these philosophic hymns. The poet states problems rather than answers them. He seems to be conscious that he is dealing with enigmas. The hymn is a long one of fifty-two stanzas and it will only be

[1] *R.V.* i. 164.

possible to outline its contents.[1] In obscure and symbolic language, the poet describes the riddle of the universe. The sun and stars of heaven, the lightnings and the fire of sacrifice, are brothers. Behind the multiplicity of the phenomenal is the one. The one bears the world, is present as the father in the starry heaven, and the sacrificial fire on earth. The one is the axle of the earth. The one is the divine spirit and the World-Father. Corresponding to the world-order are the metres of the Vedic songs and the earthly sacrifices.

To the earthly speech, the holy word of the *Veda*, corresponds the heavenly speech (*Vāch*), the heavenly cow, whose lowing is thunder, and whose milk is rain. To the earthly sacrifice corresponds a heavenly. Three-fourths of the holy speech is hidden in heaven; one-fourth only is revealed through the Vedas on earth. Then comes a verse of great importance:

> 'They call him Indra, Mitra, Varuṇa, Agni,
> And he is heavenly nobly-winged Garutman.
> To what is one, sages give many a title;
> They call it Agni, Yama, Mātariśvan.'[2]

The line 'To what is one, sages give many a title' has been described as the most important in Indian thought before the great 'Thou art that' of the *Upanishads*. It is one of the most-quoted lines of the *Ṛigveda* to-day. The hymn as a whole marks, in obscure and halting language, the transition from a polytheism in flux to a unitary conception of the real.

The Hymn of Creation.[3] Of far greater interest and beauty is the famous hymn of creation in the tenth book. In a few master-strokes the poet describes the primaeval and undifferentiated chaos. There was neither being (*sat*) nor non-being (*asat*). In the ocean of darkness only the one existed. By 'Tapas' had he been born from the void. The first meaning of 'Tapas' is warmth, and it is thus that Griffiths translates it

[1] For a full commentary see Deussen, *op. cit.*, pp. 105–19.
[2] *R. V.* i. 164. 46. [3] *R. V.* x. 129.

D

here. It suggests a hen brooding over her chickens. But in a land where heat is a hardship, by a natural transition, the word came to denote austerity, asceticism, and it is possible that this is the meaning here. Then in the fourth stanza the poet reaches the height of his argument. Something stirred in the void. It was *kāma*, desire.[1] Because of it the world was created. The next stanza is very obscure, but seems to speak of a differentiation into two. Deussen holds that the division is between the 'thing in itself', the real, and its corresponding phenomenon,[2] but this endeavour to read the Kantian distinction into this ancient hymn is surely strained. In the last two stanzas the poet confesses that the creation is to him a mystery. The creation preceded the gods. Does the one know of it, or is he, too, ignorant? As the poem is not only important but brief we quote it in full:

1. 'Then was not non-existent nor existent; there was no realm of air, no sky beyond it.
   What covered in and where? and what gave shelter? was water there, unfathomed depth of water?

2. Death was not then, nor was there ought immortal: no sign was there, the day's and night's divider.
   That one thing, breathless, breathed by its own nature: apart from it was nothing whatsoever.

3. Darkness was there: at first, concealed in darkness, this All was indiscriminated chaos.
   All that existed then was void and formless: by the great power of warmth (*tapas*) was born that unit.

4. Thereafter rose Desire in the beginning, Desire, the primal seed and germ of spirit.
   Sages who searched with their heart's thought discovered the existent's kinship in the non-existent.

5. Transversely was their severing line extended; what was above it then, and what below it?
   There were begetters, there were mighty forces, free action here and energy up yonder.

[1] The ἔρως of Parmenides.

[2] *Op. cit.*, p. 125.

6. Who verily knows and who can here declare it, whence it was born and whence comes this creation?
The Gods are later than this world's production. Who knows then whence it first came into being?

7. He, the first origin of this creation, whether he formed it all or did not form it,
Whose eye controls this world in highest heaven, he verily knows it or perhaps he knows it not.'[1]

Here we have in full power the subtle questionings of the Indian mind, and it is with no surprise that we find a modern Hindu writer claiming for this hymn that it must have been 'I will not say composed but revealed to the Ṛishi', and that 'it contains all the fundamental elements of the religious, philosophic, and scientific, consciousness of humanity'.[2]

Inevitably speculation, once begun, could not rest content with this unknown god, so we have further hymns which seek to define this mysterious one behind the many.

The Hymn of the Golden Germ.[3] There is a well-known hymn in which Indra's exploits are recounted and at the end of each verse is the refrain:

'Have faith in him, for he, O men, is Indra.'[4]

It seems to have been in conscious opposition to this hymn that there was written the hymn known as the hymn of the Golden Germ (Hiraṇyagarbha).[5] In place of Indra this poet puts the great unknown god as the doer of the mighty deeds. First in creation was the Golden Germ:

1. 'In the beginning rose Hiraṇyagarbha, born only lord of all created beings.
He fixed and holdeth up this earth and heaven. What god shall we adore with our oblation?

[1] *R. V.* x. 129.
[2] *Brahmadarśanam* by Śrī Ānanda Āchārya.
[3] *R. V.* x. 121.
[4] *R. V.* ii. 12.
[5] Macdonell points out that, although the Hiraṇyagarbha is mentioned several times in the *Atharvaveda* and the *Brāhmaṇas*, this is the only place in which the word occurs in the *Ṛigveda*. *Vedic Mythology* in *Grundriss der Indo-Arischen Philologie und Altertumskunde*, 1897, p. 119.

D 2

5. By him the heavens are strong and earth is steadfast, by him light's realm and sky-vault are supported.
By him the regions in mid-air were measured. What god shall we adore with our oblation?

9. Ne'er may he harm us who is earth's begetter, nor he, whose laws are sure, the heaven's creator,
He, who brought forth the great and lucid waters. What god shall we adore with our oblation?'

At last comes the answer. He gives the unknown god the name Prajāpati, Lord of creatures:

10. 'Prajāpati! thou only comprehendest all these created things, and none beside thee.
Grant us our heart's desire when we invoke thee. May we have store of riches in possession.'[1]

This word Prajāpati became later one of the most influential of Brāhmanic conceptions. Closely allied to this hymn are two to Viśvakarman, the all-creator.

The Hymns to Viśvakarman.[2] In the first of these two hymns (x. 81), Viśvakarman, the all-creator, is invoked as at once the high-priest and the architect of the universe. In this way the sacrificial order and the world's creation are even at this early date linked up together. The motive of the world's creation is held to be the desire for offspring.

In the second of these hymns (x. 82), Viśvakarman is acclaimed as 'mighty in word and power', 'Maker, disposer and most lofty Presence', 'the Father who made us men, the Deities' name-giver'. Then the poet asks:

5. 'That which is earlier than this earth and heaven, before the Asuras and gods had being,—
What was the germ primaeval which the waters received where all the gods were seen together?

6. The waters, they received that germ primaeval, wherein the gods were gathered all together.
It rested, set upon the Unborn's navel; that One wherein abide all things existing.'

The poet feels that none of those reputed wise can help him.

[1] *R. V.* x. 121, stanzas 1, 5, 9, 10.

[2] *R. V.* x. 81, 82.

The singers of hymns, self-absorbed and complacent, are unable to behold and declare this great mysterious One.

> 7. 'Ye will not find him who produced these creatures: another thing hath risen up among you.
> Enwrapt in misty cloud, with lips that stammer, hymn-chanters wander and are discontented.'[1]

The Hymn to Brahmaṇaspati.[2] In the Ṛigvedic religion, as we have seen, to prayer is assigned theurgic power. The gods depend on sacrifice and prayer for their well-being. It was natural then to personify *brahman*, the magic word or prayer, and make of it a god. This was done under the name of Brahmaṇaspati—or, if the metre required a shorter form, Brihaspati—the Lord of Prayer. In the earlier part of the chapter, mention has already been made of Brihaspati as one of the gods of the earth, the high-priest, the path-preparer. Gradually his importance grew in priestly estimation till at length in this hymn he is extolled as the all-creator. As a smith he forges out of the non-existent the existent, and with it the world of gods. With that love of the impossible so often found in Indian thinkers, the poet speaks of Daksha as at once the mother and the child of Aditi, the primaeval matter. The cosmogony is at the same time a theogony.

> 1. 'Let us with tuneful skill proclaim these generations of the gods,
> That one may see them when these hymns are chanted in a future age.
> 2. These Brahmaṇaspati produced with blast and smelting, like a smith.
> Existence, in an earlier age of gods, from non-existence sprang.
> 3. Existence in the earliest age of gods, from non-existence sprang.
> Thereafter were the regions born. This sprang from the Productive Power.
> 4. Earth sprang from the Productive Power; the regions from the earth were born.
> Daksha was born of Aditi, and Aditi was Daksha's child.'[3]

Then follows an account of the creation of the gods. Last

[1] *R. V.* x. 82, stanzas 5, 6, 7. [2] *R. V.* x. 72.
[3] *R. V.* x. 72, stanzas 1-4.

to be produced is the sun. This conception of Brahmaṇaspati, the Lord of Prayer, as the all-creator, marks an important stage in the development of the idea of Brahman as the ultimate principle of the universe.

The Hymn to Purusha.[1] Most famous and probably latest of all the Ṛigvedic hymns is the hymn known as the Purusha-sūkta.[2]

Here in place of personified abstractions like Prajāpati and Viśvakarman is put Purusha, man, humanity. Man, the head of creation, is made its origin. Whereas in the *Ṛigveda* the gods are primarily personifications of parts or special powers of nature, here nature as a whole is regarded as an extension of the primaeval man, and thus a metaphysical unity is realized.

The poem falls naturally into three parts:[3]

I. *The world is Purusha.* Stanzas 1–5. Purusha as more than an ordinary man has a thousand heads and eyes and feet. He not only fills the earth. He is ten finger-space beyond it in every direction. So he is greater than all that is. All living things on earth sprang from one-fourth of him, while three-fourths of him 'are eternal life in heaven'. From Purusha comes Virāj, and from Virāj Purusha again was born. Purusha is thus the first begetter and the first begotten.

II. *The creation of the world through the sacrifice of Purusha.* Stanzas 6–10 with stanza 15. The gods, the Sādhyas[4] and the Ṛishis offer up Purusha, and from that sacrifice is born all living things, the Vedas, horses, cattle, sheep and goats.

III. *The parts of the world are the organs of his body.* Stanzas 11–14. In this part of the poem occurs the first and very famous reference to the four castes—a reference which clearly proves the lateness of the hymn:

[1] *R. V.* x. 90.

[2] The main idea of the myth embodied in the poem—the creation of the world from the body of a giant—is indeed, as Macdonell says, very primitive, but 'several details in this myth point to the most recent period of the *Ṛigveda*'. *Vedic Mythology*, p. 13.

[3] See Deussen, *op. cit.*, 150-8.

[4] A class of gods.

11. 'When they divided Purusha, how many portions did they make?
What do they call his mouth, his arms? What do they call his thighs and feet?

12. The Brāhman was his mouth, of both his arms was the Rājanya[1] made.
His thighs became the Vaiśya, from his feet the Śūdra was produced.

13. The Moon was gendered from his mind, and from his eye the Sun had birth.
Indra and Agni from his mouth were born, and Vāyu from his breath.

14. Forth from his navel came mid-air; the sky was fashioned from his head,
Earth from his feet, and from his ear the regions. Thus they formed the world.'

The concluding stanza may be a later addition:

16. 'Gods, sacrificing, sacrificed the victim: these were the earliest holy ordinances;
The mighty ones attained the height of heaven, there where the Sādhyas, gods of old, are dwelling.'[2]

In this poem we feel we have already approached very near to the *Upanishads*, but before we can reach those loftiest summits of India's thought, we have first to traverse as best we may the dense and pathless jungle of the *Atharvaveda* and the *Brāhmaṇas*.

The Atharvaveda and the Brāhmaṇas. Before tracing the development of thought in this period it is necessary to speak a little of the *Atharvaveda* and the *Brāhmaṇas* from the point of view of the moral and spiritual condition which they reveal.

The Atharvaveda. The *Atharvaveda* is to-day recognized as being like the *Ṛigveda*, śruti and divine, but it was long before it obtained quite the sanctity of the other three *Vedas*, and in its present form it is clearly later. Verses from the *Ṛigveda* are quoted in it with little regard to meaning or context. In subject-matter it differs much from the *Ṛigveda*. The *Ṛigveda* presupposes magic, but looks away from it.

[1] i.e. The Kshatriya caste.

[2] *R. V.* x. 90, stanzas 11–14, 16.

The *Atharvaveda* is first of all a book of magic spells. As such, some enthusiastic admirers of the *Ṛigveda* are unwilling to admit that the *Atharvaveda* can be Āryan. Thus Madame Ragozin writes: 'We have here, as though in opposition to the bright, cheerful pantheon of beneficent deities, so trustingly and gratefully addressed by the Ṛishis of the *Ṛigveda*, a weird, repulsive world, of darkly scowling demons, inspiring abject fear, such as never sprang from Āryan fancy.'[1]

But such a theory, though permissible, is quite unproved. And they do not understand India who suppose that contradictions cannot exist side by side. Thus the vague Theism of the modern educated Hindu rarely rids him of his fear of omens and his desire to begin every new phase of his life on an 'auspicious day'. Just so, along with the brighter pantheon of the *Ṛigveda*, existed the devil-haunted world of the *Atharvaveda*. And this *Veda* is of considerable interest in that its charms reveal in ample detail the life of ancient India. Then as now every stage of life has to be consecrated by religion. So even for trivial purposes we find a charm provided. A man wishes to secure a maiden's love. A maiden seeks to win a husband. A wife desires to destroy her rival. A woman seeks safe delivery and to have only male children. A child has cut his first two teeth and for him blessing is sought. The farmer desires to speed his plough. He wishes to ward off dysentery and fever, vermin, tigers, wolves, and thieves. He is in fear of evil spirits, especially of those that molest his women, and for all these purposes there are charms. Less innocent are curses for the destruction of enemies. Fiercest of all are imprecations on Kshatriyas who dare to oppress the Brāhman and rob him of his cows. The limits of this essay do not permit quotation, and there is little need; for magic spells are the same the whole world over. Of interest as showing that strange blending of the noble and the base so often in Indian religion is the famous hymn to Varuṇa.[2] Here more than anywhere in the *Ṛigveda*, the omnipotence

[1] *Vedic India*, 3rd edit., pp. 117, 118.

[2] *A. V.* iv. 16.

and omniscience of Varuṇa is extolled; yet the prayer terminates with a terrific curse:

1. 'The mighty ruler of these worlds beholds as though from close at hand.
   The man who thinks he acts by stealth, all this the Gods perceive and know.
2. If a man stands, or walks, or moves, in secret, or goes to his lying down or his uprising,
   What two men whisper as they sit together, King Varuṇa knows: he as the third is present.
4. If any one should flee afar beyond the heaven, King Varuṇa would still be round about him.
   Proceeding hither from the sky his envoys look, thousand-eyed, over the earth beneath them.
5. All this the royal Varuṇa beholdeth, all between heaven and earth and all beyond them.
   The twinkling of men's eyelids hath he counted. As one who plays throws dice, he settles all things.
7. Varuṇa, snare him with a hundred nooses. Man's watcher! let not him who lies escape thee.
   There let the villain sit with hanging belly and bandaged like a cask whose hoops are broken.
8. Varuṇa sends and drives away diseases: Varuṇa is both native and a stranger:
   Varuṇa is celestial and is human.
9. I bind and hold thee fast with all these nooses, thou son of such a man and such a mother.
   All these do I assign thee as thy portion.'

The Brāhmaṇas. The *Brāhmaṇas* are the earliest of Indian prose writings. Of all works demanding study there are surely few less intelligible or more tedious. As Professor Eggeling, the translator of the most important *Brāhmaṇa*, remarks, 'For wearisome prolixity of exposition, characterized by dogmatic assertion and flimsy symbolism rather than by serious reasoning, these works are perhaps not equalled anywhere.'[1] The arguments used in them are often more suggestive of *Alice in Wonderland* than of the ordinary processes of human reason. Yet without some reference to

[1] *S. B. E.* xii, p. ix.

these *Brāhmaṇas*, it is impossible to trace the transition from the *Ṛigveda* to the *Upanishads*. The complex phenomena of the later religion have in many cases here their beginnings. Thus, empirically, Hinduism means to-day the observance of caste and the recognition of the supremacy of the Brāhmans. Both these conceptions are found in the *Brāhmaṇas*. Here already, as Professor de la Vallée Poussin says, we have 'the particular mentality which is characteristic of Hinduism, the medley of pantheistic gnosis, of piety and paganism, of social conservatism, and religious anarchy'.[1]

The Brāhmans, with true sacerdotal instinct, secured for themselves the monopoly not only of the cult but of education. Already we have the beginnings of the division of the Brāhman's life into the four stages (*āśramas*) of student (*brahmachārin*), householder (*gṛihastha*), hermit (*vānaprashta*), and ascetic (*sannyāsin*).[2] As the possessors of the *Vedas*, the Brāhmans were essential to every sacrifice and claimed for themselves a divine sanctity. Thus we read, 'Verily there are two kinds of gods; for the gods themselves assuredly are gods, and those priests who have studied and teach Vedic lore are the human gods.'[3] Like sacrifices to the God are fees paid to the human gods, the priests. Even at this period the Śūdra is expressly excluded from religion: 'The gods talk only to the higher castes.'

It is natural in works such as these that sacrifice should be extolled. At the sacrifice every syllable and every accent is of tremendous import. One mistake, and dreadful may be the consequences. By sacrifice the gods are not so much worshipped as subdued. The gods themselves depend on sacrifice. By it the gods obtained heaven. By it the stronger gods overcame the weaker. The sun would not rise if the priest did not offer sacrifices. In fact, as M. Barth says, 'the

[1] *Le Brahmanisme*, p. 43.

[2] Of course the 'beginnings' only. The distinction between the *vānaprashta* and the *sannyāsin* was later, and the duty of the *gṛihastha* was not at this time obligatory on all.

[3] *Śat. Br.* ii. 2. 2. 6 and ii. 4. 3. 14.

sacrifices are the true gods to which the devas, apart from the dreaded Rudra, are mere subordinate agents, abstractions, empty shadows.'[1]

As powerful as sacrifice are asceticism and prayer. Asceticism (*tapas*) is practised even when the object is to obtain in heaven most unascetic pleasures. By asceticism and prayer, men may overcome the gods. When religion is thus a theurgy, we cannot expect a lofty conception of the gods. They are depicted as drunken, and some of the stories told of them read intolerably in translation. Yet, on the other hand, the incest of the supreme god Prajāpati with his daughter Ushas is referred to as revolting to the other gods. Here and there are traces of the ethical nobility of the hymns to Varuṇa. Thus we read: 'Let him (the sacrificer) only speak the truth, for the vow indeed the gods do keep, that they speak the truth, and for this reason they are glorious: glorious therefore is he who knowing this speaks the truth.'[2] Already a man's sins are spoken of as his debts. But the doctrine of soul-wandering (*Saṁsāra*) is not yet developed. And the re-birth the wise man of a later age sought to avoid is here regarded as a reward.[3]

Such, in briefest outline, are the *Brāhmaṇas* and their religion. They reflect an age of priestly pre-eminence in which sacerdotal claims are urged with greedy cynicism. Prayer, sacrifice, and asceticism are a theurgy greater in power than the power of the gods. The age is one of spiritual feebleness, void of moral strength or beauty. Without a revival of religion, religion must have passed from feebleness to death. That revival came in the great age of the *Upanishads* and Gautama the Buddha. But the philosophy of the *Upanishads* emerged imperceptibly from the sacerdotal theosophy of the

[1] Barth, *Bulletin*, 1899, p. 30, quoted by de la Vallée Poussin, *op. cit.*, p. 46.

[2] *Śat. Br.* i. 1. 1. 5.

[3] 'For the spring assuredly comes into life again out of the winter, for out of the one the other is born again: therefore he who knows this is indeed born again in this world,' *Śat. Br.* i. 5. 3. 14.

Brāhmanic age. It is necessary, therefore, to indicate briefly the development in this period of those great conceptions to which the *Upanishads* afterwards gave classic form.

The Speculation of the Brāhmanic Age. In a famous hymn of the *Ṛigveda* already quoted,[1] Prajāpati is extolled as the great unknown god. It is around Prajāpati that most of the speculation of this period gathers. To him is assigned the world's creation. Many passages begin with some such words as these: 'Prajāpati desired, "May I be propagated and multiplied".' He uses *tapas*[2] and thus creates the world. The order and details of creation vary much in the various accounts. It must suffice to quote one of the many given in the *Śatapatha Brāhmaṇa.*

1. 'Verily in the beginning Prajāpati alone existed here. He thought within himself, "How can I be propagated?" He toiled and practised austerities (*tapas*). He created living beings. The living beings created by him passed away; they are these birds. Now man is the nearest to Prajāpati and man is two-footed; hence birds are two-footed.

2. Prajāpati thought within himself, "Even as formerly I was alone, so also am I now alone." He created a second (race of beings): they also passed away; they are those small creeping reptiles other than snakes. He created a third (race), they say; they also passed away; they are those snakes.

3. While praising and practising austerities, Prajāpati thought within himself, "How comes it that the living beings created by me pass away?"

He then became aware that his creatures passed away from want of food. He made the breasts in the fore-part of their body teem with milk. He then created living beings and by resorting to the breasts, the beings created by him thenceforward continued to exist: they are these (creatures) which have not passed away.'[3]

[1] *R. V.* x. 121.

[2] Here, as in *R. V.* x. 129, it is hard to say if *tapas* denotes 'brooding', as of a hen over her chickens, or 'austerity'.

[3] *Śat. Br.* ii 5. 1. 1–3.

These speculators do not seem to have asked that ancient question, 'Whence came evil?' From Prajāpati came not only the gods and men but the *asuras* who, in the *Brāhmaṇas*, are demons. Yet he is first of all the friend of the gods. Of the three-and-thirty gods he is the four-and-thirtieth. As this period draws to a close we can see the signs of the decline of Prajāpati's glory. Men seek a prior principle. Thus in the following passage it is stated that at first there was the non-existent (*asat*).

1. 'Verily in the beginning there was here the non-existent. The Ṛishis doubtless were the vital airs; inasmuch as before (the existence of) this universe they desiring it, wore themselves out (*rish*) with toil and austerity (they are called) Ṛishis.

2. This same vital air in the midst doubtless is Indra. He by his power (*indriya*) kindled those other vital airs from the midst; and inasmuch as he kindled (*indh*) he is the kindler (*indha*); the kindler indeed—him they call Indra mystically, for the gods love the mystic. They (the vital airs) being kindled, created seven separate persons.'[1]

Then we read that the seven persons were made into one person and that person became Prajāpati. And Prajāpati, desiring to be multiplied, performed austerity and produced the *Veda*, in which all else rests.[2] The passage is of interest not only as showing the disposition of Prajāpati, but as illustrating the strange dialectic of these *Brāhmaṇas*. Accidental assonances are treated as etymological connexions, and, on the basis of these, elaborate cosmogonies are constructed.

As the importance of the mythological Prajāpati thus grew less, speculation began more and more to gather around the two conceptions now classic in Indian thought: the Brahman and the Ātman. It is necessary to trace with some precision the meaning and history of these two words.[3]

Brahman. The origin of the word 'Brahman' is still much disputed. Its etymology is uncertain and the word is used in

[1] *Śat. Br.* vi. 1. 1. 1–2. [2] *Śat. Br.* vi. 1. 1. 3–8.
[3] For what follows see Deussen, *op. cit.*, pp. 239–336.

a variety of senses. Thus Deussen quotes from the St. Petersburg lexicon no less than seven meanings: (1) Prayer, (2) Magic charm, (3) Holy speech, (4) Holy knowledge (i.e. the Veda), (5) Holy mode of life (i.e. chastity), (6) The absolute, (7) The holy caste (i.e. the Brāhmans). It is natural to suppose that behind all these there is some unifying thought. Deussen finds this in the conception of 'prayer', and holds that the first meaning of 'brahman' is the 'will of man striving up after the holy and divine'.[1]

Prayer, he says, has two sides, 'the superindividual and the individual.' The individual side desires individual blessings and this tends to mythology and magic. But it is not this but the 'superindividual' side which he regards as the essential element in the conception of 'brahman'. The 'superindividual' side of prayer denotes the elevation of the spirit through the sense of identity with God above our individual life with its cares and sorrows. So the words of our prayer become the expression of our unity with God, and belong not to us but to the God in us who speaks through them. And in support of this view he quotes many passages which illustrate the belief that prayer is an inspiration. Thus in the well-known hymn of the *Ṛigveda* already quoted, it is stated that one-fourth only of the heavenly speech (*Vāch*) came down to dwell with men.[2] In this Deussen sees an admirable illustration of the truth that prayer is of a divine nature and is not limited to the prayers of men.

Interesting as this explanation is, it cannot be said to be probable. As Hillebrandt says, 'With no little probability, research inclines now to the view that the fundamental meaning of the word is neither "devotion" nor "prayer" but "magic".'[3] In the *Ṛigveda*, 'Brahman' is clearly the prerogative only of the few, and it is significant that the *Atharvaveda*, the *Veda* of charms belonged originally to the Brāhmans. It is very probable, therefore, that originally 'brahman' means magic, and the Brāhman was the sorcerer or medicine man, the

[1] *Op. cit.*, p. 241. [2] *R. V.* 164. 45. [3] *E. R. E.* ii. 797.

wielder of those spells of which the *Atharvaveda* is the great collection. If so, then the gradual elevation of the conception of 'brahman' affords an admirable illustration of that conservatism of the Indian mind which will not reject the past, but rather will transform a word belonging originally to the lowest stratum of religion until it becomes in the end the highest metaphysical principle of a lofty idealistic philosophy.

From the kindred conceptions of magic, prayer, and sacred speech, the word 'brahman' came to denote the sacred knowledge of the Vedas, and the Brāhmans began to be honoured, not as medicine men, but as the upholders and possessors of those sacred Vedic songs without which no sacrifice could be complete. As we have seen, Brahman was deified as Brahmaṇaspati, the priest of the gods, and, in a late hymn of the *Ṛigveda* already quoted, Brahmaṇaspati is celebrated as the all-creator.[1]

In many passages Brahman is closely connected with the sun. So we read 'the Gāyatrī is the Brahman, and as to that Brahman it is yonder burning disk'.[2] Gradually Brahman is no longer held to be dependent on Prajāpati; the two are regarded as identical, and finally Prajāpati is subordinated to Brahman. Thus in the following passage, Brahman is clearly regarded as the supreme creative principle, and the quotation is of interest also as one of the earliest instances of that explanation of the phenomenal universe, so common later, as form and name.

1. 'Verily in the beginning, this (universe) was the Brahman. It created the gods; and having created the gods it made them ascend these worlds: Agni this (terrestrial) world, Vāyu the air, and Sūrya the sky.

2. And the deities who are above, these he made ascend the worlds which are above these; indeed, just as these (three) worlds and these (three) deities are manifest, so are those

[1] *Ṛ. V.* x. 72.

[2] *Śat. Br.* viii. 5. 3. 7. Gāyatrī as the metre of the famous hymn to the sun became another name fpr Savitar, the Sun God.

(higher) worlds and those (higher) deities manifest—(the worlds) which he made these deities ascend.

3. Then the Brahman itself went up to the sphere beyond. Having gone up to the sphere beyond, it considered, "How can I descend again into these worlds?" It then descended again by means of these two—Form (*rūpa*) and Name (*nāma*). Whatever has a name, that is name; and that again which has no name and which one knows by its form, "This is (of a certain) form" that is form: as far as there are Form and Name so far extends this (universe).

4. These indeed are the two great forces of the Brahman; and verily he who knows these two great forces of the Brahman becomes himself a great force.'[1]

Of considerable importance in this connexion are some hymns of the *Atharvaveda*. Thus in one hymn,[2] Purusha, the primaeval man, is identified with Brahman, the highest principle of being. It was through the Brahman immanent in him that Purusha was able to go to his creative work. The body of man is the fortress of Brahman, the heart of man his dwelling-place. He who knows this becomes as Brahman. In another hymn,[3] Brahman, the highest principle, is said to be embodied in men like a cow in a cow-stall. Along with Brahman was the great primaeval water. From these came forth the oldest gods, Karma (work) and Tapas (austerity). From these three, Brahman, Karma, and Tapas, sprang the twofold generations of the gods—the one, the mythological gods, the other the psychological gods, the deified powers of man. The poem is very obscure, and it is hard to say how much is profound and how much meaningless, but it is noteworthy not only for its assertion of Brahman as the first principle, but for its cavalier treatment of the gods and its tendency to explain everything by psychology.

Ātman. Difficult as it is to trace the development in the conception of Brahman from a magic word to the highest principle of the universe, it is still more difficult to trace the

[1] *Śat. Br.* xi. 2. 3. 1 4. [2] *A. V.* x. 2. [3] *A. V.* xi. 8.

development in the conception of Ātman. The derivation of the word is still in dispute. It is conjectured that the word meant first 'breath', then the 'life-breath', and so the life-breath in the sense of the soul, the self. The word is thus primarily a negative one. It denotes the self in opposition to the not-self. As such it has often been compared to the τὸ ὄντως ὄν of Plato, and the *Ding an sich* of Kant. It is impossible to state with precision through what stages the thought developed until at last the Ātman came to denote the self of the universe, and, as the highest metaphysical principle, was thus identified with Brahman.[1]

It is probable that the prevalence of the cognate ideas of Purusha and Prāṇa helped to popularize the conception of the Ātman. Reference has already been made to the famous hymn in the *Ṛigveda* which speaks of Purusha, the primaeval man from whose sacrifice the world arose.[2] In an Atharvavedic hymn, Prāṇa, the breath—a conception closely allied to that of the Ātman—is hailed as the first and life-giving principle of nature.[3] In two consecutive hymns of the *Atharvaveda* an attempt is made to define more precisely this first principle of nature. This first principle is Skambha, the prop or pillar, the support of our existence. The first of these hymns[4] is noteworthy as yet another illustration of how lightly these thinkers held the popular religion. The famous three-and-thirty deities are only a part of Skambha and were created out of nothing. Even with this philosophic explanation of creation, this author is dissatisfied. To him, Skambha, Prajāpati, Purusha, and Brahman are all one. Skambha is the principle and includes in himself all space and time, the gods, Vedas and moral powers. We quote some of the more interesting stanzas:

7. 'Who out of many tell me is that Skambha,
On whom Prajāpati set up and firmly stablished all the worlds?

[1] The suggestion that 'Brahman' represents the priestly speculation and 'Ātman' the more philosophic speculation of the Kshatriyas, is interesting but very hard to prove.

[2] *R. V.* x. 90. [3] *A. V.* xi. 4. [4] *A. V.* x. 7.

13. Who out of many, tell me is that Skambha,
He in whose body are contained all the three-and-thirty deities?
17. They who in Purusha understand Brahman know him who is supreme.
He who knows him who is supreme, and he who knows the lord of Life,
These know the loftiest power divine, and thence know Skambha thoroughly.'

The following hymn[1] begins with an invocation to Brahman:

1. 'Worship to loftiest Brahman, Lord—of what hath been and what shall be,
To him who rules the universe, and heavenly light is all his own.'

In this hymn the mystic pantheism with which Skambha is described comes very near to the standpoint of the *Upanishads*. Skambha is the woman, the man, the maiden, the boy. He is the people's father and their son; the oldest and the youngest. He is the one God who men carry in their heart, he is the first-born, he is in the mother's womb.

In the last stanza of all it is asserted that this Skambha, which has already been identified with Brahman, is the Ātman. Whoso knows him, fears death no longer.

44. 'Desireless, firm, immortal, self-existent, contented with the essence, lacking nothing,
Free from all fear of death is he who knoweth that Soul (Ātman) courageous, youthful, undecaying.'

So already the Ātman, like the Brahman, is regarded as the metaphysical principle of the universe. And in one place in the *Śatapatha Brāhmaṇa*, the identity of the Brahman with the Ātman is asserted in language of which one of the most famous passages in the *Upanishads* is merely the transcript.[2]

1. 'Let a man meditate upon the true Brahman. Now man here is possessed of understanding and according to how great his understanding is, when he departs this world so does he on passing away enter yonder world.

2. Let him meditate on the Self (Ātman), which is made up

[1] *A. V.* x. 8.

[2] *Chhānd. Up.* iii. 14.

of intelligence and endowed with a body of spirit, with a form of light and with an ethereal nature, which changes the shape at will, is swift as thought, of true resolve, and true purpose, which consists of all sweet odours and tastes, which holds sway over all the regions and pervades this whole universe, which is speechless, indifferent—even as a grain of rice or a grain of barley or a grain of millet or the smallest granule of millet, so is the golden Purusha in the heart; even as a smokeless light, it is greater than the sky, greater than the ether, greater than the earth, greater than all existing things;—that self of the spirit (breath) is my self; on passing away from hence I shall obtain that self. Verily whosoever has this trust, for him there is no uncertainty. Thus spake Śāṇḍilya and so it is.'[1]

So the weary quest is over. The Ātman, the Self, is identical with the almighty power of Brahman. We have reached the great equation,

The Ātman = Brahman.

[1] *Śat. Br.* x. 6. 3.

CHAPTER III

A STUDY IN THE *UPANISHADS*

To the ritualistic *Brāhmaṇas* were added the *Āraṇyakas*, works to be studied by the recluse in the silence of the forest. As the completion of these come the *Upanishads*, the famous repositories of the redeeming mysteries of Indian philosophy.

None but special students will ever read the *Brāhmaṇas*, but the *Upanishads* have a special place and importance in the history of religion. To them, as their sacred sources, go back the dominant philosophies of India. Especially, and with right, does the Vedānta claim to be their legitimate expression. The ideas of the *Upanishads* are the very atmosphere of India. Even the simple villager, though he knows nothing of these works, is under their influence. Educated Indians declare with confidence that these venerable writings contain a wisdom which can never be superseded. Men, sincere and able, avow that in them they find the solace and strength of their spiritual life. For this philosophy is also a religion. Indeed, for many gifted Hindus it is the only religious force which is still effective. 'We go to the temple', they say, 'to please our mothers, our relations. But none know better than we do of the degradation of the ignorant priesthood and the folly of the services. But in the *Upanishads* we have all we need. They rank in value with your New Testament, and are indeed preferable to it, for whereas the New Testament gives a religion, which, as inseparably connected with one historic time and person, is local and temporary, the *Upanishads* give a philosophy which, as based on pure reason, is universal in scope and permanently valid.'

And for such claims Indians quote with zest the praise of

European scholars. Thus Schopenhauer knew the *Upanishads* only in Anquetil Duperron's *Oupnekhat*, a Latin version of a Persian translation. Yet he writes:

> 'How is every one, who by a diligent study of its Persian Latin has become familiar with that incomparable book, stirred by that spirit to the very depth of his soul! How does every line display its firm, definite and, throughout, harmonious meaning! From every sentence deep, original, and sublime thoughts arise, and the whole is pervaded by a high and holy and earnest spirit. Indian air surrounds us and original thoughts of kindred spirits. And oh how thoroughly is the mind here washed clean of all early engrafted Jewish superstitions and of all philosophy that cringes before those superstitions! In the whole world there is no study, except that of the originals, so beneficial and so elevating as that of the *Oupnekhat*. It has been the solace of my life, it will be the solace of my death!'[1]

Duperron's Persian Latin is, as Max Müller himself says, 'fearful jargon', and Schopenhauer's words savour of exaggeration. The *Upanishads* certainly do not 'display a firm, definite and, throughout, harmonious meaning'. They are not a philosophy but its rudiments. They are incoherent and self-contradictory. Yet when all deductions are made, Schopenhauer's oft-quoted words are full of significance. And his praise has been echoed by the two scholars who have done most in the West for the study of the *Upanishads*, Max Müller and Deussen. Thus Max Müller writes: 'For fitting men to lead contemplative and quiet lives, I know no better preparation than the Vedānta.'[2] And Deussen couples the *Upanishads* with the New Testament as the 'two noblest products of the religious consciousness of mankind', and holds that the characteristic doctrine of the *Upanishads* is necessary 'to put the finishing touch on the Christian consciousness and make it, on all sides, consistent and complete'.[3]

[1] *S. B. E.*, vol. i, p. lxi. [2] *Six Systems of Indian Philosophy*, p. 193.

[3] Deussen, *Philosophy of the Upanishads*, Eng. trans., pp. 49, 50. Deussen writes from the standpoint of one to whom Schopenhauer's philosophy is 'the purest form of Christianity' (*op. cit.*, p. 140). His metaphysic has thus much in common with the Vedānta, but few would accept as Christian his interpretation of Christianity.

The praise of Western scholars is of importance, as to it is undoubtedly due much of the patriotic pride that educated Indians feel in these ancient works. But such praise is somewhat academic. To Western scholars the *Upanishads* are an intellectual interest but not a religion. In India, on the other hand, and especially in the last century, many have found in the *Upanishads* their favourite study and their most sacred scripture, and to the revived interest in these writings much of what is known as the 'Higher Hinduism' is due.[1] Thus Rām Mohan Rai avowedly based his great work of reform, not on the *Ṛigveda*, but on the *Upanishads*, and saw in them not Pantheism but the purest Theism. And a man of immeasurably less spiritual genius, Svāmī Vivekānanda, the often-quoted protagonist of modern Vedāntism, writes in his exuberant way, 'This Vedānta, the philosophy of the *Upanishads*, I would make bold to state, has been the first as well as the final thought which on the spiritual plane has been vouchsafed to man.'

For the study of philosophy or religion these writings are of great historic value. To the student of Hinduism, they are of the first importance. Here in chaotic form is the essential Hinduism in which many of the noblest in India have found the explanation of life's mysteries and the solace of life's troubles.

'The study of each single religion', says Harnack, 'must never be separated from the general history of the people concerned.'[2] In the case of Hinduism, the warning is one hard to observe. The chronology of the literature is uncertain and the historical data meagre. The older *Upanishads* are generally held to date from before the time of Gautama, the Buddha, but the younger *Upanishads* are clearly later, and in

[1] Rabindranath Tagore tells us that he was 'brought up in a family where texts of the *Upanishads* were used in daily worship' (*Sādhanā*, p. vii).

[2] *Reden und Aufsätze*, ii. 167.

the elucidation of the period the Buddhist books are of considerable value.[1]

The *Upanishads* have come down to us through Brāhman editors. The tradition was oral, and inevitably the Brāhman standpoint has been dominant. But in the *Upanishads*, as in the Buddhist *Suttas*, there is clear evidence that the interest in philosophy and religion was by no means confined to the Brāhman caste. Kings invite the famous teachers of the time to their court to discuss the deepest problems. Wise men wander up and down the country eager to debate. There is something of the avidity for philosophical discussion that we associate with the age of Socrates and the Athenian supremacy. It is true that some of the discussions in the *Upanishads* are between gods and men, and so clearly mythical. Yet there seems no reason on that account to doubt the actual occurrence of the great debates convened by the princes of the time and engaged in by wandering seers. And it is significant that even in these Brāhmanically edited *Upanishads*, it is often men of the warrior caste (Kshatriyas) who are leaders in the quest for truth. The *Atharvaveda* and the *Brāhmaṇas* witness to the extraordinary degradation of the Brāhmanic religion. Many of the Brāhmans were thaumaturgists, sorcerers, but in no sense religious teachers. So in the *Sīlas*, one of the earliest Buddhist documents, reference is made to Brāhmans who, while living on food provided by the faithful, are 'tricksters, droners out of holy words for pay, diviners, exorcists, ever hungering to add gain to gain'.[2] In the *Śatapatha Brāhmaṇa*, a Brāhman can find no more contemptuous epithet for the words of an opponent than to say that they are 'like the words of a Kshatriya'.[3] But in the *Upanishads*, to Kshatriyas are assigned some of the most important passages. Thus the leading text on the doctrine of transmigration is definitely stated to be teaching given to

[1] Cp. Rhys Davids's *Buddhist India*, a fascinating attempt to read the history of the period from other than Brāhman sources.

[2] See Rhys Davids's *Buddhist India*, p. 215.

[3] *Śat. Br.* viii. 1. 4. 10.

a Brāhman by a king. And the king adds: 'This knowledge did not go to any Brāhman before you, and therefore this teaching belonged in all the world to the Kshatriya class alone.'[1] So the great doctrine of the identity of the self with the Brahman is not known to the learned Brāhman, Bālāki, who after vain attempts to explain the Brahman has to ask the king to take him as a pupil.[2] When the great Brāhman sage, Yājñavalkya, gives his doctrine of the self, the Ātman, he is mocked at by the Brāhman teachers. It is the Kshatriya king, Janaka, who upholds his doctrine and rewards him richly.[3]

Whatever be the derivation of the word *Upanishad*, its meaning is undoubtedly 'the mysterious', 'the esoteric'. In the *Brāhmaṇas*, as we have seen, the great equation had already been reached: Ātman = Brahman; the psychic principle is identical with the cosmic. But this equation was there only the occasional philosopheme of an obscure priestly speculation. It is only in the *Upanishads* that the equation becomes a great doctrine of religion. It is possible that it was in Kshatriya circles that the doctrines of transmigration and of redemption through unity with Brahman were first regularly taught, and that later these doctrines were communicated to the Brāhmans as mysteries, and hence the writings embodying them are called *Upanishads*.

The *Upanishads* are not philosophic sources in our sense of the word. They are in no way systematic or self-consistent. For the systematic exposition of the Vedānta it will be necessary to turn to Bādarāyaṇa's *Sūtras*, where the doctrines of the Vedānta are expressed in 555 aphorisms of extraordinary conciseness. These, with Śaṅkara's comments, form the authoritative dogmatic of the most influential school of the Vedānta. But in the *Upanishads*, poetry, religion, ritual, and

[1] *Chhānd. Up.* v. 3. 7. [2] *Kaush. Up.* iv. 19.
[3] See the dialogues of the *Bṛih. Up.*

philosophy are inextricably confused. To speak, then, of the system of the *Upanishads* is to misrepresent them. Yet with many variations and irreconcilable differences, there stand out clearly in the *Upanishads* the two great doctrines of the unity of the self with Brahman (*brahma-ātma-aikyaṁ*) and of transmigration (*saṁsāra*). The relation of these two great doctrines is still obscure. There is a sombreness in the Upanishadic thought strange to the *Ṛigveda*. There life is a blessing and death abhorred. Here existence is a delusion and a misery. There men hope, when death at length comes, to enjoy in the next world glad commerce with the gods. Here redemption is sought through the realization of the identity of the individual soul with the cosmic and attributeless Brahman. To explain these strange contrasts, many have thought that we must explain this cheerless doctrine of redemption by a prior belief in transmigration. Genetically this seems impossible. The Brahman-Ātman doctrine is the legitimate development of speculation which goes back to the later hymns of the *Ṛigveda*, and, as we have seen, is already found in the *Brāhmaṇas*. The doctrine of transmigration, on the other hand, is first found in the *Upanishads*, and so, if we may rely on our literary records, is thus clearly the later. Yet it may well be that it was the belief in transmigration which deepened the sense of human misery and made poignant the cry to be delivered from the bondage of the weary round of birth and death. If so, then it would be possible to ascribe to this belief in cyclic recompense, the transformation of the doctrine of the identity of the Self with the Brahman from an obscure and occasional speculation into a great message of redemption which to many souls has brought the comfort of a quiet heart. However it may have been at first, from the time of the *Upanishads* on, the supreme object of philosophy in India has been to provide a means of redemption from the flux of births. The logical *prius* of all speculation has been this doctrine of *karma*. On this account, it will be convenient to deal first with this doctrine of transmigration, and then to pass on from it to the doctrine of the identity of the Ātman with the Brahman as the means of liberation from the miserable round of birth and death.

The Doctrine of Transmigration.

The Upanishadic texts seek to trace back to Ṛigvedic times the doctrine of transmigration, but they do so only by strained and fantastic exegesis. The whole conception of transmigration is in fact alien to the genial hearty piety of the *Ṛigveda*, which has a keen appreciation of the good things of this life and a happy expectation that, for those who propitiate the gods, these good things will be in the next world continued and increased. The origin of the doctrine is still quite obscure. The belief that animals and plants have souls, not unlike the souls of men, and that a human soul may take possession of a tree or animal, is very widespread among peoples at a low stage of culture,[1] and it is probable, as Gough suggests,[2] that such a view was held by the indigenes of India, with whom more and more the Āryan invaders intermingled. This would not in itself provide the doctrine of transmigration, but we find in the *Brāhmaṇas*[3] a growing emphasis on the principle of recompense, and it is possible that the indigenous belief in the activity, after death, of the spirits of the dead, may have helped to give to this recognition of retribution the special form which it takes in the doctrine of transmigration.

It is possible that the oldest reference to the doctrine occurs in the *Bṛihadāraṇyaka Upanishad* (iii. 2), as part of the teaching of the Brāhman sage, Yājñavalkya. He had claimed the rich prize offered by King Janaka to the most learned Brāhman. The other Brāhmans challenge his claim. One of them, Ārtabhāga, questions him as to the nature of the bondage of the soul. Yājñavalkya in obscure language replies

[1] Cp. Bertholet's interesting little book on *Seelenwanderung*.
[2] *The Philosophy of the Upanishads*, p. 25.
[3] *Śat. Br.* xii. 9. 1. 1, xi. 2. 7. 33.

that the soul is in bondage as long as it ascribes reality to the organs of sense. Thus the sage may conquer death and release himself from the chain of wandering. When the sage dies his name remains, for 'the name is endless, the Viśvedevas are endless, and by it he gains the endless world'. Ārtabhāga asks about the man not thus released, but this Yājñavalkya will not answer in public. 'Take my hand, my friend,' he says, 'we two alone shall know of this; let this question of ours not be (discussed) in public.'

Then these two went out and argued, and what they said was work (*karma*) and what they praised was work (*karma*), viz. 'that a man becomes good by good works and bad by bad works'.[1] The truth so darkly hinted at seems to be this. At the death of the sage his organs of sense and motion pass into the original unity of Brahman. The soul, that has not thus won release, passes into some new embodiment: good, if its works have been good; bad, if its works have been bad. So a man's deeds determine the nature of his new birth on earth.

In the same *Upanishad*, Yājñavalkya explains more lucidly his teaching in metaphors which have become the commonplace of Indian thought. It is to be noted that in these it is the self which attracts to itself another body:

> 'And, as a caterpillar, after having reached the end of the blade of grass, and having made another approach (to another blade), draws itself together towards it, thus does this Self, after having thrown off this body, and dispelled all ignorance, and after making another approach (to another body), draw himself together towards it. And, as a goldsmith taking a piece of gold, turns it into another, newer, and more beautiful shape, so does this Self, after having thrown off this body and dispelled all ignorance, make unto himself another, newer, and more beautiful shape, whether it be like the Fathers or like the Gandharvas, or like the Devas or like Prajāpati, or like Brahmā or like other beings.'[2]

> 'Now as a man is like this or like that, according as he acts, and according as he behaves, so will he be:—a man of good acts will become good, a man of bad acts, bad.

[1] *Bṛih. Up.* iii. 2. 13.

[2] *Bṛih. Up.* iv. 4. 3, 4.

He becomes pure by pure deeds, bad by bad deeds. And here they say that a person consists of desires. And, as his desire, so is his will, and, as his will, so is his deed; and whatever deed he does, that will he reap.'[1]

So stated the doctrine may not command assent, but it is at least simple and consistent. But the new always tends to become subject to the old, and in a country so conservative as India it is rare indeed that any older teaching is entirely displaced. The early eschatology spoke of the world where Yama the first man presided over the joyous spirits of the dead. Men went there by 'the way of the Fathers' (*pitṛiyāna*). From it the evil were shut out; for them there was only the lower darkness. A higher path there was by which Agni bore the offerings to the gods (the *devayāna*), and by that path men also might ascend to enjoy the bliss of the gods. The principal source for the doctrine of transmigration incorporates with the simple doctrine of soul-wandering (*samsāra*) these earlier views. The passage occurs in each of the two oldest *Upanishads*.[2] Of these the account in the *Bṛihadāraṇyaka Upanishad* is more consistent and probably more ancient, and will be first considered here.

Śvetaketu, the son of Gautama, the Brāhman sage, is asked by the king five questions:

(1) 'Do you know how men when they depart from here separate from each other?

(2) Do you know how they come back to this world?

(3) Do you know how the world does never become full with the many who again and again depart thither?

(4) Do you know at the offering of which libation the waters become endowed with a human voice and rise and speak?

(5) Do you know the access to the path leading to the Devas and to the path leading to the Fathers?'[3]

And Śvetaketu, though a Brāhman student, has to confess

[1] *Op. cit.*, iv. 4. 5.

[2] The *Bṛihadāraṇyaka* and the *Chhāndogya Upanishads*. For an illuminating commentary and synopsis of the two accounts see Deussen, *Das System des Vedānta*, pp. 390–5.

[3] *Op. cit.*, vi. 2.

that he cannot answer any of these questions. He goes to his father, but he too cannot answer. So these two, though Brāhmans, go to the Kshatriya king and become his pupils. And the king, to reward their humility, imparts to them the knowledge which 'has before now never dwelt with any Brāhman'.[1]

The passage consists of two parts:

The doctrine of the five fires,

The doctrine of the two ways.

The doctrine of the five fires is clothed in language of the greatest obscurity. In countries where the dead are buried it is natural to think of the dead as hidden in the ground, like the seed, one day to spring up again in newness of life. But in India, where cremation is the rule, the burning of the dead is naturally thought of as a sacrifice. It is Agni, the god of the sacrificial fire, that carries the oblations to the gods.

At the burning of the body, the faith (śraddhā) of the dead man passes upwards and is five times offered in sacrifice to the gods. In these five sacrifices is depicted the descent of the soul to be re-born. Faith regarded thus as the immortal part of man passes up to King Soma. From Soma it passes into rain. From rain, through the fertilization of the ground, arises food. From food comes seed. From seed offered on the altar of the woman is formed the embryo from which in due time appears the man. Then, when this man dies once more, the cycle of ascent and descent is begun. This passage has perplexed Indian as well as European commentators. As Max Müller says somewhat quaintly in a comment on the passage as it occurs in the *Chhāndogya Upanishad*:

'The great difficulty or danger in the round of transmigration arises when the rain has fructified the earth and passes into herbs and trees, rice, corn, and beans. For, first of all, some of the rain does not fructify at once but falls into rivers and into the sea to be swallowed up by fishes and sea monsters. . . . Even if the rain be absorbed by rice, corn, &c.,

[1] vi. 2. 8.

and this be eaten, it may be eaten by children, or by men who have renounced marriage, and thus again lose the chance of a new birth.' [1]

Combined with this obscure doctrine of the five fires is the famous doctrine of the two paths.

The way of the Gods.

'Those who thus know this (the doctrine of the five fires), and those who in the forest worship faith and the true, go to light, from light to day, from day to the increasing half, from the increasing half to the six months, when the sun goes to the north, from those six months, to the world of the Devas (gods), from the world of the Devas to the sun, from the sun to the place of lightning. When they have thus reached the place of lightning, a spirit comes near them and leads them to the worlds of Brahman. In these worlds of Brahman they dwell, exalted for ages. There is no returning for them.' [2]

The way of the Fathers.

'But they who conquer the worlds by means of sacrifice, charity and austerity go to smoke, from smoke to night, from night to the decreasing half of the moon, from the decreasing half of the moon to the six months when the sun goes to the south, from these months to the world of the Fathers, from the world of the Fathers to the moon. Having reached the moon, they become food, and then the Devas feed on them there, as sacrificers feed on Soma as it increases and decreases. But when this (the result of their good works on earth) ceases, they return again to that ether, from ether to the air, from the air to rain, from rain to the earth. And when they have reached the earth, they become food, they are offered again in the altar fire, which is man, and thence are born in the fire of woman. Thus they rise up towards the worlds and go the same rounds as before.'

In the *Bṛihadāraṇyaka Upanishad* there is yet a third path. 'Those, however, who know neither of these two paths, become worms, birds, and creeping things.' [3] This account of transmigration is fairly simple. The wise pass up to the world of Brahman from which there is no return. The good ascend by the way of the Fathers to the moon, and then, after enjoying the fruit of their good works, are born again on earth. The ignorant and careless, after death, are born again as the lowest animals.

In the *Chhāndogya Upanishad* a confusing addition is made,

[1] *S. B. E.* i. 83. [2] *Bṛih. Up.* vi. 2. 15. [3] *Bṛih. Up.* vi. 2. 16.

which has, however, become an integral part of later Indian thought. A moral differentiation is made amongst those who journey along the way of the Fathers. 'Those whose conduct has been good, will quickly attain some good birth, the birth of a Brāhman or a Kshatriya or a Vaiśya. But those whose conduct has been evil, will quickly attain an evil birth, the birth of a dog or a hog or a Chaṇḍāla[1]'[2]. As retribution is thus introduced into the path of the fathers, there is no need for the third way mentioned in the *Bṛihadāraṇyaka Upanishad*, but this too is retained at the sacrifice of any consistency.

Such is the classic text for the doctrine of transmigration. Later, to the wicked before they are re-born on earth, are assigned terrifying hells, and there is thus a double retribution, in the world beyond and in a miserable re-birth on earth.[3] An endeavour is made, even in the *Upanishads*, to reconcile the inconsistencies of the great passage; and in the *Kaushītaki Upanishad* it is stated that 'all, without exception, pass to the moon. Only afterwards do the two paths diverge.' In the bright half, the moon 'delights in the spirits of the wise'. In the dark half, 'the moon sends them on to be born again'. Verily the moon is the door of the Svarga (i.e. the heavenly world). Now if a man objects to the moon (i.e. is not satisfied with life there), the moon sets him free. But if a man does not object, then the moon sends him down as rain upon the earth. And according to his deeds, and according to his knowledge, he is born again here as a worm, or as an insect, or as a fish, or as a bird, or as a lion, or as a boar, or as a serpent, or as a tiger, or as a man, or as something else in different places.[4]

However and whensoever the doctrine of transmigration arose, its influence is decisive in all later Indian thought. As Gough says, 'The sum and substance, it may almost be said,

[1] A low caste. [2] *Chhānd. Up.* v. 10. 7.

[3] The popular Śaivite manuals are particularly ferocious. Thus the *Pālapādam*, a Tamil Śaivite handbook for the use of schools, contains the most lurid description of the future torments reserved for various sins.

[4] *Kaush. Up.* i. 2.

of Indian philosophy is, from first to last, the misery of metempsychosis and the mode of extrication from it.' Not to remember this, is to 'lose the way in what will then seem a pathless jungle of abstractions'.[1] The doctrine has been praised by such Western writers as Goethe and Schopenhauer,[2] but to it the sombreness of Indian thought seems chiefly due. Within the limits of the *Upanishads* there are indeed few explicit references to the misery of the life caught in the ceaseless cycle of death and birth. And its authors are saved from pessimism by the joy they feel at the message of redemption they proclaim. Yet the futility of life seems everywhere quietly to be assumed. Men find in the world not happiness but ennui.

And in the later *Upanishads* the gloom deepens. Thus in the *Maitrāyaṇa Upanishad*[3] we have the following narrative. The king Bṛihadratha puts his son upon the throne and himself retires into the forest for meditation and penance. There he stands with uplifted arms looking up to the sun. At length a holy seer comes up to him and bids him choose a boon. The king answers, 'O saint, I know not the Self; thou knowest the essence (of the Self). We have heard so. Teach it us.' The sage replies, 'What thou askest is difficult to obtain. Choose other pleasures.' But the king, touching the saint's feet with his head, thus replies: 'O saint, what is the use of the enjoyment of pleasures in this offensive, pithless body—a mere mass of bones, skin, sinews, marrow, flesh, seed, blood, mucus, tears, phlegm, ordure, water, bile, and slime. What is the use of the enjoyment of pleasures in this body which is assailed by lust, hatred, greed, delusion, fear, anguish, jealousy, separation from what is loved, union with what is not loved, hunger, thirst, old age, death, illness, grief, and other evils.' Insects, herbs and trees, grow and decay. Mighty kings and

[1] *Philosophy of the Upanishads*, pp. 20, 21.

[2] Vide Bertholet, *Seelenwanderung*, pp. 47–53, and, for a fuller statement of the influence of the doctrine in the West, Gennrich, *Die Lehre von der Wiedergeburt*, pp. 305–48.

[3] An *Upanishad* held to be later than the *Bhagavadgītā*.

warriors disappear. Oceans dry up, mountains fall, the pole star is unstable, the earth submerges. 'In such a world as this what is the use of the enjoyment of pleasures if he who has fed on them is seen to return (to this world) again and again. Deign therefore to take me out. In this world I am like a frog in a dry well, O saint, thou art my way, thou art my way.'[1]

Emancipation.

This piteous cry for deliverance from the weary round of birth and death finds in the *Upanishads* its answer. From first to last, there comes the promise of redemption from the bondage of the seen and the temporal, and it is this which gives these works, in spite of so much that is uncouth and obscure, their permanent and priceless value. As we have seen, in the *Śatapatha Brāhmaṇa* there is already the great surmise that the Ātman and the Brahman are one. The self in man is one with the great self of the universe, and this in turn is identical with Brahman, the cosmic principle. In the *Upanishads* this equation ceases to be the recondite speculation of priestly pedants and becomes a message of redemption which to many has brought satisfaction and peace of soul. What is probably the oldest teaching of the doctrine in the *Upanishads* is assigned to the great Brāhman sage, Yājñavalkya, and it is the king Janaka whom he instructs. Janaka has already learnt the *Vedas* and been told the *Upanishads*, but he knows not whither he will go at death. Yājñavalkya promises to explain. 'The gods', he says, 'love what is mysterious and dislike what is evident.' So he first describes the Ātman in obscure physical terms. At length there comes the famous statement: 'And he (the Ātman) can only be described as No, no. He is incomprehensible, for he

[1] *Mait. Up.* i. 2–4. As Dr. Griswold says: 'A kind of pessimism has ever marked the attitude of the choicest spirits towards the world'; but whereas 'the pessimism of the Hebrew prophets is ethical, based on their theory of duty, the pessimism of the Hindu sages is speculative, and is the consequence of their theory of being'. *Brahman*, p. 64.

cannot be comprehended; he is undecaying, for he cannot decay; he is not attached, for he does not attach himself; he is unbound, he does not suffer, he does not perish. O Janaka, you have indeed reached fearlessness.'[1] In the following dialogue, Yājñavalkya proclaims that the man of full desires obtains the result of his deeds and returns again to the world of action. 'But as for the man who does not desire, who, not desiring, freed from desire, is satisfied in his desires, or desires the Self only, his vital spirits do not depart elsewhere—being Brahman, he goes to Brahman. On this there is the verse: "When all desires which once entered his heart are undone, then does the mortal become immortal, then he obtains Brahman. And as the slough of a snake lies on an ant-hill, dead and cast away, thus lies this body, but that disembodied immortal spirit is Brahman only, is only light".'[2]

Men crave this knowledge, not out of speculative curiosity, but in order to be redeemed from misery. 'Sir,' says one who knew the Sacred Books but not the Self, 'I have heard from men like you that he who knows the Self overcomes grief. I am in grief, do, Sir, help me over this grief of mine.'[3] And the sage at length gives answer: 'We must desire to understand what bliss is. The infinite is bliss. The infinite is the I, the Self. The Self is below, is above, is behind, before, right and left. The Self is all this. He who sees this, does not see death, nor illness, nor pain; he who sees this, sees everything and obtains everything everywhere.'[4]

So salvation is won, not by action nor good deeds, but by intuitive knowledge. 'And, as here on earth, whatever has been acquired by exertion, perishes, so perishes whatever is acquired for the next world by sacrifices and other good actions performed on earth. Those who depart from hence without having discovered the Self and those true desires, for them there is no freedom in all the worlds. But those who depart from hence, after having discovered the Self and

[1] *Brih. Up.* iv. 2.
[2] *Brih. Up.* iv. 4. 6, 7.
[3] *Chhānd. Up.* vii. 1. 3.
[4] *Op. cit.*, vii. 22-6.

those true desires, for them, there is freedom in all the worlds.'[1]

Apart from this knowledge of the Self, all life is vanity. Thus in a speech assigned to Yama, the ruler of the dead, it is said: 'Fools dwelling in darkness, wise in their own conceit and puffed up with vain knowledge, go round and round staggering to and fro like blind men led by the blind. The hereafter never rises before the eye of the careless child deluded by the delusion of wealth. "This is the world," he thinks, "there is no other";—thus he falls again and again under my sway.'[2] Only the Self has value. The Ātman, the Brahman, is the one reality. 'All this is Brahman.'[3] 'In the beginning there was that only which is (τὸ ὄν), one only, without a second.'[4] 'That which is the subtle essence in all that exists, has its Self. It is the true. It is the Self and thou art it.'[5] The individual soul is identical with the solitary principle of the universe.

And in the absence of any duality, all the manifest world is an illusion. Even metempsychosis is an illusion, as unreal as the snake for which the traveller at night time mistakes the rope. All deeds, good and bad alike, belong to the illusory sphere. Only he who knows the Self has stability amid the flux of things. For such, his deeds and his self with all his knowledge become one with the highest Imperishable. 'As the flowing rivers disappear in the sea, losing their name and their form, thus a wise man, freed from name and form, goes to the divine Person who is greater than the great.'[6]

And this liberation was felt to be real and blessed. 'The wise who understand this, behold the immortal which shines forth, full of bliss. The fetter of the heart is broken, all doubts are solved, all his works (and their effects) perish, when he has been beheld who is high and low. In the highest, golden

[1] *Chhānd. Up.* viii. 1. 6.

[2] *Kaṭh. Up.* i. 2. 5, 6. In the *Muṇḍaka Up.* (i. 2. 8) the words are used of those who rely on good works and sacrifices.

[3] *Chhānd. Up.* iii. 14. 1.

[4] *Chhānd. Up.* vi. 2. 1.

[5] *Op. cit.*, vi. 14. 3.

[6] *Muṇḍ. Up.* iii. 2. 8.

sheath, there is the Brahman, without passions, and without parts. That is pure, that is the light of lights, that is it which they know who know the Self. The sun does not shine there, nor the moon and the stars, nor these lightnings and much less this fire. When he shines, everything shines after him; by his light all this is lighted. That immortal Brahman is before, that Brahman is behind, that Brahman is right and left. It has gone forth, below and above; Brahman alone is all this, it is the best.'[1]

So conceived the doctrine is the purest idealism. Brahman, Ātman, is the sole reality. Our self is identical with the great changeless and eternal Self of the world, and as such is delivered from the flux of time, and the cycle of re-birth. The sublimity of this conception has won for it a permanent place in the history of the world's thought, and to many in India it has seemed a genuine philosophy of redemption. Succeeding ages have been able to add nothing to this doctrine, for it represents in one direction the limit of human speculation. Yet it is significant that this idealism has always been unstable. And this is natural, for in this doctrine of redemption are three implicates, hard to accept, and which, from the time of the *Upanishads*, have continually been modified.

(1) This world and this world's life are unreal.
(2) God and the soul are alike unknowable.
(3) Redemption, as the intuitive realization of what already is, effects no change in a man's life, and so, in most cases, can give neither peace nor power without the added means of asceticism or ecstasy.

(1) *The world and the world's life are unreal.*

Implicit in the doctrine of redemption is the assertion of the

[1] *Muṇḍ. Up.* ii. 2. 7-11. It is perhaps necessary to re-emphasize here that there is no one doctrine capable of expressing all the various teachings of the *Upanishads.* At some sacrifice of completeness, the account given in this chapter concentrates on the doctrine of redemption in the form most influential in the subsequent development of Indian thought.

unreality of the world and of life in the world. It would seem indeed that the explicit teaching that the world is illusion (*māyā*), and God the illusion-maker (*māyin*), does not occur before the late *Śvetāśvatara Upanishad*, and many scholars have followed Colebrooke in saying, 'that the notion that the versatile world is an illusion (*māyā*) and that all that passes to the apprehension of the waking individual is but a phantasy presented to his imagination, and every seeming thing is unreal, and all is visionary, does not appear to be the doctrine of the text of the Vedānta. . . . The doctrine of the early Vedānta is complete and consistent without this graft of a later growth.'[1] Against this, Gough's essay on *The Primitive Antiquity of the Doctrine of Māyā* argues strongly.[2] The conception of Māyā is implicit in the earliest statements of the doctrine of redemption. Thus the dialogue between the sage Yājñavalkya and his wife, Maitreyī, occurs in what is generally held to be one of the earliest parts of the *Upanishads*,[3] and in it, it is clearly taught that it is only on account of the Self that anything has value. Only in so far as external objects are related to the self, do they exist. The sounds of a drum have no existence apart from the drum that is struck. Just so it is the Self alone exists. Duality is apparent only. The Self alone is all that is. The Self is to be described as *neti, neti*, not so, not so. So the only reality is the unknowable and attributeless Self. So the beautiful *Īśā Upanishad* begins with the assertion that, 'All this, whatsoever moves on earth, is to be hidden in the Lord (the self). When thou hast surrendered all this, then thou mayest enjoy.' The doctrine of *māyā* is indeed implicit in the fundamental tenet of the Vedānta, 'One only without a second.' In the *Śvetāśvatara Upanishad* the teaching becomes explicit. In opposition to the Sāṅkhya philosophy, which

[1] In his essay on the Vedānta read before a meeting of the Royal Asiatic Society in 1827. (Vide Gough, *Philosophy of the Upanishads*, p. 237.) This view is supported by Jacob in his edition of the *Vedānta-sāra*. (*A Manual of Hindu Pantheism*, p. 46.)

[2] *Op. cit.*, pp. 235–62.

[3] *Bṛih. Up.* ii. 4 and iv. 5.

postulates an eternal primordial matter (*prakṛiti*), it is asserted that this *prakṛiti* is *māyā*, illusion, and that the great Lord is the Māyin, the illusion-maker.[1]

This doctrine is so alien to thought and experience that inevitably and often unconsciously the sages retrogress from it. The idealism, which denies the existence of plurality, and regards matter as an illusion, becomes a pantheism which asserts the reality of the universe and yet holds that the Ātman alone is real; for the Ātman is the universe. So the creation of the world is assigned to the projection of the Ātman. And in violent contrast to the Vedāntic doctrine, and in conscious opposition to it, we find the Sāṅkhyan philosophy, which asserts the eternal reality of the primordial matter (*prakṛiti*) side by side with a multiplicity of spirits (*purusha*). Not only is the universe unreal but, as will be shown in detail later, our moral life is also unreal. Redemption is not unto holiness, but unto an intuitive insight to which virtue and vice are without distinction or meaning.

(2) *God and the soul are alike unknowable.*

It was said of Spinoza that he was *Gott-betrunken.* In their flight from the cycle of birth and death, these ancient thinkers also were 'intoxicated with God'. They might have made their own those words of Jacob Boehme, 'I sought only for the heart of God, therein to hide myself.' Yet the God they found was a God who could never be known. He is the self. But, because there is no distinction of subject and object, neither can be known. When one asks Yājñavalkya

[1] *Śvet. Up.* iv. 10. It should in fairness be stated 'that the word need mean no more than that he is the artificer, and the world the product of his miraculous power'. So Nicol Macnicol, *Indian Theism from the Vedic to the Muhammadan period*, p. 50. Dr. Macnicol denies that the doctrine of *māyā* is found in the *Upanishads*. For a mediating view see Thibaut, *S. B. E.* xxxiv, pp. cxvii–cxxv. Thibaut holds that although 'the Māyā doctrine cannot be said to form part of the teaching of the *Upanishads* it is not an 'addition to the system from without, but only a development from within, no graft but only growth'. *Op. cit.*, p. cxxv.

to tell him 'the Brahman who is visible, not invisible, the Self who is within all', the sage replies: 'Thou couldst not see the seer of sight, thou couldst not hear the hearer of hearing, nor perceive the perceiver of the perception, nor the knower of knowledge. This is the Self who is within all.'[1] Brahman or Ātman is the subject and not the object of thought, and so essentially unknowable. He is bliss (*ānanda*), but he is not blissful (*ānandin*). The whole conception of Brahman is in fact essentially negative. It would be truer to say of him not 'he' but 'it'. Brahman is neuter, not masculine. Only one term can describe him; he is *neti, neti,* not so, not so.

Men have never been able for long to make a God of an abstraction. And in the *Upanishads* themselves there are many traces of another view of God, not personal in the Christian sense, but at the same time not quite impersonal. Thus often the neuter Brahman gives place to the personal masculine Brahmā, whilst Ātman is hailed as the creator and upholder of the world.[2] And in a late *Upanishad*, the *Śvetāśvatara Upanishad*, there is a clear endeavour to assert the existence of individual souls and of a God who can be worshipped. Thus in the following allegory, a distinction is manifestly made between the soul and God. 'Two birds, inseparable friends, cling to the same tree. One of them eats the sweet fruit, the other looks on without eating. On the same tree, man sits grieving, immersed, bewildered, by his own impotence. But, when he sees the other lord, contented, and knows his glory, then his grief passes away.'[3] And in the same section of this *Upanishad*, *māyā*, the illusion of the world, is assigned to the creation of the Māyin, the illusion-maker. And this great Lord is identified with Rudra, the Śiva of later times.[4] But this conception of Īśvara, the personal God, is obscure and ill-developed in the *Upanishads*, and the sage soon falls back on Brahman, the first principle.

[1] *Brih. Up.* iii. 4. 2.

[2] Cp. *Die Lehre der Upanishaden und die Anfänge des Buddhismus*, H. Oldenberg, pp. 103, 104.

[3] *Śvet. Up.* 6, 7.

[4] *Śvet. Up.* iv. 10–14.

Later in Śaṅkara's exposition of the Vedānta, Īśvara is regularly proclaimed as a personal God, but unreal with the unreality of the material world, our moral struggle, and the cycle of re-birth, and it is only after the time of the earlier *Upanishads* that the craving for a personal God finds passionate expression in the *bhakti* movement, where loving faith, and not cold intuition, is regarded as the means necessary for redemption.

With justice did the Buddhist teachers attack the Vedāntists for speaking so much of a Brahman of whom they knew nothing.[1] Gautama himself opened the way to all. For him there was no *rahasyam*, no secret doctrine. The criticism of Jacob, if severe, seems true:

> 'The supreme being, Brahman, is a cold impersonality, out of relation with the world, unconscious of its own existence and of ours, and devoid of all attributes and qualities. The so-called personal God, the first manifestation of the Impersonal, turns out on examination to be a myth; there is no God apart from ourselves, no Creator, no Holy being, no Father, no Judge—no one, in a word, to adore, to love or to fear. And, as for ourselves, we are only unreal actors on the semblance of a stage.'[2]

(3) *Redemption works no change in a man's heart.*

Redemption, as conceived in the *Upanishads*, is simply the intuitive perception of what already is and eternally has been. So there is in this redemption no re-birth, no new creation.

[1] 'Then you say that not one of the Brāhmans or of their teachers or of their pupils, even up to the seventh generation, has ever seen Brahman face to face. And that even the Rishis of old, the utterers of the ancient verses which the Brāhmans to-day so carefully intone and recite precisely as they have handed down, even they, did not pretend to know, or to have seen, where or when, or whither, Brahman is. So that the Brāhmans versed in the three Vedas have forsooth said thus:—To a state of union with that which we know not, and have not seen, we can show the way, and say "This is the straight path, this is the direct way which leads him, who acts according to it, unto a state of Brahman".' *Tevijja Sutta* 14. 15, quoted by Monier-Williams, *Buddhism*, p. 94.

[2] *Vedāntasāra*, p. 129. Cp. Gwatkins' words: 'The pantheist strips his deity of all the relations of reality and worships not indeed an idol but a meaningless word which he takes for the name which is above every name' (*The Knowledge of God*, i. 82).

We can obtain no knowledge of redemption, for the intuitive knowledge is redemption. So the best emblem of this redemption is deep and dreamless sleep. 'As people who do not know the country, walk again and again over a gold treasure, that has been hidden somewhere in the earth, and do not discover it, thus do all these creatures, day after day, go into the Brahman world (i.e. they are merged in Brahman, while asleep), and yet they do not discover it because they are carried away by untruth.'[1] The knowledge of the self is itself emancipation. 'If a man understands the Self saying "I am he", what could he wish or desire that he should pine after the body? Whoever has found and understood the Self, that has entered into this patched together hiding-place (i.e. the body), he is indeed the creator, for he is the maker of every thing, his is the world, and he is the world itself.'[2]

For such, this life has no further meaning. Later a distinction is made between the man redeemed in this life, and the man redeemed at death, but according to the classic teaching of the great Upanishadic passages, immediately a man knows himself to be identified with the Ātman, he is redeemed. This redemption has thus no relation to moral change. The wise man is more than the good, for good works like bad belong to that illusory sphere from which the wise man is redeemed. Deussen regards this doctrine as 'one of the most decisive and striking expressions of eternal philosophic truth'. Yet even he has to admit that this knowledge is 'like an ice-cold breath which checks every development, and benumbs all life'.[3] One does not need to be a Christian to prefer Christ's test, 'By their fruits ye shall know them.' Hindus, taught by Christianity to associate redemption with newness of character, point somewhat anxiously to those passages which speak of the moral prerequisites of this emancipating truth. Thus these words are quoted from the popular *Kāṭhaka Upanishad*: 'But he who has not first

[1] *Chhānd. Up.* viii. 3. 2. [2] *Bṛih. Up.* iv. 4, 12 and 13.
[3] *Philosophy of the Upanishads*, pp. 361, 362.

turned away from his wickedness, who is not tranquil, and subdued, or whose mind is not at rest, he can never obtain the Self (even) by knowledge.'[1] But, in spite of an occasional reference of this kind, it is impossible to read the *Upanishads* without feeling that, at the best, ethics are only at the periphery of attention. To the wise man, the distinction of good and evil has lost its meaning. 'As water does not cling to the lotus leaf, so no evil deed clings to one who knows it (i.e. the Ātman).'[2]

Sometimes there is an almost brutal emphasis on the insignificance of evil deeds. Thus, in a dialogue in which Indra, the Vedic God, is made to teach the doctrine of the Self, Indra says, 'Know me only: that is what I deem most beneficial for man, that he should know me.' Then follows an account of his heroic deeds, of the many he has slain, and then he adds, 'He who knows me thus, by no deed of his is his life harmed, not by the murder of his mother, not by the murder of his father, not by theft, not by killing of a Brāhman. If he is going to commit a sin, the bloom does not depart from his face.'[3] And, of the man by whom the Self is desired, Yājñavalkya says, 'Then a father is not a father, a mother not a mother, the worlds not worlds, the gods not gods, the Vedas not Vedas. Then a thief is not a thief, a murderer not a murderer. He is not followed by good nor followed by evil, for he has then overcome all the sorrows of the heart.'[4] Later, as in the *Bhagavadgītā*, an attempt was made to combine with the Vedāntic teaching an emphasis on duty, but that is not the Upanishadic doctrine. Redemption is intuitive, and has in it no moral power.

From the standpoint of this doctrine men should have attained peace immediately the Self was recognized. Instead, we find that artificial means were sought to produce that synthesis of the 'I' and the 'it', which is redemption. Even in the earlier *Upanishads*, reference is often made to the virtue

[1] *Kāṭh. Up.* i. 2. 24.
[2] *Chhānd. Up.* iv. 14. 3.
[3] *Kaush. Up.* iii. 1.
[4] *Bṛih. Up.* iv. 3. 22.

of the regulated breath and the calmed organs. In the later *Upanishads*,[1] the idea of *yoga* is worked out in full, probably owing to the influence of the Sāṅkhya philosophy. The sacred syllable *om* becomes the special object of meditation. By retention of the breath, a cataleptic state is sought, in which the mind shall indeed be one with the attributeless and insentient 'It'.[2] Thus an endeavour is made to realize redemption through an absorption (*samādhi*) in which all distinctions are lost and the mind actually succeeds in being without consciousness of any object. Thus this new conception of redemption leads to a vacuity without moral meaning or intellectual content. And such is the inevitable outcome of a doctrine of redemption, based on the identity of the soul with an attributeless God. For God to be more than personal is to be less. For God to be impersonal means that God and the soul are alike lost for an abstraction.

But in spite of their chaotic form and inharmonious and defective philosophy, the *Upanishads* will always retain their value. To them the student of Hinduism must continually return. In many passages there is described, with rare power, the pathetic sense of the futility of this ever-circling life. The solution reached will be displaced, but the intense yearning after reality, after the spiritual and the eternal, will at all times win for them the honour and affection of men who love religion and the quest of the unseen. And this much seems clear. Christianity will not satisfy the best minds of India until it is clearly seen that it answers to the full the craving for redemption and does indeed redeem unto the eternal. And when at last India finds in Christianity the redemption sought for, but not attained, in the *Upanishads*, men will turn back to these writings to trace in them a foreglimpse of the glory, and an answer, however mistaken and obscure, to the call of the voice of God.

[1] Such as the *Kāṭhaka*, the *Śvetāśvatara*, and the *Maitrāyaṇa Upanishads*.

[2] Cp. the minute instructions in the *Śvet. Up.* ii.

THE WAY OF KNOWLEDGE

CHAPTER IV

THE VEDĀNTA DOCTRINE

THE *Upanishads*, as we have seen, are inchoate and self-contradictory. Only if the term is used in a vague and general sense can we speak of their philosophy. As Thibaut has well said, 'Their various lucubrations on Brahman, the world, and the human soul, do not allow themselves to be systematized simply because they were never meant to form a system.'[1] They are excursions after truth, often irreconcilable, but held in some sort of unity by the common quest of ultimate reality and redemption. And in them the religious interest is predominant. It is not disinterested knowledge which is sought, but knowledge which delivers from the curse of birth.

After the creative age of the *Upanishads* had passed away, philosophy was taught for the most part by means of the aphorisms of unparalleled concision known as the *Sūtras*. Often these were mere mnemonics, intelligible only by the help of a teacher. Thus the philosophy which claimed to be the *Vedānta*, the true and legitimate expression of the teaching of the *Upanishads*, was handed down by *Sūtras* which Bādarāyaṇa is said to have written. These *Sūtras*, together with the *Upanishads* and the *Bhagavadgītā*, form the three institutes (*prasthānas*) on which any philosophy which claims to be Vedāntic must still be based.

Most famous of all commentators on these *Sūtras* is Śaṅkarāchārya, the Thomas Aquinas of Hinduism. Śaṅkara's famous work is to-day more praised than read, but it remains as the one authoritative exposition of the dominant and most

[1] *S.B.E.* xxxiv, p. cxiv.

characteristic philosophy of India, the Vedānta,[1] and with this it will be necessary to deal in detail.

It cannot be said that Śaṅkara's teaching is in all respects identical with that of the *Sūtras* he expounds, and a very different interpretation of them is given by Rāmānuja,[2] the commentator next in influence to Śaṅkara. To Rāmānuja, Brahman is not an attributeless abstraction, but a God of grace, possessed of every perfection, who redeems men to enjoy with Him at death His own attributes of bliss. And this modified non-duality (viśishṭādvaita) of Rāmānuja is not only directly opposed to the 'non-duality' (*advaita*) of Śaṅkara, but claims itself to be the one legitimate development of the teaching, not only of the *Vedāntasūtras*, but of the *Upanishads*. It is impossible here to attempt to adjudicate such claims, and unnecessary, as Thibaut, the translator of both these commentaries, has discussed the problem with great fullness, and apparent cogency.[3] If we accept his conclusions, we shall have to recognize that there is lacking in the *Vedāntasūtras*, teaching so characteristic of Śaṅkara's commentary, as the distinctions between the higher and the lower knowledge, and between Brahman and Īśvara, and also the doctrines of the unreality of the world and the absolute identity of the individual and the highest Self. Yet Thibaut holds that Śaṅkara's teaching represents, better than the *Sūtras* themselves, the legitimate development of the dominant teaching of the *Upanishads*, and he makes the very interesting suggestion that the *Bhagavadgītā* may have been the influence which caused Bādarāyaṇa 'to lay greater stress on the personal character of the highest being than is in

[1] No less than six systems claim to be Vedāntic, but Śaṅkara's system is the most influential and is often referred to as *the* Vedānta, the Vedānta *par excellence*.

[2] Rāmānuja like Śaṅkara belonged to South India. He lived from about 1050 to 1137 A.D. His name is inseparably connected with Śrīraṅgam, near Trichinopoly, where stands to-day the greatest of Vaishṇavite temples.

[3] *S.B.E.* xxxiv, pp. xv–cxxviii.

agreement with the prevailing tendency of the *Upanishads*'.[1]

Of Rāmānuja's commentary no detailed account is here given, as the Vaishṇavite theism will be illustrated from the far earlier, more famous, and influential *Bhagavadgītā*. Śaṅkara's commentary is of the greatest interest and importance, as the perfect development of the speculation most congenial to Indian thought, and of this a textual exposition is therefore attempted.

Especially in South India, Śaṅkara's is a beloved and familiar name, and the popular tradition of his life is of value in enabling us to orientalize his position and importance in Indian religion.[2]

To an obscure village in Malabar is commonly assigned the honour of his birth. His parents, long childless, had prayed to Śiva to remove this curse. Śiva, before granting this prayer, appeared to the wife in a dream and asked her whether she would rather bear a number of fools and knaves, or one son, short-lived but wise. She chose the latter, and Śaṅkara was born. Another legend connects his birth with Chidambaram, the most sacred of all Śaivite shrines. His mother was a pious Brāhman woman whose husband had renounced the world and retired into the forest for meditation. She continued for long to serve Śiva, and at length to reward her devotion he enabled her miraculously to bear a son and that son was Śaṅkara.

It is usually believed that his birth took place in A.D. 788.

[1] *Op. cit.*, cxxvi. Sukhtankar, a modern Indian exponent of Rāmānuja's system, goes far beyond Thibaut, and not only denies that 'the fundamental doctrines' of Śaṅkara's commentary 'are manifestly in greater harmony with the essential teaching of the *Upanishads* than those of other Vedantic systems' (*op. cit.* cxxiv), but claims that Rāmānuja's system is the one true Vedānta. (*The Teaching of Vedānta according to Rāmānuja*, by V. A. Sukhtankar, pp. 12, 13, and 17.)

[2] There is an interesting account of his life by C. N. Kṛishṇasvāmī Aiyer, written from the standpoint of a devout English-educated Hindu (*Śrī Śaṅkarāchārya, His Life and Times*, Natesan & Co., Madras).

His childhood was precocious and abnormal. At length the time came for marriage. He wished to shun the duty of a householder and become at once a *sannyāsin*. His mother bemoaned the loneliness that would be hers with no daughter-in-law to tend her. At length, when they were bathing in a river, a crocodile seized him by the foot. He told his mother of his plight and begged that he might even then have her permission to become a *sannyāsin*, that so he might die in peace. She granted it and he escaped from peril. Immediately he renounced all his possessions and wandered off to find a guru to initiate him formally as a *sannyāsin*. At length he found the great teacher, Gövinda, whom he served as pupil. Subsequently we hear of him in Benares, by now famous and sought after. According to tradition, he composed there not only works of philosophy but hymns of devotion to the gods. He left Benares and began a triumphal tour through India. At that time North India was free of Buddhists through the zeal of Kumārila-Bhaṭṭa, the great Hindu teacher of the way of works (*karma mīmāṁsā*). But Kumārila had committed two sins. Through him, his Guru, a Buddhist, had been killed, and in his defence of the Veda and the Vedic rites he had practically denied God. To expiate these sins he had himself burnt at the stake. Śaṅkara, eager to dispute with him, hastened to the spot, but found the fire already lit. Śaṅkara none the less wished to argue with him, but 'as he had already become half-burnt, he could not collect his thoughts'. He therefore referred Śaṅkara to Maṇḍana, another great teacher of the way of works. Śaṅkara goes to Maṇḍana and engages in a great controversy with him, with Maṇḍana's wife as umpire. Each promised, if he was defeated, to take the condition of the other. Śaṅkara would become a householder—the worst sin a *sannyāsin* could commit—Maṇḍana would take from his wife's hand the saffron robe of the ascetic. Śaṅkara was declared victor and he then debated with the umpire, Maṇḍana's wife. She found that only in the science of love was Śaṅkara ignorant. To acquire this Śaṅkara used his yogic powers, and thus enabled his spirit to enter into the body of a king who had just died. Taking the king's place he then enjoyed, and narrated in a poem still extant, his dalliance with the queens.

For long, Śaṅkara laboured to revive Hinduism. To help in this work he founded monasteries (*maṭha*), some of which are still famous and wealthy. At length his mother drew near to death. He tried to teach her his philosophy, but she could not understand. So he composed instead a hymn to Śiva. Śiva's messengers appeared, but his mother, frightened at their terrible forms, refused to go with them to Śiva's world. Then Śaṅkara sang in praise of Vishṇu. His messengers came, bright and gracious, and Śaṅkara's mother went gladly with them to Vishṇu's abode. His relatives protested at him, a *sannyāsin*, performing funeral rites. Alone he had to cremate her, cutting up the body as it was too heavy to move. For this he cursed the Nambūtiri Brāhmans, and secured that as he had done so they must do.[1]

After this we find him labouring with great zeal to put down the grosser manifestations of the worship of female deities (śakti-worship) and to unite all the sects of Hinduism in the recognition of the supreme Brahman of which the gods are the illusory phenomena. He died young, worn out by his toil, some say in his thirty-second, others in his thirty-eighth year.

Legendary as much of this tradition clearly is, it is of interest as showing the esteem with which he is still regarded. To the Hindu, Śaṅkarāchārya is not only the philosopher meditating on the infinite, he is the Yogin and the miracle-worker, the singer of hymns of love to the gods, and above all the supreme protagonist of Hinduism.

It is with Śaṅkara rather than with Bādarāyaṇa that we have here to deal. As we have seen, it cannot be claimed

[1] It is still customary for Nambūtiris to cremate their dead in their own compound, and they are said, before doing so, to touch with a knife the joints of the corpse.

that Śaṅkara's commentary is always in accord with the intention of the *Sūtras*. But it is Śaṅkara's exposition as it stands that is the authoritative expression of classic Vedāntism; and so, for the purposes of this essay, it will suffice to treat the commentary and the *Sūtras* as a whole.

In his method of teaching, Śaṅkara is essentially scholastic.[1] It is by appeal to authority that truth is found. As Scripture (*śruti*) he quotes especially the Upanishads. As Tradition (*smṛiti*) he recognizes the Sāṅkhya and Yoga systems, the *Māhābharata*, especially in its most famous episode, the *Bhagavadgītā*, and the *Law Book of Manu*. But the quotations from the *Upanishads* far outnumber all others.[2] Śaṅkara's work is indeed a sincere endeavour to give the teaching of the *Upanishads* greater unity and coherence. He recognizes their manifest antinomies but seeks to solve these by postulating a twofold knowledge, a higher and a lower (*parā vīdyā* and *aparā vidyā*), or, as he elsewhere puts it, a knowledge (*vidyā*) and a nescience (*avidyā*).

It is with this distinction that he begins his work. The metaphysical reality is the Self which, as subject and not object, is necessarily unknowable. The phenomenal world—the not I—is knowable but unreal. And Śaṅkara recognizes that this distinction does not come easily to the untutored mind. 'It is on the part of man', he says, 'a natural procedure, which has its cause in wrong knowledge, not to distinguish between the two entities.' Yet this confusion is the source of all our evil. It is the object of philosophy to remove this delusion and give to the self the sense of its unity with the infinite and alone real Brahman. So the study of the *Vedānta* has a practical end, and the introduction concludes: 'With a view to freeing one's self from that wrong

[1] The account of Śaṅkara's teaching given in this chapter owes much to Deussen's luminous exposition (*Das System des Vedānta*). *Sūtras* are in italics. Passages marked as quotations are given verbally from Thibaut's translation.

[2] Deussen (*op. cit.*, p. 32) calculates that of the 2,523 quotations in the commentary, 2,060 are from the *Upanishads*.

notion, which is the cause of all evil, and attaining thereby the knowledge of the absolute unity of the Self, the study of the Vedānta text is begun.' If Śaṅkara in his commentary had kept this distinction between exoteric and esoteric knowledge clearly marked, the exposition of his philosophy would be simple. Instead the two spheres are inextricably confused, and it is difficult in a short space to give an exposition, textual and adequate, yet clear.

Śaṅkara's work is in four parts (*adhyāya*). His order of treatment is not consistent, but for the most part he deals with his subject in the convenient order of Theology, Cosmology, Psychology, Metempsychosis, and Redemption.

Theology.

The first *Sūtra* of all runs: '*Then therefore the inquiry into Brahman.*' Śaṅkara first denies the view that the word 'then' indicates that 'the inquiry into Brahman presupposes as its antecedent, the understanding of the acts of religious duty'. Theology is one thing, Religion and Ethics another. 'The knowledge of active religious duty has for its fruit transitory felicity, and that again depends on the performance of religious acts. The inquiry into Brahman, on the other hand, has for its fruit eternal bliss, and does not depend on the performance of any acts.' An inquiry is necessary because 'there are many various opinions, basing part of them on sound arguments, and scriptural texts misunderstood. If therefore a man would embrace some one of these opinions without previous considerations, he would bar himself from the highest beatitude and incur grievous loss. For this reason, the first *Sūtra* proposes under the designation of an inquiry into Brahman, a disquisition of the Vedānta texts.' Śaṅkara then proceeds to discuss at length the various names ascribed to Brahman in the *Upanishads* and explains away whatever is contradictory to his doctrine. Amid the intricacies of his polemics his own teaching is repeatedly affirmed.

Brahman is Being (*sat*) and this Being is original. Thus

a later *Sūtra* runs: '*But there is no origin of that which is* (i.e. *of Brahman*) *on account of the impossibility* (*of such an origin*).'[1] Śaṅkara thus refutes any possible origin to Brahman. Brahman as mere being cannot spring from mere being, as wherever there is the relation of cause and effect there is a certain superiority in the cause. And it would clearly be against experience for Brahman to spring from something less general. Nor again can Brahman spring from not-being (*asat*), for not-being has no self, and besides, this is against Scripture. Nor again does the fact of the effects springing from effects imply that Brahman also would be an effect; for the non-admission of a fundamental causal substance would drive us to a retrogressus *in infinitum*. And that fundamental causal substance which, as a matter of fact, is generally acknowledged to exist, just that is our Brahman. This attribute of Brahman is thus purely negative. With it is combined the two attributes of intelligence and bliss.

Brahman is intelligence (*chit*). This Śaṅkara defends at length against the objections of the Sāṅkhyan Philosophy.[2] Yet this attribute too is negative. Brahman is not the knower but the knowing, not the cognizer but the cognition. Brahman could not from Śaṅkara's standpoint be cognitive for that would involve objects of cognition and so duality. Brahman is cognition in that, like the Self, he is spiritual in his nature.

Brahman is bliss (*ānanda*), but it is a bliss whose nearest human analogy is the bliss of deep and dreamless sleep. It is bliss 'without the fruition of happiness'.[3] It is the bliss of insensibility. Thus the famous trilogy of attributes, being, intelligence, and bliss, really leaves Brahman undefined and attributeless.[4] And it is just this that is the essence of the esoteric doctrine of Brahman. Brahman is free from all

[1] II. 3. 9. [2] *Vide* on I. 5–11. [3] See Jacob, *Vedāntasāra*, p. 5.

[4] The combined epithet *sachchidānanda* does not seem to be found in Śaṅkara's commentary (so Deussen, *op. cit.*, 228). Later it became the regular Vedāntic description of Brahman. Thus the opening words of the *Vedāntasāra* are 'to the Self, existing, intelligence, bliss'.

differences (*viśesha*), attributes (*guṇa*), limiting adjuncts (*upādhi*), or forms (*ākāra*). Śaṅkara indeed recognizes that, in Scripture, Brahman is very often differently described. Thus Brahman is spoken of as the object of man's worship and devotion. All such expressions, Śaṅkara teaches, must be assigned to the lower knowledge alone. Thus on the *Sūtra*, III. 2. 16, '*And (Scripture) declares (Brahman) to consist of that* (i.e. *intelligence*),' he writes: 'Scripture declares that Brahman consists of intelligence and is devoid of any other characteristic and is altogether without difference. Simple, non-differentiated, intelligence constitutes its nature just as a lump of salt has inside, as well as outside, one and the same saltish taste and no other taste.' In his comment on the following *Sūtra*, Saṅkara quotes a story full of interest. After pointing out that Scripture describes Brahman as *neti, neti*, 'not so', 'not so', he goes on to narrate how Bāhva answered a pupil who desired to learn the nature of Brahman. 'Learn Brahman, O friend,' replied Bāhva, and became silent. A second and a third time the pupil asked him to explain what Brahman was. At last he answered, 'I am teaching you but you do not understand. Silent is that self.' In that one sentence the difference between the Vedāntic and the Christian conception of God is well summed up. Our God is a God who seeks to be revealed. The only real Brahman is a God whose revelation is silence.

Neither by word nor deed can Brahman be revealed. Only in one way can it be known by men. 'At the time of perfect conciliation, the Yogins see the unevolved self free from all plurality.' In such ecstasy the difference between Brahman and the Soul passes away. They are not two but one. The soul is Brahman, only differentiated by our description of it, just as we speak of the coils and hood of a snake in distinction from the snake itself with which they are really one.

Cosmology.

It is not easy to relate this attributeless Brahman to the

world and its creation. Christianity, teaching that God is in essence Holy Love, can see in that love the motive of the creation. God is the antetypal Father,[1] and our human desire to have children to love and cherish is derived from that Divine Love which created a world, in which men might live who would know God as Father, and answer His love with love. But Brahman has neither desire nor love. How then should the world ever have been created? On this there are two *Sūtras*: '(*Brahman is*) *not* (*the creator of the world*) *on account of* (*being engaged in any action*) *having a motive.*'[2] '*But* (*Brahman's activity*) *is mere sport such as we see in ordinary life.*'[3] On this Śaṅkara writes: 'The word "but" discards the objections raised. We see in everyday life that certain doings of princes and other men, who have no unfulfilled desires left, have no reference to any extraneous purpose but proceed from mere sportfulness, as, for instance, their recreations in places of amusement. We further see that the process of inhalation and exhalation is going on without reference to any extraneous purpose, merely following the law of its own nature. Analogously the activity of the Lord may be supposed to be mere sport proceeding from its own nature without reference to any purpose.' Against the objection that the Lord might as well have remained at rest as created a world useless to himself and the cause of pain, Śaṅkara can only say that his nature cannot be questioned, for in consequence of his conjunction with Māyā (delusive ignorance) the creation is unavoidable. Thus the creation of the world lacks an ethical basis. It is a mere sport like the illusions of a conjurer (*māyin*).

Yet Śaṅkara is not without a theodicy. But this theodicy belongs only to the lower (and unreal) knowledge. According to this, the problem of human misery is solved by transmigration. So we have the *Sūtra*: '*Inequality* (*of dispensation*) *and*

[1] Cp. Ephesians iii. 15 R.V. marg., 'The Father from whom every fatherhood is named'.

[2] II. 1. 32.

[3] II. 1. 33.

cruelty (*the Lord can*) *not* (*be reproached with*), *on account of his regarding* (*merit and demerit*) ; *for so* (*Scripture*) *declares.*'[1] On this Śaṅkara comments: 'If the Lord on his own account, without any extraneous regards, produced this unequal creation, he would expose himself to blame, but, the fact is, he is bound by certain regards, i.e. he has to look to merit and demerit. Hence the circumstances of the creation being unequal, is due to the merit and demerit of the living creatures created, and is not a fault for which the Lord is to blame.' To the objection that previous to creation there would be no distinction of merit and demerit, the following *Sūtra* makes the answer that the world is without a beginning.[2] Hence the phenomenal world with its cycles of wandering souls is unoriginated, and so to speak of the world's creation is really from Śaṅkara's standpoint erroneous.

The world's efficient and material cause is Brahman. Brahman works without any agents, just as a spider emits out from itself the threads of its web, or as a female crane conceives without a male, or as the lotus wanders from one pond to another without any means of conveyance.[3] In accordance with Indian tradition, Śaṅkara thinks, not of a world once created, but of a world without beginning, periodically proceeding out of, and returning to, Brahman. Of this periodic emanation of the world from Brahman, Śaṅkara speaks in language borrowed from the *Upanishads.* Thus in a well-known passage of the *Taittirīya Upanishad*,[4] plants, animals, and men are said to have sprung from the Ātman through the five elements, ether, wind, fire, water, and earth. These Śaṅkara discusses at length and confutes, especially the doctrine, based on many passages of Scripture, that the ether (*ākāśa*) is eternal.[5] The ether is said to be eternal only in the sense that the gods are called eternal. So too, ether, fire, water, and earth are derivative. At the end of each age (*kalpa*) the elements retract into Brahman in the reverse order from that in which they originated; so that the earth turns to

[1] II. 1. 34. [2] II. 1. 35. [3] II. 1. 25. [4] *Taitt. Up.* II. 1. [5] II. 3. 1–7.

water, water to fire, fire to air, air to ether, and ether to Brahman.[1]

From the exoteric standpoint some sort of reality is thus ascribed to the world. So Śaṅkara ridicules the Buddhist doctrine of the absolute unreality of the phenomenal. Every act of perception makes us conscious of some corresponding external thing. Why then should we listen to a man who, while conscious through his senses of external things, yet affirms that he has no such consciousness of outward things and that no such things exist, 'any more than we listen to a man who while he is eating, or experiencing the feeling of satisfaction, avows that he does not eat and does not feel satisfied.'[2] Yet although Śaṅkara thus refutes the nihilism of the Buddhists, to him too the world is in fact unreal. Such reality as it has, comes only through nescience. It is due to the association of Brahman with illusion (*māyā*). Thus, as he says on Sūtra II. 1. 14, it is only before true knowledge comes that phenomena are held to be real, just as it is only until we awake that the phantoms of our dreams seem real. 'As long as a person has not reached the true unity of the Self, so long it does not enter his mind that the world of effects with its means and objects of right knowledge and its results of actions is untrue; he rather, in consequence of his ignorance, looks on mere effects (such as body, offspring, wealth, &c.) as forming part of, and belonging to, his Self, forgetful of Brahman being in reality the Self of all.'

Yet we are to live in the world before knowledge comes as if the world were real. 'So long as true knowledge does not present itself there is no reason why the ordinary course of secular religious activity should not hold on undisturbed.' Here Śaṅkara uses the illustration so frequent in Vedāntic writings of a man in dreams. When he awakes from sleep, he regards the objects of his dream-perception as unreal. He knows he was not really bitten by a snake, nor was he bathing in a river, but we do not on that account consider the

[1] II. 3. 14. [2] II. 2. 28.

consciousness he had of them to be unreal likewise. Thus Brahman has no real relation with the world. It is only as he is conjoined with Nescience that we can speak of him as an omnipotent Lord. 'The Lord being a Lord, his omniscience, his omnipotence, &c., all depend on the limitation due to the adjuncts whose self is Nescience, while in reality none of these qualities belong to the Self whose true nature is cleared by right knowledge from all adjuncts whatever.'

Thus the world is only an illusion, and Brahman is related to it only in so far as Brahman is allied with Nescience and as a conjurer (*māyin*) illudes.

Psychology.

The cleft between the higher and lower knowledge is particularly great in the portions of Śaṅkara's commentary dealing with Psychology. Esoterically each soul is the whole and undivided Brahman. Exoterically there is a multiplicity of souls bound in an eternal transmigration, yet emanating from Brahman. To the individual soul, as known by Nescience, belongs the gross body. This leaves it at death. But after death, and through all its wandering, there cleaves to it a subtle body to which belong the vital organs of conscious and unconscious life. With this is joined a variable element formed by the surplus of good and evil deeds. This it is which determines what sort of birth the next shall be.

Śaṅkara's teaching on the soul is given in considerable detail in a long section of the second book.[1] This we shall chiefly follow here. The fact of transmigration proves that the 'individual soul has no beginning and is not subject to dissolution'.[2] Its nature is spiritual, for it is not a product, but is nothing else than the highest Brahman. If it be argued that the essence of the soul cannot be intelligence, Śaṅkara replies that the absence of 'actual intelligizing is due to the absence of objects, not to the absence of intelligence. Eternal intelligence is the essential nature of the soul.'[3] The soul is as

[1] II. 3. 16–53. [2] II. 3. 16. [3] II. 3. 18.

small as an atom. 'Just as a drop of sandal ointment though in actual contact with one spot of the body only, yet produces a refreshing sensation over the whole body,' so the soul can be the cause of perception extending over all the body although in one small part of it.[1]

Yet the soul in the light of true knowledge is infinite. It is only in conjunction with Nescience that it is limited to the intellect (*buddhi*). So long as the soul is thus in connexion with the intellect, its limiting adjunct, so long is it implicated in transmigratory existence.[2] As such it is involved in the chain of deeds. The soul is an agent, as scripture and experience alike prove. Yet its activity does not belong to its essential nature. Were that so, no release would ever be possible. Thus there is a *Sūtra*: '*And as the carpenter in double fashion.*'[3] On this Śaṅkara comments: a carpenter, in ordinary life, endures pain so long as he is working with his axe and other tools. When he has laid his tools aside, and returned home, he enjoys ease and leisure. 'So the Self also, as long as it is joined with duality presented by Nescience, and is an agent, in the state of waking and dreaming, undergoes pain, but as soon as it shakes off its weariness it enters into its own highest Self; it frees itself from the complex of effects and instruments, and enjoys full ease in the state of deep sleep.' The soul is thus in essence identical with Brahman. Its deeds belong only to the soul as known to Nescience. To the question as to whether these deeds are free or determined, Śaṅkara replies with exemplary caution. In allotting good and evil circumstances, the Lord remembers efforts for good and evil. And although 'the activity of the soul is not independent, yet the soul does act. The Lord indeed causes it to act but it acts itself.'[4] So there is a well-balanced synergism between the two.

Śaṅkara then proceeds to discuss the relation of the soul to God. This relationship may be regarded as that of the part

[1] II. 3. 23. [2] II. 3. 30. [3] II. 3. 40. [4] II. 3. 42.

to the whole or of the ruled to the ruler.[1] As the soul is a part of God, all pain is illusory. So we have the *Sūtra*: '*(As the soul is affected by pleasure and pain) not so the highest (Lord); as in the case of light and so on.*'[2] The soul, as Śaṅkara explains, identifies itself through Nescience with the body and imagines itself to be affected by the experience of pain due to Nescience. Yet this pain of individual souls is not real. It is due simply 'to the non-discrimination of the Self from the body, senses, and other limiting adjuncts, which are due to name and form, the effects of Nescience'. If a man is told that his son or friend had died, he will be grieved. Yet that his grief is imaginary only, is shown by the fact that a religious mendicant would not grieve, knowing that he is free from such connexions. By another simile, Śaṅkara seeks to show that the Lord is not affected by the pain of the individual soul. The sun does not tremble, although its image trembles when you shake the cup filled with water in which the sun's light is reflected. Even so the Lord is not affected by pain, although pain is felt by that part of him known to nescience as the individual soul.

Just as pain and pleasure are illusory, so too are moral obligations. Through the influence of Western ideals, Hindus often endeavour to claim for the *Vedānta* not only intellectual subtlety but moral sublimity. It is worth while therefore to quote Śaṅkara's authoritative words. Commenting on the *Sūtra*, '*(The possibility of) injunctions and prohibitions (results) from the connexion (of the self) with bodies; as in the case of light and so on,*'[3] he writes: 'It is true that obligation exists for him only who views the soul as something different from the body; but fundamentally all obligation is an erroneous imagination existing in the case of him only who does not see that the Self is no more connected with a body than the ether is with jars and the like.'

It would appear that, from this standpoint, all distinction of individual souls must be obliterated. In his comment on the

[1] II. 3. 46. [2] II. 3. 46. [3] II. 3. 48.

following *Sūtra*, Śaṅkara denies this. The distinction between individual souls is preserved by their connexions with bodies. Thus the results of actions are not confused.[1] Individual souls are mere appearances of the highest Self, just like the reflections of the sun on the water. 'Just as when one reflected image of the sun trembles, another reflected image does not on that account tremble also; so when one soul is connected with actions and results of actions, another soul is not on that account connected likewise.' But all these appearances are illusory, due only to the effect of Nescience. When Nescience is removed 'there results the cognition of the soul being in reality nothing but Brahman'.[2]

In thus teaching that there is in reality one Self only, all-pervasive and indivisible, Śaṅkara seems to have gone beyond his text. Thus in the following *Sūtra*, Bādarāyaṇa clearly asserts a difference between the individual and the supreme Self: '*And the embodied soul (also cannot be understood as the internal ruler) for both also* (i.e. *both rescensions of the Bṛihadāraṇyaka Upanishad*) *speak of it as different (from the internal ruler)*.'[3] In his commentary on this, Śaṅkara has to explain away the difference as one of words. It is the soul in union with the organs of action as presented by Nescience that seems different. Really the Self is one only. The difference is illusory. Against this the objection was naturally raised that, if the individual self is thus illusory, the Lord also must be unreal. To this Śaṅkara replies: 'The Lord differs from the soul which is embodied, acts and enjoys, and is the produce of Nescience, in the same way as the real juggler who stands on the ground differs from the illusive juggler who, holding in his hand a shield and a sword, climbs up to the sky by means of a rope, or as the free unlimited ether differs from the ether of a jar which is determined by its limiting adjunct (i.e. the jar).'[4]

Thus from the point of real knowledge there is no such thing as psychology, for the 'psyche' is an illusion. Brahman

[1] II. 3. 49. [2] II. 3. 50. [3] I. 2. 20. [4] I. 1. 17

is the one reality. Such a theory vigorously pressed would make impossible any belief in the soul's responsibility and in transmigration. So Śaṅkara has repeatedly to affirm that to Nescience, the great soul is limited, and thus distinguished from individual souls. 'The Lord and the individual soul stand to each other in the relation of whole and part; yet it is manifest to perception that the attributes of the two are of a different nature.' In reality the individual soul has the same qualities as the Lord, but 'the equality of attributes, although existing, is hidden by the veil of Nescience', although for some by strenuous meditation, this veil has been removed.[1] So the soul is not different from the Lord, but its knowledge and power are obscured by its connexion with the body.[2] Thus the soul, when on earth, is nearest to the Lord in deep and dreamless sleep. In waking life and dream-troubled sleep, Brahman is hidden, but in deep sleep these hindrances are removed. 'Hence it is said the self alone is the place of deep sleep.'[3]

Transmigration.

In his teaching on Transmigration, Śaṅkara preserves and increases the contradictions of the Vedic texts. So obscure is his teaching, and incoherent, that to describe it with clearness is impossible.

As we have already seen, according to the early Ṛigvedic view, the good go at death to Yama's land, where they enjoy endless felicity with the Fathers. The evil pass into nether darkness. According to the *Upanishads* there are two ways. The wise go after death along the road of the gods to Brahman and from there they do not return. The good pass by the way of the Fathers to the moon, enjoy there the fruit of their deeds, and then descend to be born again on earth. Those who have neither knowledge nor works, pass to the third place, i. e. they are born again as plants or lower animals. This teaching of the two ways is confused in the *Chhāndogya Upanishad* by the

[1] III. 2. 5. [2] III. 2. 6. [3] III. 2. 7.

addition that the evil also go to the moon before obtaining for their sins an ignoble birth on earth. According to Śaṅkara's esoteric doctrine, all transmigration is illusory. And not only so. The wise cannot, as the *Upanishads* teach, reach Brahman and obtain final redemption by the way of the gods, for redemption is no longer to be regarded as something to be attained. It is an intuitive realization of what already is. These conflicting views Śaṅkara never succeeds in reconciling. And he is most obscure just where definite exposition would be most welcome.

The soul with all its organs is regarded as morally neutral and indifferent. If this be so, how do the effects of works determine the soul's destiny? As usual, Śaṅkara shows himself but little interested in such an ethical question, and the answer he gives is hesitating and inadequate. At death the coarse body with its organs passes away. But, until the final release of the soul through perfect knowledge, there remains with it, as its material substrate, the subtle body (*bhuta āśraya*). In language of the greatest obscurity, Śaṅkara says that, in addition to this material substrate, the surplus of its acts makes for the soul a moral substrate (*karma-āśraya*) which determines its future destiny. According to the teaching of the *Upanishads* which Śaṅkara adopts, the soul receives in the moon the first requital for good and evil deeds. It is not clear why, after that, there should still be a further birth on earth. To solve this difficulty and to connect deeds with their fruits in another birth, Jaimini, the leader of the school of works (*karma mīmāṁsā*), spoke of an *apurva* which might be viewed either as 'an imperceptible after-state of the deeds' or an 'imperceptible antecedent state of the result'. Śaṅkara is evidently attracted by this view, but, following Bādarāyaṇa, he rejects it on the ground that such a causal link between action and result is unnecessary, as it is the Lord who allots rewards and punishments.[1] But in another passage, in dark and difficult words, he speaks of faith (*śraddhā*) enveloping in the form of

[1] III. 2. 40 and 41.

an *apurva*, the souls of those who have performed sacrifices, and leading them up to the heavenly world to receive their reward.[1]

As we have seen, according to the two classic texts of the *Upanishads*, those who know the teaching of the five fires and who exercise in the forest faith and penance, pass by the way of the gods by a path of light to Brahman. From there they never return, for they attain there to the highest bliss. This doctrine of the gradual ascent (*kramamukti*) is opposed to Śaṅkara's teaching that redemption is not a becoming, but the intuitive realization of an already existent identity with Brahman. To speak of an approach to the highest Brahman is from this standpoint impossible. It is only to the effected Brahman that souls are led.[2] There they reign with the Lord (*Īśvara*) in bliss, sharing all his attributes save that of originating and ruling the world.[3] But from Śaṅkara's standpoint 'there is no permanence anywhere apart from the highest Brahman'.[4] Have these souls then after all to return to earth? 'No,' says the last *Sūtra* of the book, '(*of them*) *there is non-return, according to Scripture; non-return according to Scripture*.'[5] After the darkness of ignorance there shines upon them the light of perfect knowledge. So they know themselves one with the attributeless Brahman and are redeemed.

In one passage Śaṅkara speaks of the way of the fathers (*pitṛiyāna*), and 'the third place', just as the *Brihadāraṇyaka Upanishad* does. 'For those who are neither entitled through knowledge to follow the road of the gods nor by works to follow the road of the fathers, for these there is a third path on which they repeatedly return to the existence of small animals.'[6] Yet a little before he gives a totally different doctrine. Those who by sacrifices have earned felicity go to the moon by the road of the fathers but others go, not by the third path to be at once reborn, but to the abode of Yama, there to suffer torments in Yama's seven hells before they reascend to be born again on earth.[7]

[1] III. 1. 6. [2] IV. 3. 7. [3] IV. 4. 17. [4] IV. 3. 9.
[5] IV. 4. 22. [6] III. 1. 17. [7] III. 1. 13–15.

This doctrine of reward for good works in the moon and retribution for evil deeds in hell seems inconsistent with transmigration: why should souls be born again when already they have been requited for their deeds? This Śaṅkara discusses in a long comment on the *Sūtra*: '*On the passing away of the works* (*the soul reascends*) *with a remainder according to Scripture and tradition* (*smṛiti*).'[1] To the natural objection that souls go to the moon with the express object of receiving reward for their deeds, and that therefore none will remain over to require a newbirth, Śaṅkara replies with a curious illustration. A courtier who has joined the king's court with all the requisites of the king's service, has eventually to leave it because, after a long stay, 'all his things are worn out so that he is perhaps left with a pair of shoes and an umbrella only'. Even 'so the soul when possessing only a small particle of the effects of its works can no longer remain in the sphere of the moon'. So the soul descends with a remainder of works. Nor need we fear that the existence of a remainder of works will stand in the way of final release, since 'we know from Scripture that all works whatsoever are destroyed by perfect knowledge'.

As to the method of the soul's return to the body, Śaṅkara can only fall back on the explanation of the *Upanishads*. The soul descends finally as rain upon the ground. There it enters into plants. For those who because of their evil deeds become plants, this state is one of requital. For others the souls are in the plants only as guests waiting till they are eaten by man and obtain thus an entry into a new birth.[2] But Śaṅkara's teaching like that of the *Upanishads* on which it is based, is nowhere so confused, and indeed grotesque, as when it deals with the passage of the soul from its place of requital back again to be born on earth.

Redemption.

The soul's troubled round of birth and death has no beginning, and save for redemption can have no end. Yet in reality

[1] III. I. 8. [2] III. I. 24-7.

it is only an illusion; when true knowledge comes the soul knows itself one with Brahman and is redeemed. 'The state of final release is nothing but Brahman.'[1] This redemption can come through knowledge alone, for works, good and bad, bring with them their corresponding reward of pleasure and pain. Thus the result of deeds demands a body wherein to be requited, and so works do not redeem from transmigration but perpetuate it. So, on the first *Sūtra*, Śaṅkara wrote: 'The knowledge of active religious duty has for its fruit transitory felicity, and that again depends on the performance of religious acts. The inquiry into Brahman on the other hand has for its fruit eternal bliss and does not depend on the performance of any acts.' And later he writes: 'Release is nothing but being Brahman. Therefore Release is not something to be purified.' It cannot stand 'in the slightest relation to any action excepting knowledge'.[2]

Although works do not redeem, yet the seeker after knowledge must possess calmness of mind and subdue his senses; and sacrifices performed without hope of reward may prove a help.[3] So, though works are not a means to salvation, they are useful adjuncts in obtaining knowledge. Śaṅkara quotes from an extra-canonical book the noble words: 'Quietly devoted to his duty, let the wise man pass through life unknown; let him step on this earth as if he were blind, unconscious, deaf.'[4] As Deussen puts it, works have importance, not as meritorious, but as ascetic acts.[5] Meditation, the traditional Indian approach to religious truth, is recommended, and a *Sūtra* runs: '*Sitting (a man is to meditate) on account of the possibility.*'[6]

Modern Vedāntists, themselves influenced by Western Ideas, claim for the *Vedānta* an unparalleled universality 'There is no exclusiveness', we are told, 'about the religion of the *Vedānta*, the gates of its temple are open to all to enter. The enlightened Vedāntin is expected to make no distinction between a Brāhman, a Chaṇḍāla, a cow and a dog, between friends and

[1] III. 4. 52. [2] I. 1. 4. [3] III. 4. 27. [4] III. 4. 50.
[5] *Das System des Vedānta*, p. 444. [6] IV. 1. 7.

foes, as well as between the virtuous and the sinful.'[1] Such a claim cannot be made for Śaṅkara, its classic exponent. However much a Śūdra may desire redemption, for him it is impossible. Śaṅkara's opponent admits that a Śūdra could not sacrifice, but argues that, as redemption depends on knowledge, by knowledge he could be redeemed. Śaṅkara will not have it. As the three higher castes alone can perform the *upanayana* ceremony, they alone can qualify themselves for the study of the *Veda* and so obtain the saving knowledge which only comes to students of the *Veda*. 'Spiritual capability is required in spiritual matters, and spiritual capability is (in the case of the Śūdras) excluded, by their being excluded from the study of the *Veda*.'[2]

For those thus qualified, when this knowledge comes, life has no further meaning. The man who knows Brahman is one with Brahman, who is 'neither agent nor enjoyer'. Hence he says: 'I neither was an agent nor an enjoyer at any previous time, nor am I such at the present time, nor shall I be such at any future time.'[3] So redemption destroys all moral responsibility. Works good or evil lose their effects and produce no result to be enjoyed or expiated. But if so, why need the redeemed man linger on longer in this life? Why should he not be at once engulfed in Brahman? Not so, says Śaṅkara: the effects of deeds done before redemption remain; these have to be experienced, before death can come and redemption be complete.[4] At death the soul passes into that highest light which is the self. Between it and Brahman there is no distinction and no division. Into Brahman it flows as waters into the sea. 'Hence', as the teacher Audulomi says, 'the soul manifests itself in the nature of the true intelligence, free from all manifoldness, calm, not capable of being expressed by any terms.'[5] The self is one, without difference or distinction, with Brahman, the attributeless, sole reality.

[1] Prof. M. Raṅgāchāriar, *The Vedāntic Conception of Religion*, reprinted in *Aspects of the Vedānta*, p. 63.
[2] I. 3. 34. [3] IV. I. 13. [4] IV. I. 15. [5] VI. 4. 6.

THE WAY OF LOVE

CHAPTER V

THE *BHAGAVADGĪTĀ*

AMONG educated Hindus to-day no book is so loved, no book is so influential, as the *Bhagavadgītā*. Men speak of the *Gītā* with kindling eye. They affirm that at each new reading fresh light comes. They profess to find in it an all-sufficient guide to life. Indian publishing houses are continually issuing new translations, commentaries, and expositions. The Neo-Kṛishṇa movement,[1] especially, sees in the Kṛishṇa of the *Gītā* one worthy to be compared with the Christ of the Gospels, and works in praise of Kṛishṇa and Kṛishṇa's Song are frequent. He who would understand the religion of the educated Hindu must study the *Gītā* as no other book.

And that study is not easy. Short as the book is, its problems are among the most difficult and elusive in Indian scholarship. Questions of date and structure are usually, in the case of Hindu works, of very restricted interest. In the case of the *Gītā* their discussion is essential to the understanding and exposition of the poem.

By many devout Hindus the introduction to the *Gītā* is taken as literal fact. It narrates the actual dialogue between Kṛishṇa and Arjuna at Kurukshetra, the field on which was fought, in dim antiquity, the battle between the Pāṇḍavas and the Kurus. So the poem is indeed the Lord's song. Its counsel and its comfort are the veritable words of Kṛishṇa the All-God, and naturally the poem is regarded as of immemorial age. Such a view is, of course, uncritical and contradicts entirely the development of language and of thought. When

[1] For an account of the literature of this movement, especially in Bengal, see J. N. Farquhar, *Gītā and Gospel*, 82–92.

the *Gītā* was written it is impossible definitely to say. Its latest possible date is fixed by quotations from it in Kālidāsa, who lived about A.D. 400. And some European scholars have held that the poem was not written more than a century before that time. On the other hand some Indian scholars, including men so distinguished as Telang[1] and Sir R. G. Bhandarkar,[2] have taught that the poem was written some centuries before the Christian era. Amid the confusion of views there seems to be a growing consensus of opinion that the *Gītā*, as we have it, is not later than the first century, or possibly the second century, A. D. The date is of interest as it makes very improbable, if not quite impossible, the theory once so popular with Western scholars that the close resemblances in the *Gītā* to the Christian Gospels are due to direct borrowing. Just because the *Gītā* was written by one ignorant of Christ, its testimony of a mind 'naturally Christian' is the more valuable and striking.

It is difficult to believe that the *Gītā* was written originally in its present form. Its contradictions are not those of an occasional inconsistency. They are vital and irreconcilable. The explanation has been given that the author was a poet, and not a philosopher, and that we must not test an inspired work of poetry by the canons of rigid logic. But the explanation is insufficient. In many passages the thought of the *Gītā* soars to lofty heights, but often it is pedestrian enough. The same ideas are repeated time after time. Verses from the *Upanishads* are taken over unchanged, whilst the teaching of the three moods of the Sāṅkhyan Philosophy is a piece of pedantry.[3] The *Gītā*, for all its occasional sublimity, is thus primarily not a work of poetic genius, but a work deliberately written to support a particular religious view.[4]

[1] In the introduction to his translation of the *Bhagavadgītā*, *S. B. E.* viii.

[2] In his recent *Vaishṇavism*, *Śaivism*, &c. Against his argument for an early date see A. Berriedale Keith, *The Sāṁkhya System*, p. 29.

[3] *Sattva*, *Rajas*, and *Tamas*.

[4] Garbe, *Die Bhagavadgītā*, p. 9.

We are familiar in the *Vedānta* with the distinction of an exoteric and an esoteric knowledge. But in the *Gītā* it is no case of a higher and a lower knowledge. The parts which speak of Kṛishṇa as the sole and personal God, the succourer of those that love him, convey no suggestion at all that this is mere exoteric knowledge, and that to a higher knowledge only the neuter Brahman is real. There are then, in the poem, two essentially different strata, the one theistic, the other Vedāntic, and the question of which is original has to be met. Unfortunately to this question exactly opposite answers have been made, and the points at issue are not mere minutiae of scholarship, they involve our whole conception of the rise of the *bhakti* movement.

Thus, in his brilliant introduction to his translation of the *Gītā*, Professor Garbe argues strongly that it is the Vedāntic element that is not original. Often as the words Sāṅkhya and Yoga appear, the word Vedānta is only once found and then in the sense of *Upanishad*.[1] The poem as a whole is essentially theistic. A personal God Kṛishṇa, in the form of an earthly hero, demands, in addition to the selfless fulfilment of duty, believing love and surrender to him. He shows himself in his supernatural, but still human, form, and promises to reward all faithful love by union with him after death. Such, then, Garbe holds, is the original *Gītā*, which he assigns to about 200 B.C.;[2] later it was redacted in the interests of the Vedānta and the closely related Mīmāṁsā schools—a redaction which Garbe teaches took place in the second century after Christ. Dr. Garbe ventures to indicate these Vedāntic interpolations, which amount, in his judgement, to about one-fifth of the whole poem. Their removal, as he

[1] XV. 15: 'I am to be known by all the *Vedas*. I am the framer of the *Veda's* ends (*vedānta*), the knower of the *Vedas*.'

[2] Garbe bases his argument for this early date largely on the ignorance of the author of the B. G. of the Yoga-Sūtras of Patañjali, whom he identifies with the Grammarian who lived in the second century B.C., but, as Keith shows, this identification of the reputed author of the Yoga-Sūtras with Patañjali the Grammarian is very improbable (*vide* A. B. Keith, *The Sāṁkhya System*, pp. 30 and 57).

claims, would not only simplify the teaching but make the connexion of the poem more intimate and natural.[1]

Dr. Garbe's theory is a very attractive attempt to apply to the problems of Hindu scholarship the apparatus of the Higher Criticism, which has been so fruitful in Old Testament research, but the theory has not won many converts. It is true that Sir R. G. Bhandarkar, whose earlier researches Garbe utilizes,[2] claims that he has 'established on irrefragable evidence the existence during the first three or four centuries before Christ of a religion with Vāsudeva as its central figure, and of a school of his followers known by the name of Bhāgavats',[3] but unfortunately the evidence he adduces of this early *bhakti* faith seems not only not 'irrefragable' but ambiguous and inconsistent. The view of Hopkins and Keith seems more probable. The original *Gītā* was probably an old verse *Upanishad* written rather later than the *Śvetāśvatara Upanishad*, and worked up later into the present *Gītā* in the interests of Kṛishṇaism. In this way a means was provided for Vaishṇavite devotees to express their devotion in the terms of the philosophies of the time. Thus Vishṇu was identified with the Supreme God, the Brahman-Ātman, of the *Upanishads*, and also with Kṛishṇa, the hero of the Epic. So Vishṇu ceased to be merely one of the Hindu gods, or even a member of the so-called Hindu trinity, and became instead the Absolute, the Source of All-being. At the same time Kṛishṇa becomes the full incarnation of Vishṇu-Brahman, and receives

[1] Thus to take, as example, the first big gloss: Garbe regards III. 9–18 as a Mīmāmsā interpolation. As the text stands III. 19, 'Therefore fulfil ever without attachment the work which thou hast to do; for the man who does his work without attachment wins to the supreme,' contradicts III. 17. 18, which assert that for the man whose delight is in self 'there is naught for which he should work'. If the interpolation be removed, then III. 19 connects naturally with III. 8: 'Do thine ordained work for work is more excellent than no work. Even the subsistence of the body cannot be won from no work.' (All verbal quotations from the *Gītā*, in inverted commas, are from Barnett's translation.)

[2] Garbe, *Die Bhagavadgītā*, pp. 19, 20.

[3] Vide *Vaishṇavism, Saivism*, &c., pp. 3 and 41. He regards the *Gītā* as a theistic protest against the ascetic and atheistic tendencies of the time.

the title Bhagavān, the blessed Lord. To the familiar ways of knowledge and of works is added the way of *bhakti*, of devotion. The Vaishṇavite practice was thus justified by reason. The best and normal way of worshipping God is to worship Vishṇu in the temples. The *Gītā* was thus an attempt to unite Hindu metaphysics and practice, Hindu theology and religion. The popularity of the book to-day shows that the attempt has been as successful as it was brilliant. Irreconcilables remain indeed irreconciled, and yet sufficiently in relation to exist side by side in the minds and hearts of devout Hindus.

To give a systematic statement of the *Gītā* teaching is clearly impossible. It will be convenient to deal separately with the two chief strata, the theistic and the Vedāntic. Whatever theory be adopted of the *Gītā's* origin, it is the theistic element that is most prominent, and important, and we shall describe this chiefly, using, for convenience, Garbe's analysis, though without accepting his conclusions.

Arjuna on the battle-field hesitates to order the fighting to begin. The leaders of the hostile forces are his kinsmen: why should he be the means of their death? He appeals to Kṛishṇa for counsel, and professes his unwillingness to fight. Though they seek to slay him, he will not slay. To do so would be sin. At the destruction of a family stock, laws perish and lawlessness ensues. The women sin and, through their sin, castes are mixed and that leads to hell the family and its destroyers. No longer can ancestors receive their wonted offerings. A heavy sin then would it be 'to slay our kin from lust after the sweets of kingship'.[1] The Lord Kṛishṇa bids him lay aside this unmanly spirit, and Arjuna appeals to him for guidance. 'My soul stricken with the stain of unmanliness, my mind all unsure of the law, I ask thee—tell me clearly what will be the more blest way. I am thy

[1] I. 45.

disciple; teach me who am come to thee for refuge.'[1] The Lord replies that his grief is unfitting. The wise grieve not over death. Souls are without beginning and end. The connexion of a soul with a particular body is of no moment. Pleasure and pain belong not to the soul but to the influences of matter, and these are transitory. Those who know the truth are delivered from their power. So there is no real slaying. The soul puts off its outward body and takes another as a man puts on new clothes. Why then should we grieve over any born being? If Arjuna shrinks from the fight, he will be held a coward. If he fights and is slain, he will win paradise. If he fights and conquers, his will be the joys of earth. Let him then be resolute and do his duty.[2]

Thus much, says Kṛishṇa, is according to the teaching of the Sāṅkhya. Now let him learn the lesson of the Yoga. Works must be done but without thought of reward. So even in activity a man may preserve quiet of mind. 'The man who casts off all desires and walks without desire with no thought of a *Mine* and of an *I* comes into peace.'[3] And works belong not really to the 'I'. They are done by the moods (*guṇas*) of nature. This teaching, says Kṛishṇa, is not new. He declared it in the dim past. For his previous births had been many. Whenever need arises, once more he is born.[4] Kṛishṇa works yet is workless. Wise is the man who does the same. Those who offer sacrifices, who mortify the flesh and control the breath are not rejected, but the best sacrifice is the sacrifice of knowledge. Such a man works fetter not. He possesses his self.[5] Thus the casting off (*sannyāsa*) of works and the rule (*yoga*) of works both lead to bliss.[6] Only the ignorant distinguish between the Sāṅkhya and Yoga doctrines. The ways of Yoga are many. Some control the breath not looking around them, but the best Yogin, says Kṛishṇa, 'is he who worships me in faith with his dwelling in me'.[7]

[1] II. 7. [2] I. 28–II. 38. [3] II. 71. [4] IV. 7. 9.
[5] IV. 41. [6] V. 2. [7] VI. 47.

At length Arjuna asks Kṛishṇa to let him look upon him in his glory. So the Lord granted unto Arjuna to behold him as the Supreme.[1] His light was like the light of a thousand suns ; many were his mouths and eyes, his marvellous aspects. His form filled the mid-space between heaven and earth and all the quarters of the sky. The threefold world quaked. To him gathered all the Gods, the ancestors, the saints. Arjuna trembles at the sight. Kṛishṇa's mouths are 'grim with teeth like to the fire of the last days'.[2] In them Arjuna beholds the chief of his adversaries caught between the teeth, their heads crushed. Into the blazing mouths, the worlds too were 'passing with exceeding speed to perish'. The Lord explains that in him, Arjuna sees events to come. Already has Kṛishṇa smitten the mighty men of war, Arjuna's enemies. Let Arjuna therefore smite and fear not.

Arjuna beholding the Lord in his splendour, marvels that ever he called him friend and 'hailed him as Kṛishṇa, Yādava, or comrade, in ignorance of this, his majesty, through heedlessness or affection'.[3] He prays the Lord to show himself again as Kṛishṇa with diadem and mace and disk in hand, four-armed. And Vāsudeva does as he requests. So, with many repetitions and amplifications, the dialogue continues, and the Divine Lay concludes with a beautiful invitation to Arjuna to seek refuge in the Lord and thus be delivered from all sins. And he is promised that all those who recite or read the story of the message thus graciously vouchsafed, shall come unto the Lord. And Arjuna replies, 'My bewilderment has vanished away: I have gotten remembrance of thy grace, O, never-falling, I stand freed from doubt, I will do thy word.'[4]

Such in briefest outline is the Song of the Lord. The Bhāgavat religion is here so united with Brāhmanism, that Kṛishṇa is identified with Vishṇu and Vishṇu-Kṛishṇa is the supreme God. And this religion has found its intellectual expression in categories of the Sāṅkhya and Yoga systems.

[1] In the eleventh song. [2] XI. 25. [3] XI. 41. [4] XVIII. 73.

This Sāṅkhyan system was an atheistic[1] dualism which asserted the eternal and separate existence of a primordial matter (*prakṛiti*) on the one hand, and a multiplicity of spirits (*purusha-ātman*) on the other. Redemption consisted in thus recognizing the absolute independence of the individual soul from matter. All the activities and feelings of man are ultimately physical. The soul itself is unchangeable, inactive and impassive. The redemption the Sāṅkhya seeks by way of reflection, the Yoga seeks by way of religious practices. By regulation of the breath and the like, all the activities of the Yogin were withdrawn from external objects into the intelligence (the *buddhi*).[2] A higher path is thus made possible and through concentration (*dhāraṇā*), meditation (*dhyāna*), and absorption (*samādhi*), unconsciousness is reached. The soul, emancipated even from the intelligence (*buddhi*), is completely retracted from all connexion with the material and abides in insentient solitude. Whereas the Sāṅkhya rejected Īśvara, the Yoga accepts him as a helper of the Yogin. In the *Bhagavadgītā* these two systems are combined, and this Sāṅkhya-Yoga system is here made unmistakably monotheistic. Thus when Arjuna complains that, if he slays his kinsfolk, great will be his sin, the comfort Kṛishṇa gives in pure Sāṅkhya. 'The Body's Tenant' passes from childhood into age, untouched and unaffected by the body. It is the influences of matter which produce the 'pairs' of cold and heat, and pleasure and pain. Although matter is eternal, these influences are transitory. It is only the bodies in which the spirit dwells, that die. So Kṛishṇa says, 'This body's tenant for all time may not be wounded in the bodies of any beings. Therefore thou dost not well to sorrow for any born beings.'[3] And this independence of the soul from matter is frequently reaffirmed. All our activities are due to the moods (*guṇa*) of nature. It is only through illusive egoism (*ahaṁkāra*) that

[1] Atheism here means the denial of a supreme God. The popular polytheism was not attacked.

[2] The intelligence, or *buddhi*, itself belongs to the material.

[3] II. 30.

the self imagines *I* am the doer.[1] Of these 'Moods' there are three, Sattva, Rajas, and Tamas. Etymologically these words denote goodness, fieriness, and gloom, but really the words do not admit of translation. They denote at once qualities in external things and their correlates in the individual man. The theory is important because, in it, all deeds and traits of character are referred to purely physical causes.[2] Goodness (*sattva*) 'fetters by the attachment of pleasantness and knowledge'. Fieriness (*rajas*), 'which is in essence passion', fetters with the attachment of words. Gloom (*tamas*), which is 'born of ignorance', 'fetters by heedlessness, sloth, and sleep'.[3]

In one passage the conception of redemption does not transcend that of the Sāṅkhyan system. The spirit and nature with its moods are described as both beginningless. The Spirit (*purusha*) is born again because of the bondage of the moods of nature. But the wise man, who knows the spirit (*purusha*), and nature with its moods, is redeemed. He never again is born.[4] But such a redemption, without moral change or love, is not in accordance with the general teaching of the *Gītā*. It is a piece of Sāṅkhyan philosophy unharmonized with the Bhāgavat religion. Generally the discrimination between nature and spirit is regarded merely as a preliminary accessory to the redemption which comes through the way of loving faith in the Lord. In this way the Sāṅkhyan teaching is transfused into a religion. Instead of a multiplicity of souls in absolute independence, the human soul is regarded as a part of the divine essence. The Adorable One says: 'A portion of me is the ancient elemental soul in the world of souls.'[5] Instead of the denial of a supreme God, we have

[1] III. 27.

[2] External objects convey impressions to three internal physical organs: (1) the *manas*, which receives the impressions and conveys them to (2) *buddhi*, or intelligence, and (3) the *ahaṁkāra*, the principle of egoism, which makes the self regard the body's activity as its own. Garbe, *Sāṅkhya und Yoga*, p. 24.

[3] XIV. 5–7.

[4] XIII. 19–23.

[5] XV. 7.

the beautiful and powerful portrayal of a God mighty and merciful.

God in the *Gītā* is a spiritual being. In one passage,[1] Nature is indeed spoken of as a part of Him, but, in view of the general teaching of the *Gītā*, the reference would seem to be to God's activity in nature. 'God is beyond the Perishable, and likewise higher than the Imperishable.'[2] He is the 'unborn, the one without beginning, great Lord of worlds'.[3] From Him 'the All proceeds'.[4] He it is who at the end of each age makes and moulds nature again.[5] Transcendent, He is immanent in the heart of all born beings. In the *Gītā's* sense of selfless activity, He is the true Yogin; for He is the doer of work, and yet no worker. 'Works defile Him not. He has no longing for fruit of works.'[6] On His selfless activity the world depends. He is self-sufficient yet He works.[7] Not only does He conserve the world. In times of special need He appears on earth to succour the right and restrain the wrong. Says the Adorable One, 'Many births of me and thee, have passed, O Arjuna. I know them all; but thou knowest them not, O affrighter of the foe. Though birthless, and unchanging of essence, and though Lord of born beings, yet in My sway over the nature that is Mine own I come into birth by My own magic (*māyā*). For whensoever the law fails and lawlessness uprises, then do I bring myself to bodied birth. To guard the righteous, to destroy evil-doers, to establish the law, I come into birth age after age'.[8] Thus the God of the *Gītā* is not the meaningless cipher of the *Vedānta*. The Supreme loves men and is known of them: 'Exceedingly dear am I to the man of knowledge and he to me'.[9] Graciously He bids men come to share His grace and find in Him their refuge.

Just as the *Gītā* has transformed the theoretic teaching of the Sāṅkhya, so it has enriched and modified the practical discipline of the Yoga. The quest for salvation, by flight from

[1] VII. 4–6. [2] XV. 18. [3] X. 3. [4] X. 8. [5] IX. 7. 8.
[6] IV. 13. 14. [7] III. 22. [8] IV. 5–8. [9] VII. 17.

the world, austerity, and meditation, was too prevalent to be entirely rejected, and the old Yoga method is still enjoined. In one passage, indeed, it would appear that to the saintly man works were a mere preliminary, and calm the real means of becoming a true Yogin.[1] More characteristically, the Yoga discipline in the technical sense is recommended as a help to complete detachment from the world by the way of knowledge. Let the Yogin 'abide alone in a secret place, utterly subdued in mind, without craving, and without possessions'. Let him sit 'with thought intent, and the workings of mind and sense-instruments restrained, holding body, head, and neck in unmoving equipoise, gazing on the end of his nose, and looking not round about him, calm of spirit, void of fear, abiding under the rule of chastity, with mind restrained, and thought set on the Lord, so shall he sit, that is under the Rule (*yoga*), given over to me'.[2]

But the author of the Divine Lay puts side by side with this a new and better Yoga, which a man could practise and still remain in the world and do in the world a man's work. Let a man do his duty, but in the Yoga spirit, free from attachment to the fruit of work, and without hope of reward. It is in this teaching that the *Gītā* makes one of its greatest contributions to Indian thought. And in the verse which Indian commentators have called the quintessence of the whole poem, this way alone is taught. 'He who does My work, who is given over to Me, who is devoted to Me, void of attachment, without hatred of any born being, comes to Me.'[3] Each man's duty is clear. Let him look to the law of his caste and do it without dismay. Arjuna is a Kshatriya and as a Kshatriya must do a soldier's work unflinchingly. 'For to a knight (Kshatriya), there is no thing more blest than a lawful strife.'[4] Thus to each caste there is a special duty and this duty must be done. This teaching has been often condemned for its immorality,[5] and certainly the doctrine that

[1] VI. 3. [2] VI. 10–14. [3] XI. 55. [4] II. 31.
[5] And not only by western writers. Thus in an article in the *Social*

no man can be blamed if he fulfil the duties of his caste has been carried in India to an appalling extreme. A man's work may be to steal, a woman's, to be a temple prostitute. But it may well be doubted if the author of the *Gītā* would have sanctioned such an application of his doctrine. The strife in which Arjuna is engaged is a 'lawful strife' and it is assumed that the war is just. And in other parts of the *Gītā* a high morality is enjoined. Thus the qualities assigned to men, born to the estate of the gods, form a goodly catalogue of virtues. 'Fearlessness, purity of the goodness-mood (*sattva*), abiding in knowledge and the Rule, almsgiving, restraint of sense, sacrifice, scripture-reading, mortification, uprightness, harmlessness, truth, wrathlessness, renunciation, restraint of spirit, lack of malice, pity towards born beings, unwantoning sense, tenderness, modesty, steadfastness, heroic temper, patience, constancy, purity, innocence, and lack of overweening spirit, are in him that is born to God's estate.'[1]

Thus a man may be redeemed from the world in the midst of the world's activities. He may do his work as if he did it not. Engaged in his daily task, he may yet be a true Yogin if only he be untrammelled by his deeds. So to do, is better than to renounce activity. 'Casting off of works[2] and the rule of works[3] both lead to bliss, but of these the rule of works is higher than the casting off of works.'[4] It is in Kṛishṇa, not

Reform Advocate of Madras (Oct. 30, 1915) we read: 'Kṛishṇa is strangely oblivious, or deliberately ignores, the fact that the Kshatriya is more than a mere Kshatriya, that he is also a comrade, a master, a servant, &c., owing duties as such to others in the various relations of life. How is it that this pretended gospel of duty is silent as the grave upon these other duties of his? Verily the *Bhagavadgītā* is a scripture of ruthless cold-blooded assassination of one's own kindred, of the apotheosis of a soulless, sordid exploitation of the non-Brāhman castes by the Brāhmans. . . . He (Kṛishṇa) is a god after the Brāhmans' own heart, a proof that man makes gods in his own image. In the triumphant boom of his conch on the day of Kurukshetra, one hears the knell of India's unity and solidarity, the parting day of her imperial sway under Aśoka the Great.'

[1] XVI. 1–3.

[2] The word used is *sannyāsa*, from which *sannyāsin* is derived.

[3] Yoga.

[4] V. 2.

in sacred rites, that a man must find refuge.[1] Sacrifices lead only to the world of the gods.[2] If a man do them, he must do them without thought of advantage or reward.[3] Through the attraction of the 'mood' of nature it is hard so to act. One who does so, is a true Sannyāsin and a true Yogin.[4]

Whether a man treads the path of meditation or of selfless activity, it is only that he may be ready for redemption. And redemption comes from Kṛishṇa's grace which is appropriated by the *bhakti* of men. 'Bhakti' is a word difficult to translate. Perhaps 'devotion' is the best English rendering. This devotion to the Lord may be directed to other gods. With the tolerance so characteristic of Hinduism, Kṛishṇa is said to receive all forms of worship. It is in this way that the most degraded indigenous cults have been absorbed into Hinduism. It is in this way, too, at the other extreme, that many Hindus to-day praise Christ through worshipping Kṛishṇa, and describe the worship Christians offer to Christ as acceptable to their Lord Kṛishṇa. 'If any worshipper whatsoever seeks with faith to reverence any body whatsoever, that same faith in him I make steadfast.'[5] 'They also, who worship other Gods and make offering to them with faith, do verily make offering to Me though not according to ordinance.'[6] Kṛishṇa's grace is open to all, irrespective of character, or caste, or sex.[7] Even doers of great evil, if they worship Kṛishṇa, are deemed good because of their purpose, and speedily come to righteousness of soul. Even those who, because of their sins in former births, are born as women, or in the two lower castes (Vaiśyas and Śūdras), if they turn to Kṛishṇa, attain to the supreme path.[8] And it matters not how trifling be the offerings men bring. Kṛishṇa will accept them. 'If one of earnest spirit set

[1] XVIII. 66. [2] VII. 23.

[3] This, of course, removes the motive of the Brāhmanic rites, which are frankly based on the principle *do ut des*.

[4] VI. 1. [5] VII. 21. [6] IX. 23.

[7] So the *Gītā*, though called the 'essence of all the *Upanishads*', is only tradition (*smṛiti*) and not scripture (*śruti*); for Śūdras and women are not permitted to hear *śruti*.

[8] IX. 30–2.

before Me with devotion a leaf, a flower, fruit or water, I enjoy', says Kṛishṇa, 'this offering of devotion.'[1] So to all, Kṛishṇa gives the invitation He gave to Arjuna. 'As thou hast come into this unstable and joyless world, worship Me; have thy mind on Me, thy devotion towards Me, thy sacrifice to Me, do homage to Me. To Me shalt thou come.'[2] Of the nature of the future life of those who thus come to Kṛishṇa, the *Gītā* speaks with but little clearness. From the Sāṅkhyan standpoint, the soul, when redeemed, is completely freed from all connexion with matter and, as consciousness, becomes extinct. But the promises of the *Gītā* seem in opposition to this to denote a conscious communion with the supreme. Those who are redeemed by knowledge, says Kṛishṇa, 'become one in quality with me'[3], but this relationship seems one of likeness, not identity.

Such in brief is the teaching of the more theistic part of the *Gītā* in which the Bhāgavat religion is expressed in terms of the Sāṅkhya-Yoga doctrine.

In the *Gītā*, as it stands, this teaching is confused by the Vedāntic element. Garbe, as we have seen, would regard this as due to a late Redaction. More probably it is the original element, uncoordinated with the later teaching. Thus, in the passage in the third song already referred to, the command to Arjuna to do his own work, without attachment, is interrupted by a long passage explaining the efficacy of sacrifice. 'The gods, comforted by the sacrifice, shall give to him the pleasures of his desire. He that enjoys these their gifts, without giving to them, is a thief.'[4] So elsewhere it is said that neither this world nor the next is for him who does not offer sacrifices.[5] Of greater importance is the Vedāntic assertion that Kṛishṇa is the All.[6] He is the taste in the water, the light in the moon, the mystic syllable Om in the *Vedas*, the understanding of them that understand, the splendour of the splendid.[7] Few there are that thus know Kṛishṇa to be the All.[8]

[1] IX. 26. [2] IX. 33, 34. [3] XIV. 2. [4] III. 12. [5] IV. 31.
[6] VI. 29–31. [7] VII. 7–11. [8] VII. 19.

In a long and tedious passage Kṛishṇa is identified with the greatest of each kind of being.[1] This beginningless, supreme Brahman is described in familiar Upanishadic terms as *Om, tat, sat*.[2] To understand the doctrine of the Brahman is to enjoy the essence of immortality.[3] Kṛishṇa as the All is declared to be 'known by all the *Vedas*; He is the framer of the *Veda's* ends (i.e. the *Upanishads*), the knower of the *Vedas*'.[4] In Kṛishṇa's body, Arjuna may behold the whole universe and all else that he would see.[5] In clear contradiction to the *Gītā's* central teaching, Kṛishṇa is said to be veiled by illusion (māyā) and known to none,[6] and He, who elsewhere is declared to love men, is here described as 'indifferent to all born beings'; there is none whom He hates, none whom He loves.[7]

Whatever be the *Gītā's* origin and structure, it is the poem as it stands which is so loved in India to-day. Of a systematic philosophy it is clearly impossible to speak. The contradictions are fundamental and irreconcilable.[8] Yet to the devout Hindu, these apparently cause no difficulty. Somehow in Hinduism the 'law of excluded middle' does not seem to apply. 'A' may be both 'B' and 'not-B' and in the same sense. The very inconsistency of the *Gītā* has probably increased its popularity. Thus, in the poem as we have it, there is presented a personal God knowing and loving His worshippers. Yet this God is described, in terms of Vedāntic pantheism, as the All, the Brahman. And some such illogical compromise of impersonal pantheism and personal theism seems to be just the religion of many educated Hindus to-day. But it may be doubted whether much of the position and power of the *Gītā* is due to philosophy in the systematic sense. It is because the *Gītā* supplies, what the *Vedānta* fails

[1] X. 12-42. [2] XVII. 23-7. [3] XIII. 12-18. [4] XV. 15.
[5] XI. 7. [6] VII. 25, 26 [7] IX. 29.
[8] For a very sympathetic exposition of 'the Comprehensive Universality of the Theology of the *Gītā*' see G. Howell's *Soul of India*, pp. 425-90.

to give, that it is so highly valued. It is through its demand for selfless obedience to duty, and its portrayal of a gracious God, willing to be loved and trusted, that it has won its place in the heart of India. The true Yogin is described in words of strange and haunting beauty. 'Hateless towards all born beings, friendly and pitiful, void of the thought of *Mine* and *I*, bearing indifferently pain and pleasure, patient, ever content, the Man of the Rule, subdued of spirit and steadfast of purpose, who has set mind and understanding on Me and worships Me is dear to Me. He before whom the world is not dismayed, and who is not dismayed before the world, who is void of joy, impatience, fear and dismay, desireless, pure, skilful, impartial, free from terrors, who renounces all undertakings, and worships Me, is dear to me. One indifferent to foe and to friend, indifferent in honour and in dishonour, in heat and in cold, in joy and in pain, free of attachment, who holds in equal account blame and praise, silent, content with whatsoever befall, homeless, firm of judgement, possessed of devotion, is a man dear to Me.'[1] And in Kṛishṇa's final appeal, men have found and do find consolation. 'In Him seek refuge with thy whole soul; by His grace, thou shalt win supreme peace, the everlasting realm. Thus have I set forth to thee deepest of deep knowledge; ponder upon it in its fullness, and do as thou wilt. Hear again My supreme word, deepest of all, for that thou art exceedingly beloved of Me, therefore I will say what is for thy weal. Have thy mind on Me, thy devotion towards Me, thy sacrifice to Me, do homage to Me. To Me thou shalt come. I make thee a truthful promise; thou art very dear to Me. Surrendering all the Laws, come for refuge to Me alone. I will deliver thee from all sins; grieve not.'[2]

Words such as these are the best witness to the spiritual genius of the author of the *Gītā*. Yet in two respects he was unfortunate. The Sāṅkhyan philosophy, in which the teaching of the *Gītā* is expressed, is essentially unethical. Deeds

[1] XII. 13–19. [2] XVIII. 62–6.

belong only to the material world. It is only our ignorance which imagines that the soul is trammelled by its deeds; in reality the soul is inactive and impassive. Such a view impoverishes the conception of human personality and responsibility. From it can be easily deduced teaching which is immoral. Thus the argument that, as the 'body's tenant' (i.e. the soul) cannot be injured, there is really no such thing as slaying, is a sophistry which has been used even in recent years to justify political assassination. The author of the *Gītā* is all the more to be admired that, in spite of a philosophy so unethical, and irreligious, as the Sāṅkhyan, he, for the most part, proclaims so high an ethical ideal.

And, in its religious influence, the *Gītā* has suffered much from the fact that the Kṛishṇa it proclaims, is inevitably confused in the popular mind with the freakish, vicious Kṛishṇa of the *Purāṇas*. The Kṛishṇa of the *Gītā* is indeed nobly and beautifully portrayed, and the attempt that used to be made by Christian apologists in India to ridicule the high teaching of the *Gītā* by saying that it came from the mouth of a murderer, an adulterer, and a thief, was as unjust as it was impolitic.[1] Yet it has to be recognized more clearly than is generally done in the West that the Kṛishṇa cult which the *Gītā* did so much to further has too often been a debasing influence. It is in this association of the ideal Kṛishṇa of the *Gīta* with the Kṛishṇa of the *Purāṇas* that we have the most tragic feature in India's religious history. The Kṛishṇa of the *Gītā* is the product of a devout and elevated imagination, but imagination may be degraded and blasphemous, and, in the *Purāṇas*, Kṛishṇa is conceived by an imagination at once foul and foolish. Pornographic literature exists in Europe, to Christendom's disgrace, but it is detested by religious men and exists, not because of, but in spite of, Christianity. But here the records of Kṛishṇa's

[1] Such methods of controversy are happily obsolete among missionaries of all but the narrowest sects, but I have often heard such arguments used by Indian Christians. It is but natural that in the case of those who, as outcastes, felt the cruelty of Hinduism, there should be a reluctance to recognize its higher aspects.

sensuality, told with every salacious detail, are 'religious' stories and familiar even to children.[1] And the modern endeavour of men, who through the influence of Christianity have grown ashamed of these stories, to treat them as a spiritual allegory is only a counsel of despair, and bad, in that it continues to draw attention to tales which in the interests of Indian morality should be once for all rejected and forgotten.

Modern Vedāntists sometimes speak of the superiority of Hinduism to Christianity in not being confined to one historic figure. The history of the Kṛishṇa cult is the best answer to this argument. In the case of Christianity a silly imagination is held in restraint by historic fact. Each age is forced back again upon the actual figure of Jesus Christ as recorded in the Gospels. In the case of the Kṛishṇa cult, even the noble conception of the *Gītā*, because it was the product of imagination, and not the record of fact, is unable to provide a standard. It could not save itself from being debased and befouled through association with the lewd Kṛishṇa of the *Purāṇas*. It is through the influence of Christianity that the *Gītā* has now won its place as the best-prized book in India. And that place more than all Hindu books it deserves. Here as nowhere else in Indian literature there is depicted the high aspirations of a soul naturally Christian. Here there speaks with poignancy and power the eager craving for the revelation of a God of love, and an actual incarnate Saviour.

[1] Cp. *Vishṇu Purāṇa*, Book V. A Hindu told a friend of mine that the peculiarly vile story of Kṛishṇa's night of unspeakable debauchery had always impressed him in boyhood as a proof of divine strength and virility.

CHAPTER VI

THE LOVERS OF GOD

THE Vedic hymns, the *Upanishads*, the *Vedāntasūtras*, and the *Bhagavadgītā*, are the chief documents of the Higher Hinduism of the English educated classes. But even the briefest account of living and effective Hinduism would be incomplete which made no mention of the passionate, and sometimes exalted, devotion to the Gods, cherished, not only by those educated in Western thought, but still more by those impervious to Western culture. It is not the purpose of this chapter to give a history of this *bhakti* movement.[1] It is rather the aim to indicate by a few choice instances its religious nature. For the Vaishṇavite, this devotion gathers round the cycle of legends connected with the heroes, regarded as the two chief of Vishṇu's incarnations, Kṛishṇa and Rāma. The Śaivite devotion is directed to no incarnation of Śiva, but to Śiva himself in his various forms and attributes.

It must suffice to illustrate very briefly the Vaishṇavite devotion from the writings of Tukārām and Tulsī Dās, and then to deal at greater length with the love to Śiva as revealed especially in the works of that fine old Tamil saint and poet, Māṇikka Vāśagar.

Tukārām and the Kṛishṇa Cult.

Too much of the later worship of Kṛishṇa is vitiated by its erotic nature. The relation of the soul to God is that of a

[1] There is a most illuminating review of the Bhaktimārga (by Sir G. A. Grierson) in *E. R. E.* ii. 539–51, and more recently in Sir R. G. Bhandarkar's *Vaishṇavism, Śaivism, and Minor Religious Systems*, and for a popular description see R. W. Frazer's *Indian Thought, Past and Present*, pp. 200–70.

passionate woman to her lover, and inevitably a religion so emotional and sexual in conception, leads, as Dr. Barnett says, 'to a deep sensualism both of the spirit and also of the body'.[1] Yet Kṛishṇa too has been worshipped by pure and high-minded men, and such was Tukārām.[2]

Tukārām has himself told us the story of his conversion and 'call' to service. At famine time his wife had died of starvation, and he was full of shame. He was only a Śūdra tradesman, but he resolved to become a devotee of Kṛishṇa. He tried to preach and sing his praises, but words would not come, and so he learnt by heart speeches of the saints. At length the gift of poetry became his. 'I counted holy', he says, 'the water wherein the feet of the saints had been washed. I suffered no shame to enter my mind. I served others when the chance was given me, wearing out my body. I paid no heed to friends who loved me. I was heartily sick of the crowd. The impulse of poetry fell upon me. I embraced the feet of Viṭhobā.'[3]

He became the perfect devotee of Kṛishṇa. 'If I praise any other but thee, let my tongue rot away. If I care for any other but thee, let my head be crushed. If I find pleasure in others, surely it is sinful that very instant. If the ears drink no nectar of God's glory, what use are they? Tukā says, If I forget thee for one moment, what purpose will life serve?'[4] Prosaic as his poems sometimes seem, they express often a genuine and hearty joy in Kṛishṇa's worship. 'O Lord, thou art impatient to serve thy devotees. I have learned to trust

[1] *The Heart of India*, p. 46.

[2] Tukārām was born in 1608 in the village of Dehu, about thirty miles from Poona.

[3] Paragraph 101: quotations are from J. N. Fraser's translation. Viṭhobā is here Kṛishṇa as worshipped at the shrine of Viṭhobā at Paṇḍharpur, round which the popular Vaishṇavism of the Marāṭha country centres. Bhandarkar points out that in the religious literature which gathers round Viṭhobā, Kṛishṇa is conceived, not as the lover of Rādhā, his mistress, but as the husband of Rukmiṇī, his lawful wife, and in this way 'the Vaishṇavism of the Marāṭha country is more sober and purer' (*op. cit.*, p. 89).

[4] Paragraph 151.

thy feet; hence I have given up all other efforts. Sages and saints without number have learned what thy great purpose is. Imperishable is that bliss which thou hast bestowed on these who have altogether ceased to heed the world. Tukā says, The spirit cannot contain that bliss. I have set thy feet in my heart.'[1] And in another stanza the joy becomes ecstatic. 'As we recall thy name our throat is choked with emotion; love swells within us. Oh, bless me with that lot. My hair stands erect; sweat breaks forth from me. A flood of tears fills my eyes; my eight limbs are filled with thy love. I will consume all my body in uttering thy praises. I will sing thy name day and night. Tukā says, I will do nothing else; until the end of the world there is peace unending with the saints.'[2]

And Kṛishṇa is loved by his devotees as men love their nearest. 'I feel inward sweetness as I gaze upon my treasure of faith. God is my bosom friend; the bosom friend of this helpless creature: according to his glorious might let him adorn us with purity. Tukā says, God eats with us to give us a share in his love.'[3] And this love of Kṛishṇa makes earthly joys lose their attractiveness. 'In this mortal world there is nothing which delights us but Hari's name alone. Our mind revolts from worldly life. Our spirits are sick of it. We count gold as earth, diamonds as pebbles. Tukā says, Women will appear as bears in our eyes.'[4]

His description of Kṛishṇa's saints carries the mind back at times to the *Fioretti* and the 'little brothers' of St. Francis. 'Blessed are the pious, for their heart is pure. The saints worship the visible God. They testify that they have faith therein. They know nothing of rules and prohibitions; their hearts are filled with devoted love. Tukā says, O God, you must take a form responsive to their faith.'[5] 'They dance and clap their hands, and roll on the earth, in a transport of love. My friends are the saints, the simple, the faithful people of Hari.

[1] Paragraph 747. [2] Paragraph 749. [3] Paragraph 771.
[4] Paragraph 790. [5] Paragraph 894.

They feel no shame; they have no concern with this world. Tukā says, They feel their hearts choking. Their eyes are filled with tears.'[1]

So around the image of Kṛishṇa this Śūdra tradesman weaves his thoughts of love and service. His worship was idolatrous, and yet his idolatry was able to arouse in him a devotion and a fervour not without worth and beauty.

Tulsī Dās and the Worship of Rāma.

No story in India is so famous and loved as that of Rāma, the gracious hero, and Sītā, the type and pattern of chaste and loving womanhood. The *Rāmāyaṇa* is read aloud in many houses daily as Christians read the Bible. Of the vernacular translations the best known and most significant from the standpoint of religion is the Hindī version of Tulsī Dās.[2] In it, Tulsī Dās, taking as a basis the familiar story of the *Rāmāyaṇa*, presents to us not an earthly hero merely, but an embodiment of the divine. It is as if we regarded the *Idylls of the King* as Scripture, and saw in Arthur, not a dim figure of the legendary past, but an actual and divine Redeemer. Rāma is proclaimed as the gracious God able to sympathize with his worshippers.[3] We are bidden to love him, and the love enjoined is not the hot and passionate love of a mistress for her lover, but the calm and trustful love of a child in a wise and kindly father. This version is accessible in England in the admirable translation of F. S. Growse.

It must suffice briefly to illustrate its religious nature.

The poet begins with the usual invocation to the elephant God for wisdom, and then defends his use of the vulgar tongue

[1] Paragraph 895.

[2] The original *Rāmāyaṇa* is the Sanskrit work of Vālmīki. Many of the vernaculars have versions which are regarded as classic. Thus, that by Kamban is praised by Tamulians as of incomparable beauty. Tulsī Dās is said to have lived from A. D. 1532–1623.

[3] Sir G. A. Grierson says, 'Tulsī Dās was the first Hindu to teach that God was δυνάμενος συμπαθῆσαι ταῖς ἀσθενείαις ἡμῶν ("able to sympathize with our infirmities"), a belief which is usually considered to be peculiar to Christianity.' This he ascribes to Nestorian influence (*Imperial Gazetteer*, ii. 418).

against detractors who assert that all literature should be in Sanskrit. He hastens to proclaim the praise of Rāma, and bids us 'Place the name of Rāma as a jewelled lamp at the door of our lips and there will be light, as we will, both inside and out'.[1] The name is greater than Rāma himself. 'By incessantly and devoutly repeating his name, all the faithful may attain to felicity. Rāma himself redeemed only one woman, the ascetic's wife, but his name has corrected the errors of millions of sinners.'[2] In earlier ages salvation might be won by other means; in the first age by contemplation, in the second by sacrifice, the third by temple-worship. 'But in this vile, and impure, iron age, where the soul of man floats like a fish in an ocean of sin, in these fearful times the name is the only tree of life, and by meditating on it, all commotion is stilled. In these evil days, neither good deeds, nor piety, nor spiritual wisdom, is of any avail but only the name of Rāma.'[3]

Tulsī Dās tells us that the story he has to tell clears his own doubts 'as it does every other error and delusion, and is a raft on which to cross the ocean of existence. The story of Rāma is a resting place for the intellect, a universal delight, a destroyer of worldly impurity, an antidote to the venom of passion', 'the cow of plenty in this iron age', 'a snake to devour toad-like error, the annihilator of hell'.[4] The narrative is told as if by Śiva to Umā his wife. As Śiva speaks to her of Rāma's glory, she is perplexed. 'What, the omnipresent and omnipotent God, the creator, who has neither parts nor passions, and is no respecter of persons, whom not even the Veda can comprehend, has he taken the form of a man?'[5] Śiva tells her:

> 'Seers and sages, saints and hermits, fix on him their reverent gaze,
> And in faint and trembling accents, holy scripture hymns his praise.
> He, the omnipresent spirit, lord of heaven and earth and hell,
> To redeem his people, freely has vouchsafed with men to dwell.'[6]

[1] i. *Dohā* 25.
[2] i. *Chaupāi* 24.
[3] i. *Chaupāi* 27.
[4] i. *Chaupāi* 31.
[5] i. *Dohā* 61.
[6] i. *Chhand.* 2.

Again Umā asks, 'How can he, who dwells beneath the tree of paradise, know aught of sorrow that is born of want?' 'If a king's son and so distressed by the loss of his wife, then how the supreme God?'[1] Śiva tells her that 'the cause of Hari's[2] incarnation is not to be dogmatically defined', but this much is clear: 'Whenever virtue decays and evil spirits, waxing strong in pride, work iniquity that cannot be told, to the confusion of Brāhmans, cows, gods and earth itself, the compassionate Lord assumes some new bodily form, relieves the distress of the faithful, destroys the evil spirits, reinstates the gods, maintains the way of salvation, and diffuses the brightness of his glory throughout the world. Such are the motives of Rāma's incarnations.'[3] The plural is significant. There are many 'descents' of Rāma. Śiva tells Umā of some of the earlier of these. At length comes the story of Rāma's most famous 'descent'.[4]

The world was very evil, and terrible was the oppression of the demons. The earth, 'seeing the general persecution of religion, was terror-stricken and dismayed'. 'After some consideration, she took the form of a cow and went to the spot where the gods and saints were gathered together, and with tears declared to them her distress.'[5] Brahmā bids her 'take courage and remember Hari; the Lord knows the distress of his servants, and will put an end to this cruel oppression'.[6] The voice of the Lord Rāma is heard from heaven. 'Fear not: for your sake I am about to assume the form of a man with every element of my divinity incarnate in the glorious Solar race.' In the house of Daśaratha and Kauśalyā shall 'become incarnate four brothers'.[7] Then follows the story of their birth, common to the *Rāmāyaṇa* legend. Daśaratha sends for his three wives, and divides among them a god-given

[1] i. *Chaupāī* 108, and *Dohā* 116.
[2] i.e. Vishṇu, of which Rāma was an *avatār*.
[3] i. *Chaupāī* 121, and *Dohā* 128.
[4] The more familiar word 'incarnation' has too Christian a connexion to be a good translation of *avatār*.
[5] i. *Chaupāī* 191. [6] i. *Sorathā* 22. [7] i. *Chaupāī* 193.

oblation. To Kauśalyā he gives half, to Kaikeyī a quarter, and to Sumitrā two portions of one-eighth each. According to their share of the oblation was Hari conceived in their womb. In due time Kauśalyā gives birth to Rāma. At first he wishes to display to her his power and tell of his triumphs, but she complains that she is terrified and would fain see him as a child. He yields to her wish and becomes again a crying babe. 'Thus for the sake of Brāhmans, cows and gods, and saints, he took birth as a man in a body formed at his own will, he, who is beyond all form or quality or perception of the senses.'[1] Soon after Kaikeyī bore Bharata, and Sumitrā Satrughna and Lakshmaṇa. Rāma grows up beloved by all. Then we read of Sītā, the maiden of wondrous beauty, to be won only by the hero strong enough to break Śiva's bow. Rāma breaks the bow and wins her for his bride. There is described at length the splendour of the bridal. The book ends, 'Have a hearty love for Hari's feet, discarding all vanities; much time has been spent in sleep; awake from the darkness of delusion. Whoever with love and reverence listens to the tale of Rāma and Sītā's marriage shall be happy for ever, for Rāma's praises are an unfailing joy'. In the second book we have the familiar story of the Rāma legend. We hear of Kaikeyī's jealousy, Rāma's exile, Sītā's faithfulness, and Bharata's fraternal love. Interesting as is the story, and admirably told, it contributes little to religion. The book finishes in praise of Bharata. 'All who make a vow and listen with reverence to Bharata's acts, shall assuredly acquire a great devotion to the feet of Sītā and Rāma and a distaste for the pleasures of life.'

It is the seventh and last book which for our purposes is more important, for like the first it has little story in it and much devotion. The time of Rāma's exile has passed. Rāma returns, and there is in the royal city perfect happiness and virtue. The description of this 'earthly paradise' is not only beautiful but instructive. 'Devoted to religion, the people

[1] i. *Dohā* 204. It is interesting to note the order; Brāhmans first, then cows.

walked in the path of the Vedas, each according to his own caste and stage of life, and enjoyed perfect happiness unvexed by fear or sorrow or disease.'[1] Not only among men, but among the animals in the jungle, there was peace. 'The earth was suffused with the radiance of the moon, the heat of the sun was no greater than circumstances required, and the clouds dropped rain whenever asked, in the days when Rāma was king. The Lord celebrated millions of horse-sacrifices and conferred innumerable gifts upon the Brāhmans, approving himself the defender of scriptural usage, the champion of religion, perfect in every virtue, and the sworn foe of all sensuality. Sītā was ever obedient to her Lord, incomparable in her beauty, her virtue and her meekness, sensible of the majesty of the all-merciful and devotedly attached to his lotus feet.'[2] And this wedded king was the manifestation of the divine. 'The supreme spirit, that transcends all intelligence, speech and perception, that is from everlasting, unaffected by material phenomena, or the workings of the mind, or the properties of things, even he it was who thus exhibited the actions of exalted humanity.'[3] Śiva's main narration closes with a speech in which Rāma proclaims the nature of good and evil and bids men trust in him. 'Knowledge is difficult and beset with impediments, its appliances are cumbrous, and it has no grasp on the soul. Though a man endure endless tortures, without faith, he is no friend of mine.' How Christian it all sounds, but it goes on: 'Faith is all powerful and a mine of every blessing, but men cannot attain to it except by the fellowship of the saints. Now there is no other meritorious deed in the whole world but this one, to worship Brāhmans in thought, word, and deed.'[4] 'Devoted to my name, which is the sum of all my perfections, devoid of selfishness, conceit, and vain imagination, such a man's happiness is the very sum of transcendental felicity.'[5]

[1] vii. *Dohā* 21.
[2] vii. *Dohā* 24, with the *Chaupāi* following.
[3] vii. *Dohā* 26.
[4] *Chaupāi* following vii. *Dohā* 45.
[5] vii. *Dohā* 47.

The book ends with the poet's own confession of adoration. 'Any one who reads or hears or recites this history of the glorious son of Raghu,[1] washes out the stains of the world, and the stains of his own soul, and without any trouble, goes straight to Rāma's sphere in heaven.' 'Rāma alone is all beautiful, all wise, full of compassion, and of loving-kindness for the destitute, disinterested in his benevolence, and the bestower of final deliverance; whom else can I desire? There is no other Lord like Rāma, by whose favour, however slight, even I, the dull-witted TulsīDās, have found perfect peace.'[2] There is no one so poor as I am, and no one so gracious to the poor as you, O Raghubīr; remember this, O glory of the house of Raghu, and rid me of the grievous burden of existence. As a lover loves his mistress, and as a miser loves his money, so for ever and ever may Rāma be beloved by me.'[3]

Māṇikka Vāśagar and the Love of Śiva.

Kṛishṇa, as the *Purāṇas* conceive him, is kindly, if not holy. Rāma is a gracious and noble figure, but Śiva is a god represented usually in forms terrible and grotesque. Yet in South India there are daily sung to Śiva hymns that for warmth of feeling have not often been excelled. And this worship of Śiva has not only a beautiful hymnology. It has a subtle philosophy which gifted men still proclaim with enthusiasm as the most satisfying of world-views, and which is described by Dr. Pope, the most famous of European Tamil scholars, as 'the most elaborate, influential, and undoubtedly the most intrinsically valuable, of all the religions of India'.[4] It is hard for any but devout Śaivites to understand the passionate emotion that the adoration of Śiva thus calls forth. The god

[1] One name for Rāma is Raghubīr or 'son of Raghu'.

[2] *Chhand.* 12.

[3] vii. *Dohā* 127.

[4] The *Tiruvāśagam*, lxxxiv. Of this philosophy there is an interesting account in English written by J. M. Nallasvāmi Pillai, entitled *Studies in Śaiva Siddhānta* (Madras, 1911). In German there is the elaborate work *Der Śaiva-Siddhānta, eine Mystik Indiens.* Nach den tamulischen Quellen bearbeitet und dargestellt von H. W. Schomerus. Leipzig, 1912.

seems so unlovable, yet the Śaivite saints are intoxicated with love for him, and call him Grace itself. Incurably religious must such men have been, and richly endowed with the instincts of worship and devotion.

The endeavour will be made, if not to understand, at least in some measure to expound and appreciate, this strange, yet warm and living faith. It will be convenient to illustrate chiefly from the lyrics so finely translated by Dr. Pope, which form the 'Holy Word'[1] of that great saint and poet, Māṇikka Vāśagar.

Every year there is held in the great Śaivite temples of South India a festival in this man's honour, and daily his songs are sung, not only by the impure lips of the 'women-servants' of the god, but also by earnest and devoted worshippers. Often these poems extol Śiva for deeds which seem to us fantastic and repulsive. Yet they are the work of one devoted to religion, and are hallowed by the tears and aspirations of the many who, so feelingly, have sung them.[2] The poems express, in the first place, the penitence, the thanksgiving, and the petitions of the Śaivite saint, their author. They are as intimately personal as the letters of St. Paul, and resemble Paul's letters in this also, that in them there is frequent reference to a great conversion.

The legends of Māṇikka Vāśagar's early life vary considerably. As usual in things Indian, the chronology is quite uncertain, but it is probable that it was in the ninth century that he lived.[3] It was a time when Hinduism was hard pressed. So it is said that the gods came to Śiva and requested him to save the holy cause. He therefore ordered his holy bull to descend and be born as Māṇikka Vāśagar. He was

[1] *Tiruvāśagam.*

[2] A Brāhman student of mine, whose home adjoined one of the most important Śaivite temples in Travancore, told me that his father spent many years before his death in meditation on Śiva, and in singing with intense and often tearful emotion these ancient Śaivite songs.

[3] Many Indian and some European scholars would give a far earlier date—say the second, third, or fourth century.

born near Madura at Tiruvāthavūr, and so is often known as Tiruvāthavūrar. More commonly he is called Māṇikka Vāśagar; 'he whose utterance is rubies'. His boyhood was distinguished by an extraordinary zeal for knowledge. By sixteen he had mastered the sacred Śaiva books. The Pāṇḍyan king heard of his fame and made him his chief minister. So for long he lived in pomp and wealth, and in thraldom to the senses. Frequently in his poems he speaks with penitence of these days of worldly joys, and many are the references to women's charms, to 'jet black eyes' and 'rosy lips of tender maidens', to 'bosoms full and fragrant'. Yet already, we are told, 'like those who suffer from the intense glare of heat and seek refreshing shade, his soul dissolves in passionate longing for Śiva the loving Lord'.[1]

At length the day of deliverance draws near. The king sends him with great treasure to the seaport to buy horses from abroad. The details of the story vary much.[2] According to the *Purāṇa* here followed, on his way through Madura he went to the temple to worship Śiva. A strange emotion overcame him. 'He shed tears of joy, the hair of his body stood erect, his tongue trembled, his hands involuntarily made obeisance, his mind melted like wax in the fire, and desire passed from him.' Summoning his companions, he told them that the horses would not arrive for a month and that they need not stay. Speedily he beheld Śiva surrounded by his devotees under a gurunṭham tree. Śiva received him, taught him, and consecrated him to his service. Straightway were his sins expurgated, and Śiva bade him worship him by song. So he sang hymns of praise for Śiva's grace. Gladly would Māṇikka Vāśagar have left the earth and gone to Śiva's realm, but Śiva would not permit it. At length Śiva and his

[1] Pope, xix.

[2] Pope follows throughout the *Tiruvāthavūrar Purāṇa*. The account given above is from the Tamil life of the poet given by Anavaratha-vināyagam Piḷḷai in his edition of the *Tiruvāśagam*, and is based on the *Tiruvilaiyāḍal Purāṇa*, which is reputed to be earlier.

disciples vanished.[1] Meditating on his holy guru, with tears of sorrow, Māṇikka Vāśagar composed fresh songs, expressive of his deep longing to rejoin the god whom at last he had beheld, and many of the most beautiful of his extant poems are assigned to this time. When the temple servants came and marvelled at the sweetness of these songs he distributed to them the treasure given him by the king to purchase horses.[2] Envious ministers reported this to the king, who angrily wrote to him that he must return at once. Māṇikka Vāśagar in great distress wrote back that the horses would all be sent. When the day fixed for their return expired, the king had him tortured. The sequel of the story is clearly legendary. Unable to endure the agony, Māṇikka Vāśagar cried out to Śiva in his distress. Śiva in pity went to the Jackal village and, changing the jackals into horses, brought them into Madura.[3] The king received them with great joy, but at night-time the jackals returned to their old form and, killing the real horses, fled away. The king in natural anger tortured Māṇikka Vāśagar again. Śiva, to save him, caused the river to flood so that Madura was imperilled. Orders were given that every one should build a dam before his house. One woman found the work too hard. A coolie came and offered to serve her, receiving as wages a little cake. He neglects the work and the water at that place overflows. The king has him beaten. The coolie is Śiva himself. It is one of his sportive acts. As all things are in Śiva, the weals inflicted upon his back appear on the backs of gods, men, and

[1] Schomerus suggests that it is this story of Māṇikka Vāśagar's conversion, which to the writers of the Śaiva Siddhānta school appeared not legend but fact, which accounts for the way in which Śiva is so often said to manifest himself to his devotees, not in his divine glory as creator, sustainer, and destroyer of the universe, but as the 'Satguru', the good teacher (*Der Śaiva Siddhānta*, p. 293).

[2] Other accounts say that he spent the money in building temple shrines, or that he gave it to the poor.

[3] There is frequent reference to this in some of the poems assigned to Māṇikka Vāśagar, but it may well be doubted if he is the author of them.

beasts alike. A heavenly voice proclaims Māṇikka Vāśagar as Śiva's servant.

The king in penitence asked Māṇikka Vāśagar to reign in his stead, but he refused, and in humble guise, in poverty and well-nigh nakedness, as a *sannyāsin* wandered from shrine to shrine extolling Śiva's grace. His influence and the power and beauty of his songs contributed much to the downfall of Buddhism and the spread of Śaivism in South India. As Pope well puts it, 'South India needed a personal God, an assurance of immortality, and a call to prayer. These it found in Māṇikka's Vāśagar's compositions.'[1]

It seems clear that beneath all legendary accretions there is the record of a genuine conversion and a great renunciation, while the story as it stands may serve as an illustration of Śaivite hagiology, where saints have visions frequently of Śiva, and Śiva for his saints does strange and often freakish acts.[2]

Gratitude for his conversion provides one of the great motives for these songs. In the Miracle-Decad, which is perhaps the earliest of them, it is of this alone that Māṇikka Vāśagar sings. Śiva has redeemed him from bondage to the flesh, therefore will he praise him. The poem is called also 'the unutterable experience'. One editor, whom Pope quotes, speaks of it as 'the sobbing utterance of unspeakable and unbearable experience'. It must suffice to quote the first and the last stanzas:

1. 'By lust bewildered;—in this earthly sphere
   caught in the circling sea of joyous life:—
   By whirling tide of woman's charms engulfed:—
   lest I should sink with mind perturbed,
   He gave his sacred grace, that falseness all
   my soul might flee, and showed his golden feet,
   The truth himself,—He stood in presence there
   This matchless miracle I tell not, I.

[1] *Tiruvāśagam*, xxxvi.

[2] Cp. the legends of Śaivite saints in the *Periya Purāṇa*.

10. I gave no thought on thronging "births" and "deaths",
but dwelt on tricks and wiles, and glancing eyes
Of maids with wealth of braided tresses fair;
and thus I lay. The king, our Lord supreme,
His jewelled feet, that traverse all the worlds,
to me made manifest like clustering blooms;
He wisdom gave, and made me all his own:
This miracle of grace I know not, I.'[1]

He bids men praise the God who as a Brāhman once appeared to save him.

'Haste, haste ye, garlands of fresh flowers
Around his feet to bind.
Assemble, go around, follow hard on, leave ye no gap.
Lay hold of him, although he hide himself, avoid your gaze,
The incomparable told out his nature as it is,
That those like me might hear.
He called in grace, he made me his,
He as a Brāhman showed his glory forth,
Then, while undying love dissolved my frame, I cried;
I raised enraptured voice above the billowy sea's loud waves.
In utter wilderment, I fell, I rolled, I cried aloud,
Madman distraught, and as a madman raved;
While those who saw were wildered, who heard it, wondered sore;
More than the frenzy wild of raging elephant
Bore me away beyond endurance far. 'Twas then through all my limbs
A honied sweetness he infused and made me blest.'[2]

His conversion was due not to merit of his own but to Śiva's grace.

'To me, a dog, all things not shown before, he showed;
All things not heard before, he caused to hear;
And guarding me from future birth he made me his:
Such is the wondrous work our Lord hath wrought for me.'[3]

'Thou cam'st in grace on this same earth, didst show thy mighty feet
To me who lay mere slave—meaner than any dog,—
Essential grace more precious than a mother's love.'[4]

[1] xli, stanzas 1 and 10. [2] iii. 142-57. [3] v. 111, 112. [4] i. 59-61.

'Devoid of love for him in sooth was I,
  I know it and he knows it too,
And yet he made me his, this too all men,
  On earth shall surely see and know.
He there appeared in all his grace revealed.
  He only is my being's king.'[1]

The sincerity of these poems cannot be questioned, and even to the European unused to Indian poetry and music their pathetic beauty is unmistakable. Here, assuredly, speaks a man of religious genius and experience, and yet to the Westerner how hard his religion is to understand. The very deeds for which he praises Śiva seem often so repulsive. He is moved to tender gratitude by the remembrance of legends of him, barbaric and grotesque. There is thus in the hymns that incongruity which seems characteristic of the Śaivite temples. Thus a visitor to the great Śaivite temple at Madura feels at once the wealth of devotion shown in the erection of that enormous pile. Here are devotees who have travelled far to worship. Here are holy men chanting Śiva's praises. Yet in the inmost shrine, where only caste Hindus may enter, is the nameless emblem of the Śaivite faith, that symbol of procreative power,[2] and, in the cloisters, the innumerable statues of the gods are never sublime, but often conceived in a spirit vulgar, trivial, and at times indecent. The phrase of Luther's, 'The two belong together, Faith and God', seems here no longer to apply. The object of devotion seems so inadequate to the devotion lavished. Doubtless the conception of Śiva is syncretic. He is the Rudra of the *Rigveda*, the destroyer whom men fear and yet call gracious (śiva). His home is in the Himalayas. He is the ascetic, austere, and, because of his austerities, of incomparable power. Destroyer

[1] x. 49-51.

[2] It is interesting to note Nallasvāmī Pillai's remark that the liṅga of Śaivism is nothing but the hill-top in origin (*Studies in Śaiva-Siddhānta*, p. 339) as indicative of a modern repugnance to its phallic nature. With far greater probability Bhandarkar holds that 'the Rudra-Śiva cult may have borrowed this element of phallic worship from the barbarian tribes with whom the Aryas came in contact', *op. cit.*, p. 115.

as he is, with him is connected the mystery of birth, and his is the phallic emblem. He is, withal, the Lord of goblins dancing amid the grave-yards his fierce dance, his body smeared with ashes, his neck adorned with dead men's bones. And in the South, Śiva is not only the terrible god. He is the friendly god whose 'sports' men love to praise.[1] To his saints he appears in strange disguises and genially deceives them.[2] And even the weirdest stories of him seem able to arouse in men's hearts devotion and gratitude.

The very form of Śiva brings to Māṇikka Vāśagar the remembrance of his grace. He hails him as 'the god who wears the Ganges in his braided locks'.[3] It is a curious legend. A king Bhagīratha by long austerities induced the gods to send down into the world the heavenly Ganges, that so his ancestors, consumed to ashes through the curses of a sage, might be restored. Down fell the heavenly Ganges; but Śiva, ever gracious, fearing that it would destroy the world, caught the river on his head and kept it there, amid his braided locks, and thus the world was saved.

Often the poet refers to the tiger-skin with which Śiva's waist is girt, and to the snake in Śiva's braided hair. The story is an ancient and famous one, yet how unworthy.

Vishṇu went one day to Kailāśa to worship Śiva. Śiva complained that near by in the forest there were multitudes of ascetics who did not recognize his rule.[4] So long as they continued their austerities, not even the greatest gods could prevail against them. So at Śiva's wish, Vishṇu assumed a female form and accompanied Śiva as his wife into the jungle. So beautiful did the two gods appear that all the ascetic's wives were infatuated with Śiva and all the ascetics with

[1] There is a brief and convenient account of these legends in Dowson's *Classical Dictionary of Hindu Mythology*, 296-300.

[2] So men need to entertain with kindness every Śaivite ascetic, for he too may be Śiva in disguise.

[3] v. 256.

[4] One commentator says that they were followers of the Mīmāṁsā. The whole story seems to refer to an ancient conflict between Vedāntists and Śaivites. Pope, *op. cit.* lxii.

Vishṇu. Soon they realized that these two mendicants were gods disguised, and, ashamed of their passion, uttered against them the fiercest curses, but the gods remained unharmed. At length, to destroy them, the *ṛishis* performed with minutest care an elaborate sacrifice. In consequence a fierce tiger came out of the fire to slay Śiva, but Śiva seized it, and with his finger-nail ripped off the skin and wrapped it round his body as a garment. Again the *ṛishis* renewed their offerings, and out came a great serpent, which he put round his neck, where it still hangs. It is because of this exploit that time after time Śiva's saints address him as the deceiver (*kaḷḷan*).

One deed of Śiva the poet praises often, and with most hearty gratitude. Śiva's throat is swollen and dark blue in colour. It is the emblem of the suffering he graciously endured to save the world. The gods at one time were in sore distress and came to Śiva for assistance. He descended from Mount Kailāśa and churned the sea of milk, and from thence there issued the ambrosial food of undying joy. But first there came a stream of black *hālāhala* poison, and this Śiva drank up. His neck, thus dark and swollen, is the perpetual witness of his mighty grace. So to the gods he gave ambrosia; for himself he took the deadly poison. Thus Māṇikka Vāśagar writes in one of his poems:

'He ate *hālālam* from the sounding sea, that day arisen
With mighty din; what means this wondrous act, my dear?
Had he not eaten on that day the poison fierce, Ayan and Māl,
And all the other gods of upper heaven had died.'[1]

So in one of the most attractive of his poems, the poem called 'Forsake me not', Māṇikka Vāśagar alludes to this legend with touching effect. His conversion was all due to Śiva's grace. False was he, yet Śiva made him his. Now Śiva has forsaken him to wander in the world alone, tempted and weak. Yet disconsolate as he is, he still can be sure of Śiva's grace, for his throat is black with the poison that he

[1] xii, eighth stanza. Ayan is Brahmā, and Māl, Vishṇu.

drank.[1] Time after time he appeals to Śiva not to leave him. In the temples where he worshipped were the female servants of the god, and, through them, he found it hard to subdue his lusts. So his rapturous enjoyment of Śiva's grace passed away. He prays for Śiva's mercy, and at length in a frenzy of abandonment he says that if Śiva leaves him he will abuse him sore. Yet even his abuse is praise.

> 'Lo, thou'st forsaken me, but if thou leave, I shall abuse thee sore,
> "Madman, clad in wild elephant's skin"; "Madman, with hide for his garb";
> "Madman that ate the poison"; "Madman of the burning-ground fire";
> "Madman, that chose even me for his own".'[2]

The poem concludes with a memorable stanza:

> 'Abusing thee or praising,—crushed by sin, and grieved am I.
> Lo, thou'st forsaken me, thou brightness on red coral hill.
> Thou mad'st me thine; didst fiery poison eat, pitying poor souls,
> That I might thine ambrosia taste,—I, meanest one.'

Strange as these legends are, the worship of Śiva is a genuine religion which finds in the *Śaiva Siddhānta* a not unworthy expression. The schoolmen of that philosophy lived after Māṇikka Vāśagar's time, but in undeveloped form its chief doctrines are to be found in the poems. God is regarded not as a negative abstraction, but as personal. He loves his saints and succours them. So we have the famous stanza from Tirumūlar's *Tirumanthiram*:

> 'O ye fools that speak of the unspeakable,
> Can ye see the limits of the limitless one?
> To one whose mind gains clearness as the waveless sea
> Will appear faultless the Lord with the braided hair.'[3]

And one of the chief modern exponents of the system writes:

> 'That Śiva had no *avatārs* or births is generally known. This is the

[1] vi, seventh stanza. [2] vi, forty-ninth stanza.

[3] Quoted and translated by Nallasvāmī Piḷḷai, *Studies in Śaiva Siddhānta*, p. 272.

greatest distinction of the ancient Hindu philosophy and of the Śaiva school, making it a purely transcendental religion, freed of all anthropomorphic conceptions. . . . But this absolute nature of Śiva does not prevent him from his being (*sic*) personal at the same time, and appearing as Guru and Saviour, in the form of man, out of his great love and feeling for the sin and sorrow of mankind, and helping them to get rid of their bondage.'[1]

Whereas Hindus often ascribe to Śiva but one place in the Hindu Trinity and hold his work to be that of destruction, this school of thought regards Śiva as the supreme God performing alone the threefold task of creation, preservation, and destruction. Thus Māṇikka Vāśagar sings:

'All worlds,
Thou dost create, protect, enrich with grace,
Release.'[2]

And this almighty God is proclaimed as a God of love. Thus the gifted exponent of Śaivism just quoted refers more than once to the well-known lines:

'The ignorant say, Love and God are different.
None know that Love and God are the same;
When they know that Love and God are the same,
They rest in God as Love.'[3]

And modern Śaivites, familiar with the Bible, claim for this religion a close affinity to Christian thought. Certainly some of the Śaivite poets come extraordinarily near to Christian speech. Thus Tāyumānavar has the stanza:

'O my God Lord, the fullness of bliss, great didst thou make thy love; thou camest to save my precious soul.'

But the resemblance is more in the word than in the thought.

How Śiva's grace is popularly conceived the stories of his

[1] *Op. cit.*, p. 299. [2] i. 41-3.

[3] I give Nallasvāmī Piḷḷai's translation (*op. cit.*, p. 227), but the word he translates 'God' is not the masculine 'Śiva' (Śivan), but a neuter form (Śivam). As Schomerus says, 'the word (Śivam) probably denotes redemption, blessedness, and thus the stanza deals not with the nature of God but with the nature of blessedness'; but whatever be true of this particular verse, the thought of God's love occurs very commonly in this Śaivite literature' (vide *Der Śaiva Siddhānta*, p. 62).

Sacred Sports' well show. Joyfully he accepts the devotion of his saints, grants them the vision of himself, and by strange means fulfils their desire.[1] Often the stories seem trivial and meaningless. Sometimes they have in them a certain fantastic beauty. Thus in one of his poems Māṇikka Vāśagar confesses:

'There was no love in me like Kaṇṇappan's.'[2]

And in another poem he praises Siva's grace in accepting Kaṇṇappan's devotion, though he used his mouth for a chalice and proffered flesh for food.[3] It is a strange legend. A shepherd chieftain's son, as he hunted the wild boar, came across an image of Śiva, a phallic stone on which was carved in rough the head of the God. Enraptured with it, refusing to return home, he became its devotee, and offered to it the choicest pieces of the boar he had slain. Day after day he hunted that he might make his offerings. To the Śaivite, flesh-eating is an abomination, and the Brāhman in charge of the shrine was shocked at the awful desecration he witnessed there each morning. Overwhelmed with shame he appeals to Śiva. Śiva takes the Brāhman at night-time to the rude shrine and bids him hide behind the image. When the herdsman comes to prove his zeal Śiva causes blood to trickle down one eye of the image. In great grief the herdsman seeks for herbs to stay the blood. They are of no avail. At length he remembered that eye could heal eye. With instant joy he tore out his own eye and applied it to the bleeding eye of the image and the blood ceased to flow. But then the other eye began to bleed. To heal it, he was about to scoop out his one remaining eye but Śiva put a hand out from the image, restrained the worshipper, and promised him that he should be for ever on his holy mountain. So the Brāhman learns that love was more than ceremonial purity, and the saints sing the praises of this herdsman-devotee, whom Śiva renamed

[1] Cp. the acts assigned to him at Māṇikka Vāśagar's conversion; the turning of jackals into horses; his work as coolie; his suffering himself to be beaten.

[2] x, stanza 4.

[3] xv, stanza 3.

Kaṇṇ-appan,[1] the man who gave his eye for the God. Thus Śiva's grace was shown.

Not only through such myths as these is Śiva's grace extolled. Poets and philosophers alike ascribe to his grace the release from bondage. So in both Śaivism and Christianity there is proclaimed the grace (*aruḷ*) of God, demanding in response the faith (*bhakti*) of man. It is not surprising that modern exponents, familiar with Christianity, should say, as Mr. Nullasvāmī Piḷḷai does, that the doctrine of grace in the *Śaiva Siddhānta* 'differs in no respect from the Christian doctrine'.[2] And it is sometimes claimed that the bondage from which Śiva releases is that of sin. But in reality it is just here that the great distinction lies. Sin is not treated as the act of a responsible personality. All Śiva's grace can do is to illuminate the soul by revealing its identity with himself. This redemption means for the soul 'an absolute passivity, and this absolute passivity on the part of the soul makes it impossible to understand by this unity with God, communion with God in the Christian sense'.[3] The soul, which Śiva's grace illumines, has to gather itself apart from its threefold bond and thus gradually obtains its final emancipation. But the bond from which the soul is thus released is not that of sin but a bond partly karmic, partly material.[4] So though Māṇikka Vāśagar, in common with the other writers of this school, very frequently praises Śiva's grace, the grace thus extolled is not the same as grace in the Christian sense. Grace in Christianity denotes God's holy love seen in relation to human sin. Where God is not regarded as essentially holy, and where man is not

[1] Literally 'the eye-man', or, possibly, as some take it, 'the man who applied his eye as a poultice', taking *appan* not in its familiar sense, but as a derivative from *appu*, 'to apply as of a poultice'.

[2] *Op. cit.*, p. 355.

[3] Schomerus, *Der Śaiva Siddhānta*, p. 430.

[4] This bond (*pāśam*) is a rope of three strands: (1) *Āṇavam*, an inherent defilement which darkens the soul's light or intelligence, so that it cannot understand its true nature, its oneness with Śiva. (2) *Karma*, the effect of past deeds impelling to new births which must be neutralized. (3) *Māyā*, which in this system is not so much illusion as an elemental matter in which inhere the impurities of the soul. For a brief account see *E. R. E.* v. 27.

sufficiently responsible for his deeds really to be guilty, we cannot give to grace its Christian meaning.[1]

In spite of an inadequate conception of God and the human soul, the poems of Māṇikka Vāśagar often express with rare beauty his gratitude for God's past favour and his aspiration for perfect union with his Lord. As we have seen, at his conversion he had laid aside his princely pomp and taken the meagre garb of an ascetic. But, in renouncing the world, he had not escaped its temptations. Even to the end he seems to have found it hard to resist the allurements of the 'women servants' of the god, and in his poems are many confessions of his failure to withstand their charms. Eagerly therefore does he desire to quit the body and be perfectly redeemed.

'To cast quite off this sinful frame; to enter Śiva's home;
To see the wondrous light that so these eyes may gladness gain;
O infinite beyond compare; th' assembly of thy saints
Of old to see, behold, O sire, thy servant's soul hath yearned.'[2]

In another poem he expresses his sorrow that he must still stay on earth amid emth's distractions:

1. 'Mingling with thy true saints, that day in speechless joy I stood;
Next day, with dawning daylight, trouble came and there abode.
My soul grows old. Master, to seek the gleam of fadeless bliss
Wand'ring I went. In grace to me, thy slave, let love abound.

2. Some of thy saints have gained through plenteous love thy grace. Grown old,
All vain my griefs; of this vile corpse I see no end.
Remove from sinful me my deeds of sin; let mercy's sea o'erflow;
O Master, to thy slave give ceaseless, soul-subduing grace.

7. They've seen the sea-like bliss, have seized it and enjoy. Is't meet,
That I, low dog, with added pains and pining sore should bide?

[1] Pope's statement that 'the Tamil word *aruḷ* (அருள்) is used in every sense given to *χάρις* in the New Testament, and חֶסֶד in the Hebrew' (*op. cit.* xlviii), cannot therefore be accepted without qualification.

[2] xxv, ninth stanza.

> Master, do thou thyself give grace; I pray, I faint, I fail;
> Cut short thy work, O light, let darkness flee before thy mercy's beam.'[1]

In the poem entitled the 'Decad of the bruised heart', the grief at his severance from Śiva and his homesickness for him find beautiful and poignant expression. No virtue had he when Śiva first visited him in love. Why then should he be forsaken now? Dog as he was, Śiva had taken him for his own. Even in his desolation he is altogether Śiva's own. On him alone he meditates. In him is his solitary joy. We quote the last three stanzas:

> 8. 'Me dog, and lower than a dog, all lovingly thyself didst take for thine. This birth-illusion's thrall
> Is placed within thy charge alone. And I in sooth, is there aught I need beyond that with care search out?
> Herein is there authority at all with me?
> Thou may'st again consign me to some mortal frame; or 'neath thy jewelled foot may'st place me, Brow-eyed One.
>
> 9. Thou in whose brow a central eye doth gleam. Thy feet—the twain—I saw; mine eyes rejoiced; now night and day
> Without a thought, on them alone I ponder still, how I may quit this earthly frame, how I may come
> To enter 'neath thy feet in bliss, I ponder not; save thee, O king, should I thy servant ponder aught?
> Thy service here hath fullness of delight for me.
>
> 10. Thy beauty only, I, a slavish dog, desire, and cry aloud. O Master, thou didst show to me
> Thy sacred form in lustre shrined and didst accept my service. Thou my glory, mine august abode,
> In ancient days assured, thou now withholdest; and so, O beauteous Lord, Thou of the glorious mystic word,
> My king—sorely indeed hast thou bruised my poor heart.'[2]

But at the end his devotion seems to have become more untroubled. Thus in the poem called 'The Decad of the Tenacious Grasp',[3] he speaks as one who, though on earth, is yet redeemed and already one with Śiva.[4] Śiva has kept him

[1] xxxii, stanzas 1, 2, and 7. [2] xxxiii, stanzas 8–10. [3] xxxvii.
[4] A *Jīvan-mukta*, to use the technical phrase.

safe through the long years. Greater by far is Śiva's love than love of a mother for the child she suckles. Rapture, Śiva gives, and sweetness. Śiva is the wealth of bliss and the splendour of grace. All bonds for him has he removed. In his servant's vile body Śiva deigns to dwell as if in a shrine of gold. In the refrain of each verse the poet triumphantly declares, 'I've seized thee now, I hold thee fast'.

The last of his hymns is called 'the Wonder of Salvation', or 'Joy ineffable'. He records with penitence his many failures, but thankfully confesses Śiva's all-sufficient grace. In successive verses he hails Śiva as Father, the Mystic Dancer, the Guru, the High and Lofty One, the Master, the Last One and the First, the Mother of all:

1. 'To me who toiled and moiled 'mid fools that knew not way of final peace
He taught the way of pious love;[1] and that old deeds might cease and flee,
Purging the foulness of my will, made me pure bliss, took for his own;—
'Twas thus the Father gave me grace; O rapture, who so blest as I?

3. Me trusting every lie as truth—plunged in desire of woman's charms,—
He guarded that I perished not with soul perturbed,—the Lord Superne,
On whose left side the Lady[2] dwells—He brought me nigh his jewelled feet,
'Twas thus my Guru gave me grace; O rapture, who so blest as I?

10. With those that knew not right or good, men ignorant, I wandered too.
The first, the primal Lord himself, threefold pollution caused to cease;
Even men he took as something worth—like dog in sumptuous litter borne.
'Twas thus the Mother gave me grace: O rapture, who so blest as I?'[3]

[1] The Tamil word is *bhakti*.

[2] Umā, the consort of Śiva, or, in philosophic language, his Śakti or power.

[3] li., stanzas 1, 3, and 10.

Wonderfully successful as Dr. Pope's translation of these poems is, no translation can express in a language so dissimilar to Tamil as is English the power of the original. To those whose ears have grown accustomed to Indian music and rhythm these poems have a strange and, at times, even a haunting beauty. But their chief interest is not as literature but as religion. Here is expressed the penitence and the joy, the loneliness and the ecstasy, of a man of religious genius and vivid spiritual experience. Unworthy as the God he worshipped seems to receive such devotion, unattractive as so many of the legends he uses are, we can understand the Tamil saying, 'He whose heart is not melted by the *Tiruvāśagam*, must have a stone for a heart'.

Cardinal Barberini, we are told, dedicated his translation of Marcus Aurelius's *Meditations* 'To his soul, to make it redder than his purple at the sight of the virtues of this Gentile'. And as we read the works of these Indian saints we may well bid our souls blush crimson at the virtues of these true lovers of God, and inevitably we look forward to the day when the devotion so lavishly bestowed on Kṛishṇa, Rāma, and Śiva shall be given in full measure to the crucified and perfectly holy Saviour of the world.

PART II

CHAPTER VII

JESUS CHRIST AND HIS GOSPEL

HE who desires to know of Jesus Christ must turn first to the writings of His immediate followers. There in the New Testament he will find a literature in every way unique. Written by men without literary ambition, and for the most part devoid of literary gift, it yet pulsates with energy and strength. The classic writers of the time have the weariness which marks an age's end. These men have the vigour of a new age. Differing in their approach, they are one in their central theme. It is not so much that they feel they have a new truth to proclaim. It is rather that a great event has happened which has changed not only their lives but the world they live in—nay, more, has brought heaven to earth and endowed weak men with the power of the life to come. That event is Jesus Christ. Jews, regarding as blasphemy the slightest infringement of God's unique, and transcendent, supremacy, here claim, with calm confidence, that the Man, with whom some of them had lived for long in the closest intimacy, was none other than the eternal Son of God. Yet these men who write are not fanatics. They have learned from Jesus a moral realism and vigour unsurpassed in ethical literature. And their presentation of His character has a unity in difference, a power, and an attraction, which no fictive genius could invent.

Yet to the great world at Rome, as reflected in its literature, how contemptible these Christians seemed. Nero could think to avert from himself the suspicion of having set Rome afire by placing it upon them as men capable of any crime.

Though the great historian Tacitus recognizes that this charge was false, yet all he knew of the Christians is that they were a class hated by the common people for their secret crimes; and of Jesus he says only that 'Christus, from whom their name had its origin, suffered the extreme penalty in the reign of Tiberius at the hands of our procurator, Pontius Pilate; and a most mischievous superstition, thus checked for the moment, again broke out not only in Judaea, the first source of the evil, but even in Rome, where all things hideous and shameful from every part of the world, find their centre and become popular'.[1] A little later, and the younger Pliny writes from Bithynia to the Emperor Trajan about these troublesome Christians. He has put to death many who refused to curse Christ and offer incense to the statue of the Emperor. He is a humane man and manifestly he is uneasy. The superstition, he says, has infected not only the town but the villages and the country. He has endeavoured to get the truth by torturing two deaconesses, but all he could find in their confessions was a depraved superstition. No true Christian, he complains, will ever recant. Those who did so were men who for long had ceased to be Christians. And these said that the sum of their offence had been that on fixed days they sang a hymn to Christ as God and took an oath to commit no crime.[2]

Before the end of the second century Tertullian, though he has still to repudiate shameful accusations brought against Christians by the populace, can yet boast of the vast extent and power of the Church in the West, and, in his vehement way, can bid defiance to the Roman power. A little later, in Alexandria, Clement and Origen can seek, in their own words, 'to bring all learning into the Gospel net', and the despised

[1] Tacitus, *Annals*, Bk. xv, Church and Brodribb's translation, page 304. Tacitus was a boy of nine in A. D. 64, when the fire of Rome took place.

[2] *Letters*, x. 97. These pagan witnesses are of considerable importance from the standpoint of this essay. Not unnaturally many Hindus answer the modern criticism, which resolves so much of the Kṛishṇa story into a legend, by a *tu quoque*, and in turn deny the historicity of Jesus with the help of Western books.

cult of Christ becomes in their hands not only a religion, but a sublime philosophy, able to challenge the best wisdom of the Greeks. It is to-day the commonplace of history that no human life can approach Christ's in importance. Through the centuries He has brought both peace and a sword. He has been to multitudes their strength and joy. He has been the great disturbing and revolutionary force demanding of man incomparable sacrifices, and exacting an obedience which men will only give to God. Such a one cannot be ignored. The most important question in religion is still: Who was Jesus Christ? What does He mean to us?

And the importance of this question is increasingly recognized in the East, and to it the East claims, with justice, the right to express its answer in its own way. When Rām Mohan Rai, the founder of the first Brāhma Samāj, was shown a picture of Christ, he complained that the artist had given to Christ a European countenance. And this complaint has in various forms been often repeated. 'England', said Keshab Chandra Sen,[1] 'has sent us after all a Western Christ. It seems that the Christ who has come to us is an Englishman, with English manners and customs about Him, and with the temper and spirit of an Englishman in Him; why should Hindus go to England to learn Jesus Christ? Is not Christ's native land nearer to India than to England? Are not Jesus and His apostlesand immediate followers more akin to Indian nationality than Englishmen?' And Mozoomdar, his disciple, and in a sense his successor, has described in language that makes painful reading, the contrast between the 'Western' and the 'Eastern' Christ. 'The Western Christ' he speaks of is surely a caricature of some harsh-spirited and intolerant missionary. It is hard for any Christian to recognize in the picture any likeness to Jesus Christ.

'He insists upon plenary inspiration, continually descants on miracles, imports institutions foreign to the genius of the continent, and, in case of non-compliance with whatever he lays down, condemns men to eternal

[1] In his lecture, *India asks who is Christ?* given in April, 1879.

darkness and death. He continually talks of blood and fire and hell. He considers innocent babes as the progeny of deadly sin; he hurls invectives on other men's faith, however truly and conscientiously held. No sacred notions are sacred to him unless he has taught them. All self-sacrifice which he does not understand is delusion to him. All scriptures are false which have grown up outside of his dispensation, climate, and nationality. He will revolutionize, and denationalize, and alienate men from their kith and kin. Wherever he goes, men learn to beware of him. He is a Mlecha to Hindus, a Kaffir to Muḥammadans, a rock of offence to everybody. He is tolerated only because he carries with him the imperial prestige of a conquering race. Can this be the Christ that will save India?' . . . 'When we speak of an Eastern Christ we speak of the incarnation of unbounded love and grace, and when we speak of the Western Christ we speak of the incarnation of theology, formalism, ethical and physical force. Christ we know is neither of the East nor of the West, but men have localized what God meant to make universal.'[1]

The accusation has to be admitted, in part, with sorrow. Yet it may be doubtful whether Mozoomdar's interpretation does not go as far to one extreme as the view of Christ he so vigorously denounces does to the other. The mystic *sannyāsin* he depicts could have no message for the West. That perhaps matters little. What is more serious is that his interpretation does not bring to the East 'the ethical force' which is not a Western misconception, but an essential attribute in the character of Christ as given in the Gospels and received by the Church. In truth, this distinction between a Western and an Eastern Christ seems to be of little value. It is indeed true that a man's estimate of another is a revelation of himself, and it has to be admitted that racial differences are more real than home-staying folk can realize. As it has been truly said, 'we may say beauty is only skin-deep, but as a matter of fact there are few deeper things than skin; it represents, not so much a physiological or racial difference, as an intellectual, a moral,

[1] Pratāp Chandra Mozoomdar, *The Oriental Christ*, pp. 43 and 46. The whole history of the Brāhma Samāj is from this point of view very instructive. Vide *E. R. E.* ii. 813-24, and J. N. Farquhar's *Modern Religious Movements in India*, pp. 29-74.

and a social cleavage between man and man'.[1] The saints of the East do not win the enthusiasm of the West. The ideals of the West seem often noisy and vulgar to the East. Yet Christ transcends such limitations. An Oriental, He has gained the worship of the West which forgets His Eastern birth; preached to-day by men of Western blood and speech, He is loved by men of many a race who think of Him as theirs. An Asiatic, He yet belongs to the world, and the history of the Church has shown that men of every clime and colour can find in Him their congenial Lord.

To the men of His own age, Jesus was in the first place a teacher and a healer of diseases. In days when men have been overawed by the claims of science, the belief in His miracles has often been abandoned; but in His character of Teacher, He has been always and almost universally admired. It is convenient, therefore, to deal first with the message which He brought.

It is His transparent sense of God that conditions all His teaching. God is for Him both Father and King. So around the two foci of God, the Father and the kingdom of God, all His teaching gathers.

Through Christ it is that the Fatherhood of God has become the commonplace of religion. Old Testament saints had indeed spoken of a God who pitied like a Father,[2] and comforted like a Mother,[3] but such glimpses of God's love are only occasional and transitory. It is true that in some of the earliest of Āryan hymns 'Father-Heaven' is extolled, but it is in conjunction with Mother-Earth, and 'Father' here means little more than 'Fertilizer'.[4]

Nowhere has Jesus defined God, nowhere does He describe

[1] A. M. Fairbairn, *The Philosophy of the Christian Religion*, p. 369.
[2] Psalm ciii. 13.
[3] Isaiah lxvi. 13.
[4] In six hymns of the *R. V.*, Dyaus Pitar (Father-Heaven) and Prithivī (Mother-Earth) are hailed as the universal parents, but there is nothing in common between this idea of the impregnating sky, referred to as the roaring bull, and the holy Heavenly Father of the Christian.

His attributes. Never was a religious teacher less a schoolman than Jesus. In homely speech, in aphorism and parable, Jesus made God real to His disciples and taught them who He was. It is not because God created man that Jesus calls Him Father. It is because He loves men with an unmerited love, and watches over them and defends them with a Father's care. Fatherhood, as Christ conceived it, is thus a moral and not a physical relationship. And God's gratuitous and forgiving love requires as its complement our childlike trust and receptivity. God is eternally the Father. He loves all men, and to all men alike He shows His bounty. Thus God does not become the Father but we have to become His sons,[1] to learn by the way of faith to trust in Him and reflect His character. In words that all the world has learned to love, Christ speaks of God's pursuing grace. Evil-doers are not to God the hopelessly accursed. As a woman seeks her lost money *until she find it*, so does God seek the lost. Over the restoration of every sinner there is joy in heaven, and to the prodigal is given the glad welcome of forgiveness. For God each soul of man is of immeasurable worth. The Heavenly Father cares for us each one, counts the hairs of our head, knows when a sparrow falls. Yet we should wrong Christ's teaching in regard to God if we dwelt only on its graciousness. The glad and tender message is yet incomparably stern. Our Father is the Father in Heaven, the almighty, and infinitely exalted, God. The proper attitude before Him is one not of love and trust only, but of fear.[2] God demands of His children that they should be dissatisfied with the imperfect and seek to be perfect as He is. And this means that a ruthless self-discipline is necessary. Thus to renounce all cherished sins may mean a mutilation of our desires as violent and painful as any mutilation of the body. We are the servants of God as well as His children. And God demands an undivided

[1] Wendt, *Teaching of Jesus*, i. 194: 'God does not become the Father, but is the heavenly Father even of those who *become* His sons.'

[2] Cp. Titius' suggestive words, *Jesus Lehre vom Reiche Gottes*, pp. 104, 110.

service, and His service seems at times exacting. Jesus knew full well how hard it would be for His disciples to share His glad confidence in the Father's love. Often God would seem as callous as the unjust judge, as reluctant to help as a selfish neighbour at night-time. Yet Jesus recognizes such doubts only to dispel them. Of His disciples He demanded a faith which no circumstance could daunt. Fearing God we need fear nothing and no one else. Even in persecutions His little flock could still be brave. Was it not their Father's good pleasure to give them the kingdom?

So with Christ's message of God as Father is inseparably connected His proclamation of the kingdom of God. God as Father gives His best gifts to His children. The best gift of all is the kingdom. This is the treasure, this the pearl which above all else we must seek. Yet the kingdom is not earned by men, but given by God's grace. Already men may rejoice in God's forgiveness, know Him as Father, and, as His servants, find themselves redeemed, not only from sin, but from the strain and pressure of the world. So Jesus calls His message not a law but a gospel. Membership in the kingdom meant at that time for many persecution and death. Yet joyfully He bade men enter it, knowing that thereby they would find not loss, but gain. He who bade men follow Him to the scaffold was no ascetic. Joyous was the life of the man of sorrows. Joy and peace are meant to be the inalienable right of His disciples.

Men have often asked whether the kingdom of God as Jesus knew it was a present or a future conception. Such a question fails to understand His teaching. For Him the 'future has become present and the present is projected into the future. The future salvation has become for us present, and yet has not ceased to be future.'[1] Only in heaven, in the sphere of the eternal, is God perfectly known and His will completely obeyed, yet in part the powers and blessings of the kingdom may already be ours. To Christ they completely belonged. His consciousness of the Father was clear. He did at all times

[1] J. Kaftan, *Dogmatik*, p. 472.

the Father's will, and rejoiced always in His full communion with Him. So He could tell the Pharisees that already the kingdom of God was in their midst. So, though Christ bade men pray 'Thy kingdom come', He did not merely wait for a distant boon. Already was the realm of blessing available for men. The miracles of healing that Jesus wrought were thus the signs of the kingdom's presence.[1] To Him and to His disciples belonged already the powers of the eternal world.

It is this sense of the supremacy of the eternal that defines Christ's attitude to this world's life. With the East to-day, Christ held that the finite could never satisfy the soul of man. The rich farmer, intent only on building bigger barns, was in God's sight a pitiable fool. To lose our true life to gain this world was not only wicked, it was stupid.[2] Yet with the West, He made the distinctive note of life not inactivity but energy. As it has been well said, 'Thought, desire, will were not to be disowned in despair, through the overpowering sense of their futility. Life was not to be reduced to zero through their renunciation, but raised to infinity through their affirmation and satisfaction'.[3] Though the disciple felt in the world a home-sickness for the beyond, it was not for him to flee the world. Christ bade men pray not only for spiritual good, but for daily bread. The love which he enjoins is to be shown not only in forgiveness and intercession, but in the active philanthropy of the good Samaritan. And Christ could appreciate not only service to those in such desperate need; He valued the tender kindness of hospitality, and praised, as no austere man would do, the woman who 'wasted' in her love the precious ointment.[4] So, to Christ, detachment from the world did not mean renunciation of it. He himself was free, not only from sin and guilt, but from bondage to the finite. How could two years have held

[1] Cp. Luke vii. 22.
[2] Mark viii. 36. [3] Du Bose, *The Gospel in the Gospels*, p. 19.
[4] Mark xiv. 6–8. Cp. Titius, *op. cit.*, p. 61.

more sorrow than did those of Christ's ministry? Poverty, contempt, treachery of friends, malice of foes, anguish of body, loneliness of soul, all these were His: yet He lived not as the victim but as the master of His circumstances. Sure of His Father's favour, He met with courage and steadfastness His incomparable sorrows and triumphed over them, and over death the last enemy.[1] And His peace He offers to His disciples. Theirs is the kingdom. They too may in fortitude and love show themselves redeemed from the pressure of the painful and the finite.

Such in briefest outline is Christ's message. No other has spoken of God to us with such beauty and tenderness; no other has made so clear God's purpose for the world. And this much, most men would admit. In East and West alike few would dispute His supremacy as teacher, or deny His unique spiritual insight and moral vigour. Yet to go so far only, seems to be impossible. As soon as we begin to look with greater care at Christ's teaching in regard to God or the Kingdom, we find implicit in it the assumption that His message is inseparably connected with His Person. But if this is so, either we are compelled to go beyond the recognition of Christ as the greatest of teachers, or, if not, we have to deny His assumption, and in doing so we seriously compromise our belief in the wisdom or even the sanity of His teaching.

In a few scanty paragraphs we have seen with what vividness and confidence Christ spoke of the Father in heaven and His love for men. Yet He preaches the good tidings, not as a prophet speaks of his God, but as a son speaks of his father. It is not so much that Jesus calls Himself the Son. It is rather that He speaks as only the Son can do. The filial consciousness of God is, with Him, perfect, permanent, and normative. As a child, He can speak of His Father's house. The voice which proclaimed at the Baptism and Transfiguration 'This

[1] Cp. Bornemann, *Unterricht im Christentum*, pp. 83, 84.

is My beloved Son' brought to Him no new message. He bade His disciples say 'our Father'. He said 'My Father' and 'your Father'. Familiarity often robs these words of their meaning. Yet clearly Christ places Himself in a unique relationship with God. In the parable of the husbandmen, He is the Son, and not the servant. It is true that in the first three Gospels, though He accepts, He does not use the phrase 'Son of God'. Yet all that the word involves He makes His own, and so it is probable that the frequent use of the expression in the fourth Gospel is not the product of later reflection, but a genuine echo of the Master's words, remembered by one who by greater insight could receive more of His meaning. Certainly, not even in John's Gospel, have we a clearer record of Christ's filial consciousness than is given us in Matthew and Luke.[1] The seventy disciples had returned from their mission, full of gladness at its success. Jesus, in grateful and exultant joy, praises the wisdom of God in suffering men, weak and ignorant, to receive truths the wise reject. And, in His profound emotion, He enables us to get a glimpse of those deep things of His soul which usually He concealed from men's gaze. 'All things have been delivered unto Me of My Father: and no one knoweth the Son save the Father, neither doth any know the Father save the Son, and he to whomsoever the Son willeth to reveal Him.'[2] This, it is true, is 'not a claim to universal domain, but a confession of entire dependence'.[3] Yet the words reveal a unique and perfect intimacy with God. As only He so knew the Father, only through Him could the Father be known. And so, in His colossal consciousness of Sonship, He could bid men, weary and fainthearted, come to Him to find a yoke that was easy and a burden that was light. Their refreshment would be Christ. In Him would they find peace for their souls. Only in the Son could the Father be thus known.

[1] Luke x. 17-22. Matthew xi. 25-30. [2] Matthew xi. 27.
[3] A. E. Garvie, *Studies in the Inner Life of Jesus*, p. 311.

As Christ's revelation of the Father was perfected, not through His teaching, but in Himself, so His proclamation of the Kingdom assumed that, in it, His position was unique. He was the Son of Man.[1] His vocation it was to found the kingdom of God, and, with Him, 'vocation and personality were absolutely coincident'.[2] That Jesus thus knew himself to be the Messiah may be regarded as certain. To deny this, as Kaftan says, is 'to write history not as it is or as it was, but as it ought to be'[3]—in the judgement of rationalizing critics. That He hid His secret from the people was inevitable. Their hopes were political, and had He called Himself the Messiah, they would only have misunderstood the worse His meaning. Yet all the functions of the Messiah He assumed, and, when He entered Jerusalem to die, He made explicit to all His claim.

If Jesus thus thought Himself to be the Messiah, then He believed Himself to be the goal of this nation's history, and the vehicle of God's salvation to the world. And this belief is implicit in all His teaching. Often men who praise Jesus as the supreme teacher only, speak of 'the simple teaching of the Sermon on the Mount', and contrast with this the later developments of Christian thought. It is a strange phrase, for the Sermon on the Mount is not 'simple'. Its moral ideal is so exalted that if Christianity were teaching only, we would have to pronounce its demands to be intolerably exacting and oppressive. And in this programme of the Kingdom, Jesus speaks of Himself in a way that no wise teacher could do unless he were something more. He revises without hesitation or apology the Jewish law, which men held to be the very word of God. He bids men to be perfect as their Father in heaven is perfect, and does so with no suggestion that He Himself was imperfect. He identifies Himself with

[1] It seems fairly generally agreed that the phrase does not mean 'representative man', but goes back to Dan. vii. 13, and possibly to the *Similitudes of Enoch*, and denotes the 'establisher of the kingdom of God'.

[2] H. R Mackintosh, *Person of Jesus Christ*, p. 31.

[3] *Jesus und Paulus*, p. 16.

the cause of righteousness. To be persecuted for His sake is the same as to be persecuted for righteousness' sake.[1] In His hands is man's eternal destiny. The future and eternal kingdom of God will be opened to men only by His Word. He assumes with unquestioning confidence that, at the final judgement, men will plead that they have done great works in His name, and, if their lives are evil, He will say, 'I know you not'. And such a word will mean exclusion from final blessedness.[2] And in a subsequent utterance this claim is re-emphasized. 'Every one who shall confess Me before men, him will I also confess before My Father which is in heaven. But whosoever shall deny Me before men, him will I also deny before My Father which is in heaven.'[3] As Dr. Denney says, 'It is impossible to exaggerate the solemnity of this utterance or the greatness of the claim it makes. It says, as clearly as language can say, that fidelity to Jesus is that on which the final destiny of man depends.'[4] So it is with no surprise that we find that His intercourse with His disciples was marked as much by aloofness and reserve as by kindness and sympathy. They could call no man teacher, no man master. One was their Master, One their teacher.[5] And because He thus identified Himself with God's saving purpose for the world, He, the meek and lowly, could demand of men the severest sacrifices. To be His disciples, men must, if necessary, renounce the dearest ties of blood and kin. They must be willing to follow Him even to the criminal's death. The future of the Kingdom is His future. By His return He shall consummate the Kingdom's glory.

He mediates the blessings of the Kingdom in a way no man could do. Thus, at the outset of the earliest Gospel,[6] is given an account of the healing of the paralytic. As this passage occurs also in Matthew and Luke, it surely satisfies the most finicking shibboleths of criticism. And Jesus here

[1] Matt. v. 10, 11. [2] Matt. vii. 21–3. [3] Matt. x. 32, 33.
[4] *Jesus and the Gospel*, p. 225. [5] Matt. xxiii. 8.
[6] Mark ii. 1–12.

with final certainty declares that the man's sins are forgiven. Those to whom sin is a trifle may minimize the incident, but those who have been taught by Christ Himself to regard sin as the one intolerable evil, cannot so do. A man, who thus pronounces sin's forgiveness, puts himself unmistakably by the side of God. This passage alone would be sufficient witness to Christ's sense that He was divine, and so could forgive sin as only God could do.[1]

This connexion between Jesus and His Gospel is shown most clearly in regard to His death. He had come to seek and to save the lost. The Son of Man came, not to destroy men's lives, but to save them.[2] And, towards the end of His life, He explained the manner of that salvation. The Son of Man had come, not to be ministered unto, but to minister, and to give His soul a ransom for many. He would deliver men from their slavery to anxiety and sin. He would free men, not by money, but by the giving of His life. So His Kingdom would come, not by the way of drastic conquest, but by the way of apparent failure and sacrificial love. His sovereignty over souls would come through the ignoble cross.

It is natural to contrast the dying words of Gautama, the Buddha, with those of Christ. When Gautama felt the end was near, he turned to Ānanda and said: 'O Ānanda, I am growing old and my journey is drawing to its close. I have reached eighty years, my sum of days, and just as a well-worn cart can only be with much care made to move along, so my body can only be kept going with difficulty. It is only when I am plunged in meditation that my body is at ease. In

[1] Cp. Schaeder, *Zur Trinitätsfrage*, p. 16.

[2] Harnack points out that there are eight prime passages in the Synoptics beginning with the words 'I am come'. This is a Messianic phrase, and Harnack regards these verses as programmatic. It is significant that of these eight, four deal with Christ's saving work. *Zeitschrift für Theologie und Kirche*, Jan. 1912, pp. 1–30.

future be to yourselves your own light, your own refuge: seek no other refuge. Hold fast to the truth of your refuge; look not to any but yourselves as refuge.' And just before his death he further said: 'It may be, Ānanda, that in some of you the thought may arise, "The words of our Master are ended; we have lost our Master"; but it is not thus. The truth and the rules of the Order which I have founded and preached, let these be your teacher when I am gone.'[1]

But Christ before His death speaks not at all as one who, having taught, has done His work and desires only that His teaching be remembered. He looks to the work before Him, not to the work behind. On the eve of His betrayal, He institutes the feast that should keep Him in the perpetual remembrance of the Church. He saw in His death, not the symbol of failure, nor the cessation of His work, but the God-given way to perfect victory. It was the beginning of a new covenant between God and man. His death was for 'the forgiveness of sin'.[2]

But a confidence so entire could spring only from the clear and certain consciousness that His life was perfectly at one with the will of God. Only one who needed not to repent for His own sins could forgive sins and proclaim His death as the means of a new covenant of grace. So, to the Christian gospel, the belief in the sinlessness of Jesus is not accessory but essential. To renounce belief in the sinlessness of Jesus is to make ineffective every blessing that He brought. It would be useless in that case to admire Him for His supremacy as teacher. If He spoke as one sinless and yet was a sinner we might well prefer to turn to humbler guides who bade men look, not at themselves, but at their message. Strange indeed would it be, and unspeakably tragic, if He, who has done more than any other teacher to unmask

[1] *Mahā Parinibbāna Sūtta.*

[2] Matt. xxvi. 28. The authenticity of the phrase has, of course, been much attacked, but the rite in its Old Testament connexion can only have that meaning.

hypocrisy and pretentious virtue, should so terribly have misjudged His own worth. Because of what Christ has shown us of God's perfection, the sense of unworth and failure, of gratitude for God's pardon, and of aspiration after a truer life, has become the normal sign of the Christian character. We say with Luther, 'He that is a Christian is no Christian'. We know that the greatest saints are the greatest penitents. Yet in Christ's consciousness there is no trace of sin. Nowhere does He crave for Himself forgiveness. He acts, as we have seen, as no sinner could do. He was terribly deluded or He was sinless.

Yet the word 'sinlessness' may easily be misunderstood. It is negative, and may be thought to denote the absence of evil rather than the presence of triumphant good. It is better therefore to speak of the absolute holiness of Christ. And that holiness was not given ready-made. We cannot penetrate into the secret of His inner life. 'His person is beyond all psychology, and its key is in God's hands alone.'[1] But it is clear that His life, like ours, was one of moral conflict. He was tempted, yet His temptations were to acts nobler than other men's best deeds. Thus the temptations of the wilderness concerned not His personal ambition but the cause for which He lived. Let Him do His work in the popular way; let Him utilize His vast powers over nature to satisfy men's material needs; let His attitude to the spirit of the world be one of compromise; let Him dazzle the people by showing them a conspicuous and drastic miracle: so would His work for God be prosperous and successful. His holiness was thus an act. It came through inner conflict. He chose by the whole force of His soul to do always the Father's will. His sinlessness, then, was not the harmlessness of the feebly good. It was the strong and continuous deed of a great and vigorous soul. The attempts in literature to depict a perfect character have failed. Instead of a saint there has been a prig. What

[1] P. T. Forsyth, *Person and Place of Jesus Christ*, p. 113.

literary men have failed to do, the simple chroniclers of Christ's life have done. There in Jesus Christ is the perfect union of sinlessness and strength, and that picture no genius could invent.[1]

If we were asked why we revered the great teacher of our student days, or why we so love and honour those dearest to us, father, mother, or wife, we would know how poor our answers were, how little they expressed the secret of their personalities or of our own devotion. Immeasurably harder would it be to describe the character of Jesus of Nazareth. The diversity of the attempts shows their failure. Men have spoken of Him as if He were gentle always, averse to conflict, calm and quiet. Others have emphasized His indignation against wrong, and spoken as if stern strength were His most conspicuous characteristic. His character has none of the simplicity of those whose lives flow smoothly in the shallow way.[2] Each estimate is false only in what it omits. In truth, in Him are moral qualities so vast and so opposed, that only His great soul could have contained them without rupture.

Nowhere do the Synoptic writers praise Jesus, or attempt to express their estimate of His moral worth and beauty. They are content with artless simplicity to portray His words and deeds. As we read the Gospels we share with them their knowledge. We see Him with the children gathered around Him. We notice His genial kindness. He is a lover of flowers and birds and the country-side. Devoted as He is to His great vocation, it is not with the fierce concentration of the fanatic,

[1] Tennyson said on one occasion to a young man, 'Be ye therefore perfect as your Father in heaven is perfect', and then added, 'But don't be a prig' (*Memoir* by his son, one vol. edit., p. 267). Yet many would be inclined to think that in his ideal picture of Arthur, he has failed to obey his own injunction.

[2] Cp. A. Ritschl: 'It is no mere accident that the subversion of Jesus' religious importance has been undertaken under the guise of writing His life, for this very undertaking implies the surrender of the conviction that Jesus as the founder of the perfect, moral and spiritual, religion belongs to a higher order than all other men.' *Justification and Reconciliation*, p. 3.

blind to the life round him. He sees the children playing at 'weddings' and 'funerals' in the market-place, the farmer in the fields, the merchant from a distant country seeking treasure. He is one interested in life's homely tasks. For long He laboured to support His mother. When at last He began His public mission, it was obscure men whom He summoned to His service. The poor and the outcast felt they had in Him a friend. He despised no man for ignorance or stupidity. The Gospels show, in their unconscious touches, His infinite patience and His adaptability to His disciples, who so persistently misunderstood. And even when death drew near, how marvellous is His self-forgetfulness. On the eve of His trial, He partakes with His disciples of the Last Supper, and, for their comfort, makes of it a memorial feast. Even in this time of tragedy, with pitiable triviality, His disciples are striving as to who 'should be accounted the greatest'. His rebuke to them is one of love. He girds himself with a towel that He may do the menial task of washing these men's feet. Unworthy as they are, He trusts them to continue His work after His death. He speaks to them of the new covenant of His blood that, when He is dead, they may know that He is with them still, and discover that His death was gain, not loss; victory, not defeat. In the bitter anguish of the Garden, He remembers His disciples' need. They will not pray. They will not realize their peril. He prays for them. When at last His enemies appear, He offers Himself to them at once, that His disciples may go free. He heals the ear of one of the rude band of His arresters. Even in the time of cruel mockery He remembers Peter's need, and gives him the look that means his restoration. On the way to death He can sorrow for the woes that must befall the daughters of Jerusalem. When stretched in agony upon the Cross, He prays for the rough soldiers who nailed Him there, that they may be forgiven, for they knew not what they did.[1]

[1] For much in this paragraph see a fine passage in Du Bose, *op. cit.*, p. 125.

Yet, as we have seen, with this self-forgetfulness there was the dignity, not regal but divine, of one who knew Himself to be the Son of God and the vehicle of God's salvation. Sympathetic, He is yet aloof. Tender as the gentlest woman, He can be terribly stern. Careful to provide food for the multitude that had come to hear Him preach, bidding men pray for daily bread, He yet demanded of his followers unparalleled denials. Poor and despised, He claimed and won a devotion which no king has ever obtained.

And this man belongs to the past only as we adopt towards Him the attitude of the critic unconscious of any need. We begin by judging and admiring Him, but soon we find we cannot do so. It is He that is judging us. Spiritual experience is incommunicable. We can but hint of what we know. But it is the central and authentic fact of Christian experience that in Christ men have apprehended God. We feel that we have seen God, and know that the God of 'all this unintelligible world' is the God whom Christ called Father, and whose grace and love He in His own life perfectly revealed. As one of our greatest Christian teachers has written: 'We know that in Christ we meet with God, and we know what sort of meeting this is. We know that this God gives us comfort and courage to face the world, joy in meeting the demands of duty, and, with all this, eternal life in our hearts.'[1] So for us Jesus is no longer an 'historical problem but the Reality before which we bow'.[2] He has brought to us God's full redemption. He mediates to us the Father's mercy. He speaks to us and claims our allegiance, not as a dead saint but as a living Lord.

And such a one we may not ignore. To admire Him is only in a refined way to reject. He demands a faith and an obedience as complete as the salvation He bestows.

[1] Herrmann, *Der Verkehr des Christen mit Gott*, p. 143; *The Communion of the Christian with God*, p. 173.

[2] *Op. cit.*, p. 165. English trans., p. 200.

CHAPTER VIII

CLASSIC CHRISTIANITY

THE APOSTOLIC EXPERIENCE OF CHRIST AND HIS GOSPEL

WHEN Jesus died, the faith of His disciples died too. His resurrection meant the new birth of their hope and courage. From hesitating followers of a Master whose ways they could neither understand nor praise, they became the glad evangelists of a gospel, the proud ambassadors of a risen and regnant Lord. And these early leaders of the Church, though they differed in many matters of polity and doctrine, were one in the central content of their faith. What has been called the first Christian creed, expresses not Paul's distinctive teaching but the common tradition of the Church. The Gospel which Paul preached, and his converts believed, was, he tells us, the message which he himself had received from the Church at his conversion. Its content was simple and sufficient. 'Christ died for our sins according to the scriptures and hath been raised on the third day.'[1] Or as von Harnack paraphrases it, 'Christ died a sacrifice for our sins and He lives'.[2] And the religious life which thus finds expression is not something solitary and unique. It is the classic Christian experience. To understand it, is to enter into the genius of Christianity and to be able to appreciate all that is central and permanent in the Christian salvation.

The New Testament, as has often been remarked, is not in the first place a manual of doctrine, and its unity is not theological but religious. Its writers preserve their idiosyncrasies and express in their own way, from the standpoint of

[1] I Cor. xv. 3, 4.

[2] *Das Wesen des Christentums*, p. 98.

their own experience, the faith that is in them. So in the unity there is a rich variety of thought and feeling. It must suffice for our purpose to glance at the conceptions of Christianity connected with the great names of Peter, Paul, and John.

Peter.

The speeches of Peter in the first chapters of *Acts* have a peculiar interest as the immediate and unformulated expression of the earliest Christian faith. Peter's worst fears had been realized. The death he could not endure to think of had befallen his Master in its most shameful form. Yet he comes before the people not as a disappointed but as a confident and exultant man. He has a fact to preach which is a Gospel. That fact is the Resurrection of Jesus Christ. Him whom they had crucified and slain God had raised up.[1] As a Jew speaking to Jews, inevitably he construed his message in terms of Jewish prophecy. The Jesus whom they had done to death was the Christ, the Messiah, the chosen vehicle of God's salvation. And the death which once seemed impossible for the Messiah to die, he now saw to be a necessity. This Jesus was the suffering Servant of the Lord of whom the noblest prophecy of the Old Testament had spoken.[2] Risen, He was strong to save. Once Peter had thought much of earthly pre-eminence; now he can rejoice in suffering, scourging, and dishonour for his Master's sake.[3] Like the rest of these earliest disciples, Peter was conscious of the power of the Risen Lord, and, rejoicing himself in the realization of a completely adequate salvation, could bid men repent and partake of its benefits.

It is probable that the *First Epistle of Peter* was written after the Epistles of Paul, but it, too, represents the primitive and rudimentary type of teaching. It is written to give hope

[1] Acts ii. 23, 24.

[2] Acts iii. 13, 26, iv. 27, 30. In all these cases 'Servant' (not 'son' or 'child') is certainly the right rendering, as the word (παῖς) goes back to the servant passages of the Exilic Isaiah and especially to Isaiah liii.

[3] Acts v. 41.

to men in suffering. The Cross of Christ, once a problem, is now to Peter the key to life's mysteries. *Via crucis, via lucis.*[1] The way of the cross has become the way of blessedness. Christ has shown us how to suffer. Ours it is to do so, gladly and bravely. Peter's interests are pastoral, not didactic. He does not explain; he exhorts. Yet he too dwells mostly on the death and resurrection of Jesus Christ. Not having seen Christ, we yet may love Him, and, because of our faith, rejoice with joy unspeakable and full of glory.[2] To the Christians he addresses has come a great salvation. Before, their life was engrossed in the futility, the *māyā*, of the world. Now they were redeemed 'through the precious blood of Christ'.[3] Let them therefore 'show forth the praises of Him who called them out of darkness into His marvellous light'.[4] And men who had received so great a salvation could bear, with equanimity, persecution. The reward of well-doing at that time would probably be suffering.[5] But they had before them the example of Jesus Christ. In words that go back to the fifty-third chapter of *Isaiah*, Peter describes, with power and pathos, Christ's suffering for us. He did no sin, neither was any guile in His mouth. When reviled, He reviled not again. 'In His own self, He carried up our sins in His body to the tree.'[6] To one like Peter brought up in Judaism, the tree, the gallows, was an accursed place. Through human sin, Christ had died on the shameful cross. What sin did to Christ, that Christ did to sin. He took up our sin to the place of shame.[7] By His death He condemned sin, exposed it in its horror. And the object of it all is this, that 'we may live unto righteousness, healed with His stripes'.

There is little theory, but there is much religion, in all this. Clearly Peter felt that he owed everything to Jesus Christ. So, though Christianity meant persecution, and for many death, he could proclaim it as the greatest blessing earth could

[1] Cp. Stevens, *New Testament Theology*, p. 295. [2] i. 8.
[3] i. 19. [4] ii. 9. [5] ii. 20. [6] ii. 24, R.V. margin.
[7] Cp. A. Seeberg, *Der Tod Christi*, p. 292.

give. Because of the joy that would be theirs, even in suffering men might rejoice. The Epistle is significant as the work of one who, perhaps best of all the apostles, represented the average opinion of the Church, then, as now, less interested in theology than in religion.

Paul.

At the conversion of Paul, Christianity gained its greatest Apostle. It would be difficult to exaggerate the importance of his missionary labours, but it is possible to over-estimate his significance to the Church's thought. To regard him, as some have done, as the second founder of Christianity, is to misunderstand both his teaching and the Gospel. As we have seen, the two facts for which he stood, the saving death and the resurrection of Christ, were the common property of the early Church. In his Epistles, Paul has to rebut many false and defective estimates of Christianity. Nowhere does he refer to any within his churches who reject these central doctrines. He does indeed speak of men who are 'the enemies of the Cross of Christ',[1] but he is referring not to heretics but to libertines,[2] and in his essential teaching he knew himself to be at one with the rest of the Church. Indeed, as one of his most brilliant modern biographers has said, to think of Paul simply as a theologian would be as little justifiable as to remember Frederick the Great by his histories.[3] He was a man of action, interested in the expression of Christian truth, only that the converts of his missionary labours might share with him the fullness of the new life in Jesus Christ. So his teaching is occasional and disconnected, and often hard to understand. But of the Christian experience he is the greatest interpreter.

It is impossible to appreciate fully Paul the Christian without some reference to Saul the Pharisee. Born at Tarsus, where Greek culture was known and honoured, having the

[1] Phil. iii. 18. [2] Cp. A. Seeberg, *Der Tod Christi*, pp. 180-1.
[3] H. Weinel, *Paulus*, p. 222.

suffrage of the Roman citizen, and trained in the strictest, most orthodox and zealous Judaism, he had the freedom of the three worlds of Greek speech, Roman rule, and Jewish religion. But it was the last alone that won the ardent devotion of his young life, and none entered deeper than he into the best aspirations of his race. To such a one the Christian preaching of a crucified Messiah would be offensive in the extreme. The Messiah would come, but He must come in glory. To say that He died on the tree was blasphemy. 'Accursed is every one that hangeth on the tree.'[1] So he was the fiercest enemy of the early Church, and doubtless for long he felt he had in Judaism all he needed. No impersonal narrative would be so passionate as the seventh chapter of *Romans*, and if we may regard that as autobiographical, then we have there Paul's own account of his discovery that his own religion could not suffice. The tenth commandment, 'Thou shalt not covet' (or 'lust'), bade him control not only deeds but thoughts, and that he could not do. Yet from the Pharisaic standpoint, to transgress the law in anything was to transgress in all; for righteousness before God could no longer be claimed. Yet he persecuted, as he says, 'hyperbolically' the Church of God.[2] At last the crisis came. He saw the risen Christ, and knew Him as Lord, and that experience made of the persecutor, the Apostle. 'The old things had passed away. He was in Christ Jesus and a new creature.'[3]

This 'new creation' meant for Paul far more than the purification of the old habits and the ennoblement of past aspirations. It changed his whole attitude to God and the world. God had forgiven him. He was God's child. That brought to him joy and peace, 'newness of life'. The darkness had passed away, the light now shone. But it was more than a new vision which Paul gained. It was new power. He felt

[1] Gal. iii. 13.
[2] Gal. i. 13 καθ' ὑπερβολὴν ἐδίωκον. Cp. A. B. Bruce, *St. Paul's Conception of Christianity*, p. 35.
[3] 2 Cor. v. 17.

that there had come to him, not a mere change of character but a new personality, over which ruled, not the old 'ego' with its selfish cravings, but the risen Lord. No natural explanation would account for it. His break with the past was so radical that it could only have been effected by God's creative power. St. Paul's life as a Christian was to him a miracle of God.[1]

As a Jew the supreme problem of religion had been to acquire and maintain a 'righteousness before God'. Now, still using the Jewish phrase, he rejoiced to accept a 'righteousness' God-given. Religion for him was thus no longer legal but filial, and 'recompense' ceased to be the 'ultimate principle of the world's moral order'.[2] He no longer asks, 'How shall I satisfy the demands of my Lawgiver?' but 'How shall I show my gratitude to God for His unspeakable mercies?' God had become for him the Father of our Lord and Saviour Jesus Christ, a God of grace. And the supreme proof of God's love, Paul saw in God's gift to the world of a crucified Saviour. Because of that love, he now could rejoice in God's forgiveness and be sure of His Fatherly care. We have in Tamil a proverb, 'Whoso has given the elephant, will he not also give the goad?' And so to Paul, God's greatest gift carried by implication all the rest. 'He that grudged not His own son but delivered Him up for us all, shall He not also with Him freely give us all things?'[3] Confident of God's grace, he could dedicate his life unreservedly to the Christ who had loved him and given Himself for him. And this crucified Jesus was the risen Lord whom he had seen, and whose power he daily felt. Christ informed his thought and directed his will; in Him he shared already the life that was supernatural, eternal, and triumphant.

Such in briefest outline was Paul's religious life, of which all his theology is only an attempted expression. Paul was no systematizer. His theology was made for missionary use

[1] Cp. P. Gennrich, *Die Lehre von der Wiedergeburt*, p. 22.
[2] *The Religion and Theology of Paul*, by W. Morgan, p. 84.
[3] Rom. viii. 31.

and apologetic purposes. Yet he has sufficiently indicated in a few great passages the interpretation that he gave to the death and resurrection of his Lord.

In the most elaborate of his Epistles, that to the *Romans*, he deals with the problems of religion avowedly from the standpoint of divine and human righteousness.[1] Man's sin is universal; as universal therefore is his need of salvation. To one of Paul's intense moral nature, the bare proclamation of God's forgiveness would not have sufficed. But in the death of Jesus he found an answer to his deepest need. In that violent death, sin is not passed over. It is condemned; shown up for what it is. God, in seeking that we may be righteous, exhibits His condemnation of sin that we may condemn it too. God is revealed as the 'just and the justifier of those who accept this salvation through faith in Jesus'.[2] God forgives us, and at the same time brings us into a communion with Himself in which faith can make actual our 'righteousness'. The terminology of the passage is of course Jewish, and may sound archaic to modern ears, but its meaning is an essential part of Paul's interpretation of Christianity. Sin in being forgiven is condemned. And inadequate as explanations are, only here has been found a sufficient answer to what is less a speculative question than a moral problem. 'How can sinners be forgiven and God's own righteousness, His inviolable self-consistency, be maintained?' Paul knew well enough that his message of the Cross would seem to many scandalous and foolish. But he knew also, as Christians in every age have found, that in it was God's power and wisdom.[3] And it was of the Cross he boasted. This was the ministry of reconciliation which God had given him. He was God's ambassador, beseeching men to be reconciled to God.[4]

It was not enough for Paul to say, 'In Him, I am forgiven'. Inevitably, with a man so earnest, the question had to be faced, 'How can I become holy as He was?' And the

[1] Rom. i. 16, 17.
[2] Rom. iii. 22-6.
[3] 1 Cor. i. 23, 24.
[4] 2 Cor. v. 18-20.

answer he found in faith's power to enter into, and share, Christ's death and resurrection.[1] 'I have been crucified with Christ,' he writes; 'my life is no longer mine; it is Christ who lives in me; the life I now live in flesh. I live in faith, in the Son of God who loved me and gave Himself up for me.'[2] So, as Dr. Denney says, 'The whole of the Christian life is a response to the love exhibited in the death of the Son of God for men. We cannot point to anything and say, "See, that is Christian, that is good in God's sight," without saying at the same time, "That has been generated in the life of man by the tremendous appeal of the cross".'[3] So he bids the Roman Christians reckon themselves dead unto sin but alive unto God in Jesus Christ.[4] And for himself he rejoices to fill up that which is lacking in the afflictions of Christ,[5] and to die for the Church a daily death.

Yet Christ was to him, not the dead, but the living Lord, and the Christian life meant not only a co-dying but a co-resurrection with Him. It was the vision of the risen Lord that had transformed Paul's life. Christ belonged, in Jewish phrase, 'to the age to come'.[6] He dwelt in the eternal, and His resurrection opened up for His followers the powers and forces of that supernatural and eternal world. So Paul felt that, by his faith, he had risen with Christ. He would seek the things that were above. It was not only righteousness; it was redemption that he sought and found.[7] And, through the resurrection, he was redeemed; the future and glorious age had become for him a present and experienced reality.

To express his intimate and vital relation with the risen Lord, he used, time after time, a phrase which probably he

[1] Cp. A. B. Bruce, *op. cit.*, p. 213. [2] Gal. ii. 20.
[3] *The Death of Christ*, p. 151. [4] Rom. vi. 11. [5] Col. i. 24.
[6] ὁαἰων μέλλων.
[7] As J. Kaftan, in his very suggestive essay on the *Significance of Christ's Death for Paul*, points out, the Judaism of the time had two foci, Nomism and Messianism. The first was concerned with righteousness. The second sought redemption from the trouble of this world. Both these aspirations were transformed and satisfied in Paul's Christian experience. *Zur Dogmatik*, p. 271.

coined. He was 'in Christ Jesus'. No phrase is more characteristic of his thought.[1] It denotes 'the most intimate communion thinkable between the Christian and the living Christ'.[2] He calls himself 'a man in Christ'.[3] In Christ, amid the sorrows of the time, God leads him in triumph.[4] It is in the Lord he witnesses.[5] In the Lord he teaches.[6] In the Lord has he the seal of his apostleship.[7] So too he bids his readers be strong in the Lord,[8] walk in Him,[9] and labour.[10] It is in Christ that they are blessed with every spiritual blessing.[11] In Him are all the treasures of wisdom and knowledge.[12] In Him may we be rich in all things.[13] God will fulfil every need in Christ Jesus,[14] in the Lord we rejoice,[15] in the Lord we hope,[16] in the Lord the dead sleep.[17] In the Lord will they be made alive.[18] And the phrase does not denote a mere vague relation of faith to Christ. The risen Lord, dwelling in the eternal, was to him the element in which he lived. In Christ he felt himself already redeemed in principle from the transitory as from the evil. His activities were in Christ. In Christ the eternal had become for him already a present reality.

Yet his life in the eternal was not one of complete detachment from the world, in actionless absorption (*samādhi*). He was no recluse nor dreamer, but the practical statesman of the early Church. His was a life of disappointment, conflict, and physical suffering. This patriotic Jew was inevitably regarded by his countrymen as a traitor to his race, and the most influential of the Christians treated him with coldness.

[1] Deissmann, in his elaborate essay on *Die neutestamentliche Formel 'in Christo Jesu'*, shows that of the 196 times the phrase occurs in the New Testament 164 are in Paul's writings, and of the rest 24 are in the late Johannine writings.

[2] Deissmann, *op. cit.*, p. 98. [3] 2 Cor. xii. 2. [4] 2 Cor. ii. 14.

[5] Eph. iv. 17. [6] Eph. iv. 21. [7] 1 Cor. ix. 2.

[8] Eph. vi. 10. [9] Col. ii. 6. [10] Rom. xvi. 12.

[11] Eph. i. 3. [12] Col. ii. 3. [13] 1 Cor. i. 5. [14] Phil. iv. 19.

[15] Phil. iii. 1. [16] Phil. ii. 19. [17] 1 Cor. xv. 18.

[18] 1 Cor. xv. 22. For the full list of passages see Deissmann, *op. cit.*, pp. 118–24.

This high-strung, over-sensitive, fully-educated man laboured chiefly for ignorant, and partly servile, congregations, who could not appreciate him, and often gave him little confidence. Called to a life of hardship, his was not a perfectly healthy frame. It is possible that 'the thorn in the flesh' which so distressed him was of nervous origin. He knew what it was to have added to the 'fightings without' 'fears within'.[1] He can speak without affectation of daily death, and take to himself the prophetic word, 'For thy sake we are killed all the day long'.[2] He could hold himself the most miserable of men, if Christ had not risen, and all he had done had been for a delusion.[3]

Such a one will not speak lightly of this world's troubles nor regard the present as the perfect. He knew too well what sorrow was. Forgiven, he yet found that the power of the flesh was with him still. In strong phrase he says he 'beats his body black and blue, lest it shall get the mastery, and he, who has summoned others to run the heavenly race, shall himself be disqualified to run'.[4] He knew that as yet he had not attained. He looked forward eagerly to the future and complete redemption. To faith, he added hope. But this hope did not produce in him a quietism, content to leave to God's future catastrophic act, the world's salvation. It showed itself rather in a glad endurance which gave strength, not weakness, to his activities. Already he shared the power and illumination of God's Spirit. That Spirit was the gift of the risen Lord; to use the phrase Paul borrowed from the market-place, the spirit was the 'pledge',[5] the part sum paid in deposit, as a guarantee that all the rest would eventually be given. Thus, with the presence of the Spirit of God in his heart, and with his intimate communion with the Master, the future glory was already partly his. So this hope was to him an actual, positive, and present blessing. In this hope he

[1] 2 Cor. vii. 5.
[2] Rom. viii. 36.
[3] 1 Cor. xv. 19.
[4] 1 Cor. ix. 27.
[5] Eph. i. 14. The English version gives 'earnest'.

rejoiced;[1] it was his best possession.[2] He was redeemed from the world, yet in the world he laboured. His self-sacrifice was great but it was not world-flight, world-denial. His life in the eternal did not make paltry the duties of the present. On the contrary the interests of the Churches dominate his thought. For them he rejoices and fears; over them he yearns as a father over his children. For them he prays that they may witness by their life to the Gospel they profess. He would present them to Christ as a spotless bride to her husband. So, in countless ways, he reveals that the Christian life is essentially connected with character and conduct. It means 'bringing forth fruit unto God'.[3] It is governed in all things by God's will.[4] It means obedience to God and service to man. Thus faith works through love. And Paul's conception of the ideal Christian is nowhere better expressed than in his famous hymn to love. It is impossible not to suppose that when he so described love, he had in mind the character of Jesus Christ.[5] In that love, patient, kind and long-suffering, rejoicing only in the good, and enduring to the end, we have the pattern of the Christian life. It is a life not of law, but of grace, governed not by precepts, but by principles. Its character is best described by the three words, faith, hope, and love, which in this world and the next abide.

Christ thus met for Paul every need of religion. That is the fundamental experience on which all his theology is based. And this much-travelled missionary, this citizen of the vast Roman Empire, could think of Christianity with a breadth of view impossible for smaller men. In his later Epistles especially, the massiveness of his conception of Christ and the Gospel is unmistakable. Because of his sense of the fullness of the salvation in Christ, he is sure that Christ is the ultimate goal of the whole world's history. 'God', he writes,

[1] Rom. xii. 12.
[2] For much in the paragraph see A. Titius, *Der Paulinismus unter dem Gesichtspunkt der Seligkeit*, pp. 87, 88.
[3] Rom. vii. 4. [4] Cp. Titius, *op. cit.*, p. 131. [5] 1 Cor. xiii. 4–7.

'has showered grace on us in Him who is the Beloved, the Bringer of the great emancipation, which is wrought by His death and which delivers us from sin. He has allowed us to know His secret, the hidden purpose which underlies all and interprets all. Long ago His good pleasure was determined; now, as the times are ripening, He is working out His plan. And the issue of all is this, the summing up, the focusing, the gathering into one, of the whole universe in Christ.'[1] So the meaning of history is clear. It is Christ. It is no wonder that, with such a gospel, he prays for his readers that 'they may have strength enough to claim their share in the knowledge which belongs to the holy people, to comprehend the full measure of the Divine purpose; to know, though it is beyond all knowledge, the love of Christ, and so to attain the Divine completeness, to be filled with all the fullness of God.[2] Paul was not primarily interested in philosophy, yet with this gospel he could face the philosophies of his day unabashed, conscious that in Christ he had the answer to their quest. Thus, in the *Epistle to the Colossians*, he is confronted with the vague mysticism, and the cosmological speculations, of a syncretism of Greek and Oriental thought. He appropriates the categories of his opponents and applies the highest possible to Christ. He is the image, the visible representation of the unseen God. Not in time only, but before time, is He God's agent. 'In Him the whole world was created. His supremacy is absolute and universal. He is first and He is last. Through Him, as the mediatorial Word, the universe has been created, and unto Him, as the final Goal, it is tending. In Him is no before or after. He is pre-existent and before all worlds. And in Him as the binding and sustaining power, universal nature coheres and consists.'[3] Thus the 'poverty' of the earthly Jesus was the poverty of

[1] Eph. i. 6-10, from Armitage Robinson's paraphrase *comm. in loc.*, p. 142.

[2] Eph. iii. 18, 19, *op. cit.*, p. 173.

[3] Col. i. 15-17, Lightfoot's paraphrase *comm. in loc.*, p. 142.

One infinite and divine.[1] His earthly humiliation was self-chosen. Of His own will He divested Himself of His glory, to come on earth in the form of a servant, and, for our sakes, to die upon the cross.

So the Christ who redeemed Paul was no dead hero-god, nor one of many incarnations of the Godhead; He was the one perfect expression of God's revealing love. His saving power Paul knew in the present. The humility of His earthly life was the manifestation of His eternal grace.

John.

The writings of John [2] fitly conclude this brief study of the Apostolic experience of the Christian salvation. Like Peter, he had lived in closest intimacy with Jesus during His earthly ministry. Like Paul, he was a man of consummate spiritual genius, and able to express the deepest thoughts with a simplicity of language to which Paul only occasionally attained. No writer moves more quietly and easily among the sublimest truth; none is more at home in the sphere of the eternal. Yet the eternal is not for him the indeterminate. The truth of the eternal world has been revealed in time in Jesus Christ, and its perception is made to depend on the performance of life's ordinary duties.

In the Gospel it is John's aim to show that Jesus is the Christ, the Son of God. In that earthly life, so humbly lived, he shows us the glory of the Divine. In the Epistle it is the converse that is shown. The Christ is Jesus. The heavenly Lord is inseparable from the historic Person with whom John once lived.[3]

The *Gospel of John* presents to the student of the New Testament his most difficult problem. In it reminiscence and reflection are inextricably interwoven, and if, as is often pointed

[1] 2 Cor. viii. 9.

[2] I assume that John wrote the 1st Epistle assigned to him, and that the Gospel is at any rate substantially his. As it is not necessary in so brief a sketch to deal with the book of *Revelation*, the question of its authorship fortunately does not arise.

[3] Cp. Westcott, *The Epistles of St. John*, xliv.

out, it is impossible to separate his reminiscence from his reflection, it is equally impossible to separate his reflection from his reminiscence.

No portrait could be more human than that which John gives us of Christ in his Gospel. Jesus knew hunger and thirst, and mixed freely with the humble and the despised. Yet He was the only-begotten of God. His miracles are 'signs' of His divine nature. He is perfectly one with God, and, as such, men find in Him the Light and Life of the world. He is bread to the hungry, water to the thirsty soul; He was sent that those who believed on Him might have eternal life. A good shepherd, He would lay down His life for the sheep.[1] It was as lifted up that He would draw all men unto Him.[2] In his account of Christ's last long conversation with His disciples before the crucifixion, John lets us see clearly how he thought of his Lord. Disciples would be as dependent on Christ, as Christ was on God. Their life was to be in Him. Without Him, they could no more live than could the severed branches of the vine. The risen Christ would come again to them. He would give them His spirit. Theirs should be His peace. Theirs already was eternal life. 'This is eternal life to know God and Him whom God did send.'[3] Knowledge of God comes, not from philosophemes, but from obedience. It means communion with God, and 'eternal life is the blessedness, the increasing perfection which flows from that communion'.[4] So men would be in the world, and yet 'not of the world'.[5] In tribulation they could share their Master's joy. He had overcome the world.[6] His victory would be theirs, and they would behold the glory of their Lord.[7]

John was not an 'objective historian', and, in his history of the earthly life of Jesus, his own faith is clearly seen. In the Prologue,[8] he states explicitly his conception of Christianity. In the first words of the Gospel he bids us look, not to the

[1] x. 11. [2] xii. 32. [3] xvii. 3.
[4] G. B. Stevens, *The Theology of the New Testament*, p. 230.
[5] xvii. 16. [6] xvi. 33. [7] xvii. 24. [8] i. 1–18.

manger at Bethlehem, but to the eternal glory of the Son of God. Both in Jewish and Greek thought, men spoke of the Word of God.[1] John uses the expression as one familiar to his readers, and capable of receiving a definitely Christian meaning. 'In the beginning was the Word.' In contrast to the Vedāntic view that God is silence,[2] John thus declares that to reveal, belongs to the essential nature of God. Yet all this is no mere metaphysic of the infinite. It is an interpretation of the concrete and the historic. In the earthly Jesus, whom John had known, we can see, in temporal projection, the eternal Word of God. He is the Agent of the world's creation. He 'was God', and He 'became flesh'; eternity and time are reconciled in Him. He was with God, and He tabernacled amongst us, and to Him John bears his own witness. 'We beheld His glory, the glory as of the only-begotten of the Father, full of grace and truth'.[3] Those that received Him became, through Him, children of God. So Christ is the visible of the invisible God. He is the interpreter—to transliterate John's Greek—the exegete of the Father.[4]

In his Epistle, with strange brevity John has made very clear what Christianity meant to him. He writes to a Church enjoying a temporary respite from persecution. Gnosticism, that weird amalgam of Greek and Oriental mysticism, was, in a Christianized phraseology, proving very attractive to the Christians of the time. And Gnosticism was a most suggestive philosophy. Grotesque and unethical as many of its tenets were, it had one great advantage—it was keenly interested in redemption. These early Gnostics regarded spirit and matter as eternal and distinct realities. As matter was essentially evil, from matter the spirit had to be redeemed. Redemption came through this knowledge (*gnosis*), that matter and spirit were thus eternally distinct.[5] For earnest men, this meant an ascetic life

[1] The Memra of Palestinian and the Logos of Alexandrian Judaism.

[2] Śaṅkara on Bādarāyaṇa's *Sūtras*, iii. 2. 17. [3] i. 14. [4] i. 18.

[5] It is interesting to compare the very similar Sāṅkhyan conception of redemption as embodied, for example, in parts of the *Bhagavadgītā* (*B. G.* ii. 13–30 and often).

as an aid to the liberation from the body. For others it meant licence. If deeds belonged only to the material, how could they affect the spirits of the redeemed? Naturally from this standpoint, belief in the incarnation of the Son of God was impossible. Yet the Christian Gnostics retained the Christian vocabulary. They too spoke of the heavenly Christ. But the heavenly Christ was for them distinct from the earthly Jesus upon whom He descended at the Baptism, and whom He left before the crucifixion.[1] No more stimulating heresy has ever claimed the Christian name, and John's answer is full of illumination.

John makes the object of his letter plain at once. As one who had actually lived with and known the incarnate Word, he writes that his readers may share his fellowship. 'Yea and our fellowship is with the Father and with His Son Jesus Christ.'[2] 'These things', he concluded, 'have I written unto you that ye may know that ye have eternal life, even unto you that believe on the Name of the Son of God.'[3] So the object of the Epistle is not only to controvert the Gnostic heresy and affirm the true incarnation in Jesus of Christ, the Son of God. It is also to provide an 'apparatus' of tests, an 'adequate set of criteria', by which readers may satisfy themselves that they have eternal life and are thus God's children.[4]

To Christian faith, then, Jesus was not merely a good man on whom the divine Christ descended. He was the true incarnation of the Son of God. And our victory over the world is dependent on this faith. Christ was not the radiant manifestation of God's love, Himself untouched by sorrow. The divine Christ was one with Jesus, not only at the Baptism but on the Cross. It was the Son of God that died for us. Our salvation is a tragic thing, completed only through anguish and sacrifice.[5] It is through Him that we know God, and, in

[1] So Cerinthus, John's great adversary: Irenaeus, *Ad Haer.* i. 26.

[2] i. 1–3.

[3] v. 13.

[4] R. Law's *The Tests of Life*, 2nd edit., p. 6, an exposition of the Epistle to which this brief account of it owes very much.

[5] v. 5, 6.

the end, to refuse to believe in the incarnation of the Son, makes impossible the belief in the Fatherhood of God. 'He that denieth the Son the same hath not the Father.'[1] The love of Christ is itself a revelation of God's love. The absolute of love, says John in one place, is to be seen in Christ's death for us.[2] In another place he sees love's absolute in the love of God, who sent His Son to suffer for us.[3] So the sacrifice of Christ is the sacrifice of God. The death of Christ reveals that even God cannot save sinners, such as we are, without sorrow.

To describe God, John uses a few simple but very significant words. He is righteousness; He is love; He is life, original and self-communicative; He is light. His property it is to reveal Himself, to shine in the darkness, and make Himself known as the truth. So although the word 'eternal' is often on John's lips, it is not an infinite abstraction that John calls God. This holy, loving, personal Being may be known. He has been made known to men in the incarnate Son. There may we see God's righteousness, love, and mercy, and have fellowship with Him. And this fellowship means for us already eternal life. He who has eternal life stands firm amid the flux of time. For such a one the world has lost its glamour. The selfishness, ostentation, and vainglory,[4] which are the marks of the 'world', belong not to the Father, and can no longer attract those who have learned to love Him. In John's majestic phrase, 'the world passeth away and the lust thereof, but he that doeth the will of God abideth for ever'.[5]

And eternal life does not mean merely everlasting life. It is the highest life, the life which is like the life of God. It is God's gift, and through communion with Him alone can it be ours. So its characteristics are those of the divine, and by this we may know whether we have already this eternal life.

[1] ii. 23.
[2] 'Hereby know we love, because He laid down His life for us,' iii. 16. The words 'of God' of the Authorised Version are a gloss.
[3] iv. 10.
[4] 'The lust of the flesh, the lust of the eyes, the pride of life,' ii. 16.
[5] ii. 17.

Thus, although eternal life means redemption from this world, it is manifested not by mystic ecstasies, or sublime speculations, but by our daily and ordinary deeds. The criteria of this life are righteousness, love, and truth. We know that we know Him, if we keep His commandments.[1] If we say we abide in God, we must walk as He walked.[2] There is no need to say who the 'He' is. For John there is only one 'He'. Christ filled all his thoughts. The whole object of the manifestation of the Son of God was, that he might take away sin. Sin is simply 'inadmissible' in the man who abides in God.[3] He that does not righteousness is not of God. As with righteousness, so with love. The world-old commandment of love has taken a new and perfect meaning in Christ's love and sacrifice.[4] There is no eternal life where love is not. Because He laid down His life for us, we ought also to lay down our lives for the brethren. But such a demand is remote from everyday experience, for the call for such sacrifice is rare. So immediately John adds the homely test, 'Do we succour our brethren in their needs?'[5] It is easy for men to indulge in rapturous emotion at the thought of God, but that will not suffice. Our brother is visible before us. If we do not show love to him in his patent necessity, it is useless for us to claim to love much the God who is invisible.[6]

To the tests of righteousness and love, John adds the test of belief. Our eternal life has come to us through the historic revelation of God in Jesus Christ. Only for him who accepts that revelation are its resources available. For such, every spiritual aspiration, and every demand of the conscience, finds in the Gospel its answer. Old man as he is, John himself has not ceased to wonder at the wealth of God's grace. There is the accent of rapture in his words. 'Behold what manner of love the Father hath bestowed upon us that we should be called the children of God, and such we are.' Not yet is our full salvation, but 'we know that when He shall be manifested we shall be

[1] ii. 3. [2] ii. 6. [3] iii. 6.
[4] ii. 7, 8. [5] iii. 15–17. [6] iv. 20.

like Him, for we shall see Him as He is'.[1] It is typical of the Epistle that even here there follows at once the ethical demand: 'And every one that hath this hope in Him, purifieth himself even as He is pure.'[2]

Where outside the words of the Master is there to be found such a combination of simplicity and sublimity, spirituality and ethical vigour?

As in brief outline we thus study the types of Christian experience represented by the three greatest names of the early Church, we are struck less by their difference than their unity. The practical counsels of Peter, the ratiocinations of Paul, the lofty intuitions of John, reveal men of very different mental habits and temperament. But their gospel is the same. It is the gospel of a living and all-powerful Saviour whose service to them was joy, though it meant persecution; and freedom, though it meant imprisonment. About the centrality of Christ in Christianity none of these men has any doubt. Nor do they limit His significance to the Church. All are at one in seeing in Him the world's final, because perfect, Redeemer, the complete expression of the Father's love and grace.

And their experience is not of mere historic interest. It has been not only classic but normative to Christian faith, and able to reproduce itself in countless Christians. And men to-day are able to read their words and find in them the best expression of their own personal and living faith. And these Epistles are not *Forest Books*, or *Upanishads*, to be read only by occasional students with a special interest in religious speculation, and with the rare opportunity of spending long years in uninterrupted meditation. They are the property of the ordinary Christian, and the religious experience they represent is found

[1] iii. 1, 2. As Dr. Arnold said in his last Rugby sermon, 'The mere contemplation of Christ shall transform us into His likeness'.
[2] iii. 3.

not only, or chiefly, in the writings of professed scholars and theologians. It may be studied as well in what has been called the layman's manual of Theology, the hymnaries of the Church. The hymns most universally prized and sung in the most sacred and awful moments of life are hymns which, in modern words, express, however imperfectly, the same experience as we have studied in the classic documents of Christianity, the writings of the great Apostles. It is the experience of a salvation adequate to every need. In the death of their Saviour there is brought home to men God's solemn forgiveness. In union with their risen Lord, men find themselves, in spite of daily failures, redeemed from the tyranny of the sinful and the transitory, to share already something of the power of the life that is eternal.[1]

[1] It may be said that the above presupposes a fuller Christianity than that of the average Christian. But in this sense the average Christian is not the normal but the sub-normal Christian. The experience described is not restricted to men of peculiar spiritual genius, but is reproduceable in any Christian who will take his religion whole-heartedly.

CHAPTER IX

CHRISTIANITY AND THE DOCTRINE OF CYCLIC RECOMPENSE

'THE greatness of man is great', says Pascal, 'because he knows that he is miserable. . . . His very miseries prove his greatness. They are the miseries of a king deposed.'[1] When men are thus conscious of their misery an unreflective optimism becomes impossible. Men begin to ask, 'Whence came evil?'

To deny the problem is not to solve it. To say with Pope:

> 'And, spite of Pride, in erring Reason's spite,
> One truth is clear, whatever is, is right,'

is to mock a misery we do not feel. There is a shallow cheerfulness which deserves well the fierce rebuke of Schopenhauer. 'To me, optimism, when it is not merely the thoughtless talk of such as harbour nothing but words under their low forehead, appears not merely an absurd, but also as a really wicked, way of thinking, as a bitter mockery of the unspeakable sufferings of humanity.'[2] Why should one man be leprous or crippled and another clean and strong? Why should one man be born to privilege and wealth, another to misery and poverty? Such questions must arise in the minds of all who have sufficient leisure to think, and sufficient imagination to feel the cruel inequalities of life. Before the mystery of unmerited suffering, men in the West have been for the most part content to stand dumb. It is not easy 'to justify the ways of God to man'.

[1] *Pensées et Opuscules* publiés par M. L. Brunschvigg, p. 509.

[2] *The World as Will and Idea*, English trans., i. 420, quoted in *E. R. E.* vi. 321. But Schopenhauer's own pessimism is as extreme and as unconvincing as the optimism of Leibnitz which Pope was versifying. As Prof. James Ward says, 'If the rosy pictures of the one are not decisive, neither is the gallery of horrors of the other,' *The Realm of Ends, or Pluralism and Theism*, p. 324.

We need to remember Bishop Butler's warning, 'What men require is to have all difficulties cleared. And this is, or at least for anything we know to the contrary, it may be, the same as requiring to comprehend the Divine nature, and the whole plan of Providence from everlasting to everlasting.'[1] If perfect knowledge is required to solve the problem, then we must pronounce it insoluble, for our knowledge is imperfect and fragmentary.

To Hinduism the problem seems not insoluble, but solved. There is in the world no injustice. Events and causes are linked together by inviolable law. At a man's death, the effects of his deeds remain and determine his destiny in his next birth. So a man's condition is always the result of his own acts. The outcaste in his degradation, the virgin-widow in her loneliness, the maimed and the suffering, are all alike atoning for the misdeeds of a previous life. Through cycles of birth and death, acts, good or bad, work out in reward or retribution. With such a theory, Hindus justly claim that, whereas other men confess themselves baffled, they can explain with confidence all those things in the world which seem unjust. And what was once the obscure philosopheme of a few isolated thinkers has become in India, not only the logical *prius* of all speculation, but the almost universal conviction of the common people, so firmly held that the calamities and inequalities of life appear no longer as mysteries but are regarded as the natural and inevitable consequence of previous deeds. The theory is in many ways an attractive one. As a recent traveller to India has said: 'There is an undeniable dignity in the Hindu conception of the soul pursuing its long pilgrimage through decaying worlds until at length it reaches home in the endless sea.'[2]

The importance of the doctrine thus seems to be twofold:

1. It provides a theodicy easily understood and generally accepted.

2. It secures the recognition of the principle of retribution.

[1] *The Analogy of Religion*, Part II, Chap. viii.

[2] J. B. Pratt, *India and its Faiths*, p. 106.

Clear and consistent as the doctrine of *karma* at first appears to be, it seems doubtful if its simplicity is more than superficial. That there is a connexion between sin and suffering, most men would admit. We reap, for the most part, the crop we sow. As the Indian proverb says:

> 'Who plants mangoes, mangoes shall he eat;
> Who plants thorn-bushes, thorns shall wound his feet.'[1]

Or, as the *Mahābhārata* puts it, 'As among a thousand cows a calf finds its mother, so the deed previously done follows after the doer'.[2] But it is one thing to recognize the principle of retribution. It is another to make of deeds and their effects a mathematical equation: so much surplus of good deeds equals so much happiness; so much surplus of evil deeds equals so much misery. Such equations deal with deeds, good or ill, as if they were so many counters, to be added to, or removed at will. Deeds are not thus separable from personality. Punishment to be just should deal not so much with the deeds as with the doer.

Such is not the view of Indian philosophy. The consequences of deeds act on without reference to their doer. Nor indeed with its defective psychology could it be otherwise. As Deussen says, 'As the natural consequence of the Indian view which places the essence of the soul in knowing, not in willing, the soul, with all its organs, is a quite neutral thing, devoid of all moral distinctions'.[3] It is not easy, then, to see how the effects of deeds determine the soul's destiny, and it cannot be said that the classic texts of Hinduism give us here much guidance. The account in the *Upanishads* is, as we have seen,[4] obscure and confused. Why, after requital in the next world, rebirth is needed here is not explained, and the description of the descent of the soul to be born again is certainly more curious than convincing. Nor does Śaṅkarāchārya help us here.[5] So far from removing the contradictions of the

[1] Cp. Gal. vi. 7.
[2] Quoted in Macdonell's *Sanskrit Literature*, p. 388.
[3] *Das System des Vedānta*, p. 404. [4] See Chapter iii, pp. 58–63.
[5] See Chapter iv, pp. 92–5.

Upanishadic texts, his more formal and didactic exposition only makes them more obvious. The illustration he gives of the courtier, who leaves the king's court before he is quite penniless, does not really help us to see why, if the effects of deeds operate in the next world, they still require to be worked out in this. And there is a prior difficulty, The soul is not only morally neutral. It is an unconscious entity. Few but theosophists (usually of European extraction) claim to remember their previous existences.[1] What connexion is there then between the deeds of one birth and their effects in the next? Śaṅkara, as we have seen, is here not only obscure; he is self-contradictory. In one place he assumes that there exists a causal link between deeds and their effects (*apūrva*).[2] In another passage he expressly denies this, and does so, because only so can he leave room in his system for the activity of Īśvara, the effected (and unreal) Lord.[3] But the Gods themselves are under *karma* and involved in the cycle of birth and death, and the work assigned to Īśvara is otiose. In truth, the doctrine of *karma*, accepted with thoroughness, leaves no place for personality, whether human or divine. So we find that the Sāṅkhyan philosophy, in which the transmigration theory finds its most congenial expression, is atheistic, and assigns the whole karmic process to the material sphere; [4] whilst Gautama the Buddha, regarding as axiomatic

[1] It is only by his divine omniscience that Kṛishṇa can say to Arjuna, 'Many births of me and thee have passed, O Arjuna, I know them all'. And he adds at once, 'but thou knowest them not'. *B. G.* iv. 5.

[2] iii. 1. 6. *S. B. E.* xxxviii, p. 109.

[3] iii. 2. 38. Modern theosophy is, of course, able to explain. It is the four 'Mahārājahs, who choose for the composition of the etheric double, the elements suited to the qualities that are to be expressed through it, and this etheric double thus becomes a fitting karmic instrument for the Ego, giving it alike the basis for expression of the faculties it has evolved, and the limitations imposed upon it by its own past failures and wasted opportunities. This mould is guided by the Mahārājahs to the country, ther ace, the family, the social surroundings, which afford the most suitable field for the working out of the *karma* allotted.' *Karma*, by Mrs. Besant, p. 47.

[4] This atheism (nirīśvara-vāda) does not affect the belief in the popular gods. As we have already seen, redemption in this system consists in

the belief in cyclic recompense, ignores as meaningless this belief in a useless God and an insentient soul.[1] Many and persistent have been the endeavours in India to reach Monotheism, yet somehow all have failed. Has not their failure been the inevitable consequence of this recognition of a karmic law to which even the gods are subject, and from which the highest Brahman is only exempt because He refrains from all purposed activity? Thus, as we have seen, in Śaṅkara's system, Īśvara, the arbiter of men's destiny, is active but unreal. The highest Brahman, the sole reality, is without attribute, action, or desire. And in Rāmānuja's elaborate attempt to legitimatize in the Vedānta a more theistic faith, the same necessity seems to be recognized, of removing the highest Brahman from the sphere of action, lest He too come under the karmic law. At times, Rāmānuja speaks of the highest Brahman as if He were at once personal and real. 'We know from Scripture', he writes, 'that there is a Supreme Person whose nature is absolute bliss and goodness, who is fundamentally antagonistic to all evil; who is the cause of the origination, sustentation, and dissolution of the world; who differs in nature from all other beings, who is all-knowing. who, by His mere thought and will, accomplishes all His purposes; who is an ocean of kindness, as it were, for all who depend on Him; whose name is the highest Brahman.. And, with equal certainty, we know from Scripture that this Supreme Lord, when pleased by the faithful worship of His Devotees, frees them from the influence of Nescience, which consists of *karma*, accumulated in the infinite progress of time and hence hard to overcome; allows them to attain to that supreme bliss which consists in the direct intuition of His own

knowing the absolute distinction of the soul from all the material world to which belong the organs of our mental and moral life.

[1] In the Buddhist view, 'The new person formed after death is one's karmic soul, but it is not one's identical ego. It is to save from sorrow this son of one's act, that one should seek to find the end. But there is no soul to save.' Hopkins, *Religions of India*, p. 322.

true nature;'[1] and, in other passages, Rāmānuja speaks of Brahman's all-comprehensive rule.[2] Yet in his discussion of the *Sūtras* dealing with the 'creation' of the world, Rāmānuja has no better solution than Śaṅkara gave. The highest Brahman made, or rather, 'arranged', the world in motiveless 'sport',[3] and Rāmānuja's discussion also assumes that God must be without motive and desire, or He too would fall under the karmic law. True, in the passage we have quoted, Brahman seems to be regarded as Redeemer, yet His part in redemption is one of mere passivity. Hindu *bhakti* has craved a living God, and its saints have sung of the gracious deeds, the active love, of their God; but such belief has been more the hope of the heart than the conviction of the mind, and the ardour of emotion has found it hard to withstand the chill of the conviction that God, if free from *karma*, must be inactive. If active, he will be under the karmic law. Real and meaningless, or meaningful and unreal. It is a harsh alternative. But such seems to be the inevitable consequence of this belief in *karma*. In truth the karmic law leaves no adequate room in the universe for the living God. It is a theodicy which has little use for a 'theos'.

This explanation of the world's sorrow has not removed but increased its burden. From the time of the *Upanishads* on, how sombre has been the Indian view of life, how poignant the sense of life's misery and futility. And, general as has been the acceptance of the doctrine of *karma*, it has never been able quite to displace the older views. Men still continue to sacrifice, and pray, and hope thus to obtain, in spite of *karma*, deliverance from calamity and abundant wealth and offspring. Ascetics have not ceased to strive in this present life by their austerities to gain supernatural powers unearned by the deeds of their previous birth.[4] The belief in cyclic recompense

[1] On *Vedāntasūtras*, iv. 4. 32. *S. B. E.* xlviii, p. 770.
[2] E. g. *op. cit.* on ii. 4. 14, p. 576. [3] *Op. cit.* on ii. 1. 33, p. 477.
[4] Cp. J. N. Farquhar, *The Crown of Hinduism*, p. 148.

provides no consolation to the sufferer, and no motive to the happy to relieve his suffering. The Brāhman may be pleased to regard his advantages of caste and opportunity as the due reward of his merit in a previous birth, but it does not help the Pariah to be told that the degradation which makes his very presence 'contaminating' to the Brāhman, is the fit and inexorable result of misdeeds done in a life of which he has no knowledge and no recollection. For the miserable, it is no gospel to hear that 'the Good Law is working with undeviating accuracy, that its agents apply it everywhere with unerring insight, with unfailing strength, and that all is therefore very well with the world and with its struggling Souls'.[1] Actually the universal Hindu view is that all is *not* very well with the world and with its struggling souls. In the working out of *karma* the world is getting steadily worse. The golden age was at the first; the present age is the last and most evil of all. The deeds of previous births hold men in an imprisonment more cruel than that of any dungeon, for it lasts not for one, but innumerable lifetimes.

A man may indeed improve his *karma* by good works. Thus the Benares text-book says: 'A man has only to desire, to think, to act, and he can make his *karma* what he chooses. Thus the Gods have risen to their high estate, and thus many others rise.'[2] But in this there is little consolation. Even if we could assume that the human will were strong enough to trample over difficulties, and, unaided, do good in a bad environment, the *karma* would in this life remain unchanged. The outcaste would still be an outcaste, and the leper a leper. The good *karma* gained would only be effective in a future life with which this present life has no personal and conscious connexion. And if a man can do but little for himself, he can do less for his neighbours. The Benares text-book indeed informs us that it is a 'mistake to say respecting a sufferer, "He is suffering his *karma*; if I help him I may be interfering

[1] Mrs. Besant, *Karma*, p. 50.
[2] *An Advanced Text-book of Hindu Religion and Ethics*, Central Hindu College, Benares, p. 117.

with his *karma*". Those who thus speak forget that each man is an agent of the *karma* of others, as well as an experiencer of his own. If we are able to help a man, it is the proof that the *karma* under which he was suffering is exhausted, and that we are the agent of his *karma* bringing him relief. If we refuse to carry the karmic relief, we make bad *karma* for ourselves, shutting ourselves out from future help, and some one else will have the good *karma* of carrying the relief and so ensuring for himself aid in a future difficulty.'[1] Even with this modernized, and modified, view of *karma*, the incentive to kindness seems strangely circuitous and ineffective. And this is inevitable. The quiescent compassion we feel for the criminal justly expiating his crimes is very different from the energetic help we desire to render the unfortunate; but, if the karmic view be true, the leper and the cripple, the blind and the bereaved, are all to be regarded as criminals undergoing punishment for misdeeds done in former births. Has it not been this belief which, among a people kindly and humane, has stayed the course of pity and allowed harsh customs to survive unchecked? How otherwise, for instance, could there be added to the bereavement of the widow the ignominy of the shorn head, and the poor clothes, and the deprivation of her jewels? It is this belief in *karma* which makes of the unhappy the accursed.

To the doctrine of *karma* may be not unjustly assigned the static nature of Indian society. When Christian missionaries began their work among the outcastes, they were told their work would be in vain; the ignorance, degradation, and semi-servitude of those for whom they laboured were the inevitable and inexpugnable results of past sins done in previous lives. Experience teaches; and the Hindu view has been found false in fact. The large, and long-established, Christian communities of South India have revealed how effectively Christian education can break the power of an evil past. Thus very many of the Shānar Christians have shown themselves well able in intellectual

[1] *Op. cit.*, p. 118.

ability to compete with the privileged Hindus of the highest castes, and even among the Pariah Christians there are increasingly those of Christian character, education, and refinement. Defective environment provides a more adequate explanation for the degradation of the outcaste than does the law of *karma,* and experience shows how greatly spiritual forces working in an improved environment can change men even in their present life. Through the success of Christian missions and in emulation of them, Hindus have begun to realize their responsibility for those whom they formerly regarded as outside the pale of sympathy and help. The quest of political freedom has made the social tyrant an anomaly. Stable Home Rule is possible only for a nation, not for a congeries of severed castes. So long as outcastes are regarded as accursed, Hindu leaders must not complain because the outcaste communities prefer that their destinies should be in the hands of aliens, rather than of those who regard them not as fellow countrymen, but as 'untouchables', void of the dignity of common manhood. There are now 'Depressed Classes Missions' whose endeavours are earnest and admirable. But it is hard to reconcile such work with the belief that in the present life a man's *karma* is unalterable. If an outcaste must, in any case, work out in this life the *karma* of his previous birth, such missions lose their motive. We can only strive with enthusiasm to save those whom we regard as salvable.[1]

[1] A Syrian Christian friend once remarked to me that Hindus needed to embrace Christianity in order to rid themselves of their belief in *karma*, and in caste as determined by *karma*, which makes all social work so ineffective. I replied, 'Surely there is needed for social service also the constraint of Christian love in order to arouse that spirit of self-sacrifice and patience which all who labour for the degraded need'. He answered, and with very much truth: 'That would be true in Europe, but in India from the time of Gautama, the Buddha, there have always been very many who would think nothing of self-sacrifice if it were in the pursuit of what they recognized as a spiritual end.' It is significant that the most prominent members of the Depressed Classes Mission have been members of the Prārthanā Samāj, and in this Samāj the doctrine of *karma* is treated as an open question and practically rejected by many of its members. *Vide* J. N. Farquhar's *Modern Religious Movements in India*, p. 78.

Justly proud as India is of its venerable history, its best minds are looking not to the past but to the future. They believe that the best is yet to be, and have before them the glorious vision of a repristinated India able to take its place among the most spiritual and enlightened of the nations. But the doctrine of *karma* sounds the death-knell of all such noble hope. The good time has come; it is not coming. The history of the world is one not of progress, but of retrogression. The first age was golden and in it virtue was perfect and entire. In the two succeeding ages virtue became weak and mutilated. In the age in which we live (the *kali yuga*) virtue is well-nigh dead, and evil, already supreme, must increase and increase until at last the universe is totally destroyed and reabsorbed into Brahmā. There is no message here for a rejuvenated India.

Thus the doctrine which was to solve the problem of evil has increased its burden. And not only so. From what has been said it is clear that, for all its emphasis on retribution, the doctrine has tended to weaken rather than to strengthen the moral nexus between sin and suffering. A man is not born with the experience gained in a previous existence. He has no sense of his past failure, no accumulation of wisdom learnt from his past folly. Against the cruder forms of the *karma* theory [1] the old criticism of Herder is still apposite. If a tiger in human form is born in the next life an actual tiger, how is that an expiation? A tiger has no conscience and can now ravage and kill without remorse.[2] And in its more subtle forms, too, the karmic law fails to

[1] Cp. *The Laws of Manu*, section XII.

59. Men who delight in doing hurt (become) carnivorous (animals); those who eat forbidden food, worms; thieves, creatures who consume their own kind.

62. For stealing grain, (a man) becomes a rat; for stealing honey, a stinging insect; for stealing milk, a cow.

63. For stealing meat, a vulture.

67. For stealing fruits and roots, a monkey; for stealing vehicles a camel. *S. B. E.* xxv, p. 497, 498.

[2] See P. Gennrich, *Die Lehre von der Wiedergeburt*, p. 343.

establish any moral connexion between the sins of the past and the sufferings of the present, for of the past we have no memory. And the *karma* theory gives no hope of a gradual ascent through moral struggle to freedom from sin and evil. And this is inevitable. It is beyond man's unaided powers to reach communion with God. That can come only by God's act. Re-birth will not suffice. It is the new birth which can so transform the personality as to make it, in Paul's words, 'a new creature', influenced indeed by the effects of past deeds, but no longer in bondage to them because of the great inrush of God's creative power.

The best criticism of a doctrine is its history, and history clearly teaches that the effect of the karmic doctrine has been to compel men, in revolt at the inexorable tyranny of the past, to seek to sever themselves completely from the effects of their deeds.

As we have seen, from the time of the *Upanishads* on, the classic philosophy of India has been chiefly concerned with redemption from the karmic process. And the nature of the redemption sought is full of significance. Its very one-sidedness shows the one-sidedness of the conception of the *karma* from which men sought so eagerly to be redeemed. According to the doctrine of *karma*, the individual soul must wander on from birth to death, and death to birth, bound to its deeds as with chains of steel. Surely it is in reaction against this excessive emphasis on the effect of deeds that, as we have seen, the most influential school of Indian thought proclaims a redemption which removes the soul entirely from the results of its activity, and asserts its identity with the attributeless and inactive Brahman. For the man whom knowledge has thus redeemed, the creation and Īśvara, the Creator, are alike illusory. For such a one, deeds have no effect, and retribution no meaning. Not only the deeds of the past life, but the deeds of this life also, are of no importance to the redeemed. For him, moral distinctions no longer exist, and the sense of guilt is known to be illusory.

We have seen that the importance of the doctrine of *karma* is twofold. It provides a theodicy easily understood and generally accepted. It secures the recognition of the principle of retribution. As a theodicy, in explaining sorrow it has destroyed hope. In its recognition of the principle of retribution, by its externality and over-emphasis, it has led to a view of redemption which ignores altogether the effect of deeds.

In the last two chapters the endeavour was made briefly to describe the Christian Gospel as it is revealed in Christ Himself and in the classic experience of the greatest Apostles. It remains here to indicate what answer Christianity gives to the problem of evil, and what recognition it accords to the principle of retribution.

The higher our thought of God, the more mysterious seem the world's sin and misery. If there were many gods, then chaos would occasion no surprise. If God be attributeless, unable to see or feel, then sorrow and inequality may be due to chance, or to the working of an inexorable law. But if God be the holy and almighty Creator, Sustainer, and Ruler of the universe, then surely all things must be obedient to His will and reveal His mercy. What are we to say then of the earthquake which engulfs a city, or of the pestilence which devastates a countryside, and may snatch from a man in one day all his loved ones.[1] For some, the sense of the evils of creation has become an intolerable obsession. 'In sober truth,' wrote Mill, 'nearly all things which men are hanged or imprisoned for doing to one another, are nature's everyday performances. . . . Nature impales men . . . and has hundreds of other hideous deaths in reserve such as the cruelties of a Domitian never surpassed.'[2] Such words seem too emphatic. Nature is not only hostile. The very severity of its laws is often kindness in disguise. Disease has often proved the only

[1] As cholera will often do in India.

[2] J. S. Mill, *Essay on Nature.*

effective teacher of cleanliness and regard for the poor, and, if men could abuse their bodies without punishment, the race would not be happier but more miserable. The most fertile countries, in which men get food with little labour, have not usually been the homes of the most robust nations. It is necessity which has taught invention. Strength comes from opposition. But worse and more perplexing than physical evil is moral. It is not merely the existence of evil men ; it is their prosperity which seems to challenge our faith in a righteous God. Thus in war, the greatest suffering may fall not upon the aggressor, but upon a peaceful and neutral nation whose only offence it is that it is too small to beat back force with force. And the permission of such colossal crimes is hard to reconcile with our trust in a God of love. It is with no surprise that we find that so much of the greatest literature of the world is concerned with the tragedy of the world's injustice.

The discussion of the problem in the Old Testament is peculiarly instructive. The pious Israelite, in his emphasis on God's righteousness, for long believed that God requited accurately the good and the bad. To those that obeyed Him, came in this life, prosperity ; to those that disobeyed, trouble and adversity.[1] Thus the Israelite, like the Hindu, looked upon sorrow as the result of sin. If, as in the case of a child born a cripple, or afflicted, the sufferer could not himself be accused of sin, then the suffering was assigned to the sins of his forefathers working out in retribution. Such a theory was more easily tested by experience than the more subtle and elusive doctrine of *karma,* and experience showed that it was inadequate to the facts. But there was no other theory to put in its place. The book of *Job*, the one book in the Old Testament devoted entirely to this problem, shows that the current solution is not true ; suffering is not always due to sin. But it has no explanation to give instead. Even the devoutest of the Jews found that the fact of unmerited suffering bore

[1] Cp. *The Book of Deuteronomy*.

heavily on their faith in God, and their faith is expressed at times with a passionate intensity which shows how nearly it had become doubt. Though the wicked prosper and the innocent suffer, yet the innocent still have God. God will be the strength of their heart and their portion for evermore.[1]

In the New Testament all is changed. For its writers the problem is not so much solved as removed. The Jewish explanation Christ expressly rejected. The victims of Pilate's cruelty were not more wicked than other Galileans.[2] Unlike His disciples, He refused to assign the blindness of the man born blind either to his own or his parents' sin.[3] He gave no explanation of the man's affliction, but declared that even such misfortune might 'make manifest the works of God'. After Christ's death and resurrection, the disciples lost their perplexity. They had been troubled at the blindness of a stray beggar. Now they bear without complaining or surprise their own now heavy sorrows. The Christians were scourged, imprisoned, put to death, but the Church saw in these events, not the working of retribution, nor the failure of God to do justly, but opportunities of glorifying God, and found in these persecutions nothing that could take away from them their joy and sense of triumph. In His lifetime Christ had proclaimed His twofold message of God the Father and the Kingdom of God. His disciples would not understand. Only when He was dead and risen did they obtain the invincible confidence which belongs of right to those who in Christ know God as Father, and share already in the blessings of that Kingdom which is present and eternal.

The two great facts of God's Fatherhood and Kingdom are still the inalienable possession of all true Christians. Through

[1] Psalm lxxiii. 26. [2] Luke xiii. 2.

[3] John ix. 2. The disciples' supposition that a man might be born blind through his own sin is curious. The suggestion that they had in mind some such doctrine as that of *karma* seems improbable. A few Jewish teachers may have been acquainted with that doctrine, but not laymen. More probably it is based on a current Jewish view that a babe, while still in the womb, may have emotions that are sinful.

these facts, the problem of evil, though not speculatively solved, loses its urgency and bitterness. For the Christian, the world is not the domain of fate or blind necessity. Whatever be the explanation of its mysteries, he is sure that the world was created and is ruled by the almighty God whom Jesus has bidden us call Father. And because of this faith, he is confident that the creation furthers, and does not thwart, the purposes of love. And the fact of human sin and misery does not refute God's Fatherhood. The motive of fatherhood is love, but love has only meaning among those whose natures are akin. Only persons can be loved or love. And because the men whom God created are persons, and not things, they have the power of choice, and this implies the power of mischoice. If so crude a phrase may be permitted, God 'had to take the risk'. It is the same risk as every human father takes, and if a man knows that he will love and cherish whatever children are born to him, we do not say that he should not call into the world new lives because there is the possibility that, in spite of his nurture and care, they yet may choose the wrong. To complain of the creation of fallible men is to complain of any creation at all; it is the utter pessimism of those who, like Schopenhauer, regard non-existence as better than existence, and who would prefer to have in place of the rich and varied life of humanity with all its movement, its joys and sorrows, the stillness and silence of the uninhabitable waste.

The Christian confidence in God's love springs not from speculation but from faith. And such a confidence is inadequate to our needs unless it can become as real to us as the actual sorrow of our own lives and the patent misery of the world around. It is the witness of innumerable Christians that in Christ just such a certainty has been found. He spoke, in life and death, as one who knew perfectly the Father, and we believe His witness to the Father's love. But to the Christian, Christ is not chiefly the prophet or the teacher. He is the visible of the invisible God. His holy and indomitable love is the projection in time of the holy love of God. We may be certain of the Father's love because we have seen it in Jesus Christ. Such a confidence may be troubled but not be overthrown.[1] It is not a denial of the sombre evils of life. It is a victory over these evils which is compatible with the bitterest experience of them. It was one whose life was a daily death who spoke with such impassioned eloquence of the love of God from which nothing in life or death could ever separate him. The man certain of God's love can afford to be uncertain of much else, and be content to know that love does all things for the best.

> 'Love understands the mystery, whereof
>   We can but spell a surface history:
> Love knows, remembers: Let us trust in Love:
>   Love understands the mystery.'[2]

To stop here would be to misrepresent the attitude towards suffering of classic Christianity. The Fatherhood is only half Christ's message. He proclaimed with it the message of God's Kingdom. If the blessings of the Kingdom were blessings, temporal and material, then the New Testament teaching that sorrow and suffering need not be evil is obviously untrue. The blessings of the Kingdom were spiritual and yet present. Thus the apostles felt that already they shared in the joy and stability of blessings that were eternal. True, their experience of these blessings was as yet but partial, yet, in spite of their afflictions, it sufficed to fill their lives with gratitude and hope. They felt no impulse to speculate on 'the burthen and the mystery', 'the heavy and the weary weight of all this unintelligible world'. They were content instead to thank God for His unspeakable gifts. Yet these men had, if not a philosophy,

[1] It is from this point of view that we can understand the Divine Omnipotence. As Prof. Pringle-Pattison says, 'The omnipotence of God' means 'neither the tawdry trappings of regal pomp nor the irresistible might of a physical force. The divine omnipotence consists in the all-compelling power of goodness and love to enlighten the grossest darkness and to melt the coldest heart. It is of the essence of the divine prerogative to seek no other means of triumph—as, indeed, a real triumph is possible on no other terms.' *The Idea of God*, by A. Seth Pringle-Pattison, p. 411.

[2] Christina Rossetti, *Songs for Strangers and Pilgrims.*

yet an interpretation of evil. The suffering of the world was closely connected with its sin. Its miseries were punitive to those who identified themselves with the sin from which the worst misery arises. But there was no attempt to equate sin and suffering. How could there be when it was the confession of Christ that brought upon many their greatest hardships? Even in such sorrow they found a discipline which strengthened and enriched their characters, and, like Paul, they are certain that to them that love God, all things work out for good.

Such a solution can be verified only in experience. *Solvitur ambulando—cum Deo.* The Christian finds, as he reviews his own life, that sorrow was necessary to him, that God has been doing all things well, and he believes that the God, whose love he has experienced, is a God who loves the whole world. And from the Christian standpoint, suffering is not purposeless. It may be vicarious and remedial. The world's saviours have often been men of sorrows and acquainted with grief, wounded for the transgressions and bruised for the iniquities of those they sought to serve. The Holiest died upon the cross. It is not strange that those who seek to follow Him should have to suffer. Such suffering has not been counted punishment but privilege. It is a witness to the love of God. It is a continuation of the work of Christ.

So, in spite of evil, the Christian is certain that a Father rules. Through his membership in the Kingdom he already has an eternal life which takes from sorrow its bitterness, and fills his life with hope. He does not expect to realize on earth his perfect happiness; he desires that even his suffering should help to make God's will be done, His Kingdom come. So Christianity, too, has a theodicy, but it is a theodicy which is not a universal theory but an individual achievement; a theodicy to be won not by speculation but by trust and obedience, by moral conflict and participation in God's purposes.

But the doctrine of *karma* is not only a theodicy. It is

significant also in its recognition of the principle of retribution. Christianity, as we have seen, declines to equate sin and suffering, or to explain in every case a man's misfortune by his misdeeds. But, if this is so, does not Christianity ignore the principle of retribution? Such an accusation may perhaps be sustained against some presentations of Christianity, but it would certainly not be true of any Christianity which is true to type. Christ spoke most distinctly of punishment, and in figurative language referred to the few stripes and the many.

The great principle that, whatsoever a man sows, that shall he also reap, is regarded as a truism in Christianity. The belief in a divine judgement, however interpreted, has always formed part of accepted Christian truth. But retribution is not regarded as an end in itself. Punishment and sin are not mathematically adjusted. The penalty is not made proportionate to deeds irrespective of the doer. It is with guilt that punishment must be related, and guilt depends not so much on the act as on the moral responsibility of the agent. Judgement for judgement's sake, judgement which works on irrespective of the sinner, is, from the Christian standpoint, meaningless. Even criminal justice, rough and imperfect as it is, does not think itself an end independent of the well-being of the State.[1] Its purpose is subsidiary, not final. In most modern states an endeavour is made to prevent the law working as a mere machine. The judge is allowed considerable discretion, and is expected to take into consideration the degree of responsibility in the offender. Yet, even so, our criminal justice works but clumsily, and inevitably thinks more of the deed than of the doer: The Christian conception of punishment is not thus juridical. The doctrine of *karma*, as we have seen, gives no sufficient room for an active Ruler of the world. The Christian doctrine instead proclaims a living God, the Father of all His creatures. Nature indeed does not speak to us of forgiveness. Sins

[1] Cp. A. G. Hogg, *Karma and Redemption*, pp. 52–60.

which transgress the laws of nature receive automatically their punishment. The vicious and the self-indulgent pay in their bodies for their misdeeds. Unless the law of nature were thus uniform enough to be noted and relied on, ordered life would be impossible, and human affairs would have to cease. But such inevitable consequences cannot be regarded as the just recompense of sin. The laws of nature are as often broken in ignorance as in vice, and the ignorant may suffer in this way more than the depraved. To drink unboiled water in cholera time may have more serious physical consequences than drunkenness or gluttony. If nature does not speak to us of forgiveness, neither does it speak to us of retribution which is just.

As the correlate of the Christian doctrine of the divine Fatherhood is the belief that every soul of man has before God an infinite value. It is with the self that retribution has ultimately to do. The worst effect of sin is not on our circumstances, but on ourselves. In this sense it is true that each man makes his own destiny. Our characters are chiefly of our own creation. Outer deeds are, from this point of view, important as expressions of inner acts of choice. Among presented motives the will chooses with which motive it will identify itself. The self is not an aggregate of independent states, nor is it an insentient substratum. It has a history and a character. As it wills, it largely is. Ultimately holiness is blessedness, and if any man chose always to do evil, his will would become evil, and, in a universe ruled by a holy God, such a one would inevitably be shut off from blessedness. The wages of sin is death.

The Christian gospel proclaims as its first message the forgiveness of sins. It assumes that men who in the past have chosen evil can receive God's forgiveness and with it a new transforming power. It was with this confidence that Christ bade men enter the Kingdom of God, to share in the joy of God's children and the obedience of His servants. He spoke as one who offered men, not new teaching, but new pow r. He assumed that, for all alike, to receive this message would mean a break with the past, drastic and radical. Hinduism speaks of a rebirth necessitated by the activities of past lives; Christianity speaks of a new birth, of the possibility of an inrush of divine power great enough to change the direction of the will and transform the personality. And such a new birth is not only possible but necessary. 'Never', it has been well said, 'does Christ gloss over the difference between those with whom He came in contact. He never groups them together in any rough-and-ready estimate as if they constituted one uniform mass. He seeks to find every one individually in his individual isolation from God.' He knew that there were religious as well as sinners, whole as well as sick. Yet He assumes that, in all alike, there was a perversion of the will. Men are prevented from receiving the good gift of the Kingdom, 'not by some weakness which could easily be got over, but by a false strength which a man alone could not overcome'.[1] Except a man be born again, he cannot enter the Kingdom of God. All alike need forgiveness, for the wills of all are turned away from God, and this forgiveness is a great creative act. Christ calls us to a communion with God which changes our ideals and re-creates our personality. Some there are who, brought up in Christian homes, have at all times felt the appeal of Christ, and been responsive to it. Such experience the impact on their personality of divine power, and know that, in proportion as they trust God and do His will, they live a life which is not one of bondage to past deeds, but the work of the re-creating power of God. But the 'new birth' is more conspicuously seen in those who in a moment have had the whole direction of their lives changed. Thus men who through selfish choices tend to selfish choosing, may be brought through the realization of God's love in Christ to lives of unselfish service. Men, slaves to sense, learn temperance and self-sacrifice. To all

[1] T. Haering, *The Christian Faith*, Eng. trans., p. 439.

men alike, the Christian gospel comes with the offer of forgiveness and the promise of new power.

But does not such a message of forgiveness violate just what is true in the doctrine of *karma*, its recognition of the principle of retribution? If, with those who hold the *karma* doctrine, we understand retribution only in a juridical sense, that would be true. But Christianity thinks of retribution, not from the juridical so much as from the moral standpoint. Its best analogy is not the practice of the law courts, but the wise discipline of a well-ordered home. Punishment may be deterrent and exemplary for others, but for the wrongdoer himself its object is thus not retribution chiefly, but rather the recognition of the holy law he has transgressed. Through the contumacy of the offender, punishment may become for him vindictive only, but, in so far as this is so, punishment has failed in its chief work and is fulfilling only an inferior function. It has been well said 'the truth of penalty is penitence'. And forgiveness means far more than an amnesty. An amnesty is granted without any regard to its effect on the characters of those who are 'let off'. But forgiveness means reconciliation. The divine forgiveness means the reconciliation of men with a holy God. Forgiveness thus means far more than the cancellation of a debt or the closing of an account. It is a relation between persons; a man cannot be forgiven unless he is forgivable.[1] So long as a man identifies his will with evil, he is unforgivable. Yet nothing is harder than to repent. Our repentance has mostly to be repented of. It is not sufficient that we should be sorry for the wrong deed in which we have been discovered. Such sorrow is too often concerned not with guilt but penalty. So long as a man is shrinking more from the consequences of sin than from the sin itself, we cannot speak of him as penitent. To 'let men off', and ignore their sin, would not solve but aggravate the moral problem. It is forgiveness that we need, and, if the

[1] Cp. the fine chapter on Forgiveness in Moberly's *Personality and Atonement*.

forgiveness is to be adequate, somewhere, somehow, there must be a vindication of righteousness and a recognition of the guilt of sin.

In classic Christianity the forgiveness of sins has not been proclaimed as an isolated doctrine, but in connexion with the death of Christ. As we have seen, the first article of the primitive Christian confession was this, 'Christ died for our sins'.[1] As Jews, accustomed to offer up to God sacrifices which should cover their iniquity, the early disciples naturally saw in Christ's death the one perfect sacrifice. And the history of the Church shows that even in lands where animal sacrifices have long been offered, directly the Christian Gospel has been accepted such sacrifices have completely ceased; the truth that they stood for has been expressed completely in Christ's death.[2] To us to-day, unused to the sacrificial system, to say that Christ's death was the propitiation of our sins is to mystify rather than to explain; yet for us, too, the forgiveness of sins is inseparably connected with the death of the Saviour.

To our holy God, sin cannot be a matter of indifference. He is our Father. He has endowed us with the power of choice that so as persons we may respond to His love with ours. So He saves us from sin, not by coercion, but by moral means. How He loves, and how He saves, Christ's death has shown. Of human parents it is true that they cannot save the greatly-erring child, unless they are willing to enter into the misery of his sin, and make its effects their own; if they would save, then they must suffer. And Christ in entering into our human need, and submitting Himself to the worst curse and sorrow of our humanity, has revealed to us, perfectly and finally, the power and meaning of redemptive love. Here is love's absolute. He died for us. And this love of Christ is to the Christian but the temporal projection of the eternal love of God. His death speaks to us,

[1] See Chapter VIII, p. 159.
[2] Cp. Harnack, *Das Wesen des Christentums*, p. 99.

more clearly than His life, of the love of God which loves us even in our sin and, to save us, loves to the very end. Here the penitent, doubtful if he is forgiven, experiences the certainty that God does forgive. Yet it is a forgiveness which, instead of diminishing, increases our sense of the guilt of sin. If we could believe that 'we needs must love the highest when we see it', we could hold a better view of ourselves and of the race. Actually it was not so. When the Highest came and lived on earth, men rejected Him and hated Him, and in the end had Him put to a death terrible and disgraceful. The curse of sin is nowhere seen as clearly as here. And in that sin, in that rejection of the good and choice of evil, we feel we take our share. The emblem of God's love is also the emblem of human hate. The certainty of God's forgiveness speaks to us from Christ's awful death. It is impossible to think that sin is a trifle, and forgiveness a matter of course.

And not only is there revealed to us divine love and human sin. In the death of Christ there is made most clearly manifest the actual fact of holiness. To the end, and in the extremest agony, Christ did the Father's will, and offered to Him His perfect obedience. And the forgiveness, so closely connected in Christian thought with the Saviour's death, carries with it the pledge and promise of the obedience of all who believe on Him. His love constrains men, and His Spirit is powerful to transform men's lives. So His death not only speaks to us of God's forgiveness. It is also the surety to God of a new humanity, the earnest of that Kingdom in which men, receiving God's mercy, shall do His will and serve Him in humility, confidence, and love.

Thus the truth for which punishment stands is recognized. Its purpose is fulfilled. Men learn the guilt of sin and come to hate it. Retribution is regarded as a means but not an end. We believe in the forgiveness of sins, and this forgiveness is not a fiction but a creative act. For the crucified and risen Christ, through whom has come the solemn and certain word of our forgiveness, is also the present Saviour able to deliver us from sin and weakness.

So in the face of sorrow, Christianity asserts that God is love, and that, for the Christian, suffering may be a form of service. In the face of sin, Christianity recognizes the principle of retribution and yet proclaims unfalteringly its message of God's forgiveness, brought home to us in Christ who died for us and lives to save. And this answer, much as it differs from the doctrine of *karma*, is yet in closest accord with aspirations of Hinduism, which the doctrine of *karma* itself ignores or even contradicts.

Thus, that most prized of Hindu books, the *Bhagavadgītā*, speaks of a love of God which seeks from men love in return, and upholds before men a moral ideal of selfless activity. The doctrine of *karma* that all deeds, both good and bad, fetter the doer with new chains, had naturally led to the view that men should be inactive, doing neither well nor ill. This aspiration after contemplative inactivity was too inveterate for the writer of the *Gītā* entirely to abandon, but it is his new and better way for which he chiefly cares. He bids us act, but to act without thought of self-advantage. He who is not thinking of the effect of deeds, will be untouched by them, and for him the 'rule of works' will be higher than the 'casting off of works'.[1] God Himself is ever active and yet is untouched by the effect of deeds. It is a most suggestive teaching, but one for which the doctrine of *karma* is inadequate. And this teaching seems itself tentative, incomplete. It speaks of God's love for us and the love He requires in return. It bids us work without hope of reward. But it stops there. It does not take the further step and bid us, in love for God, labour in love of man, without thought either of winning reward or of shunning the effect of deeds.

The karmic doctrine carries individualism too far. It would

[1] *B. G.* v. 2.

appear that it is this which prevents even the *Gītā* substituting for its selfless activity the unselfish service of God. To speak as if the effect of deeds was on the doer only, is false to life, and most false of all to Indian life, where, more than in the West, the bond of blood and kin is so intimate and lasting. Ought we not to broaden the conception of *karma* and say that the *karma* of a man's deeds does not affect himself alone? The shame of a son's deeds may press more heavily on his father than on himself. The greed and arrogance of one country, may bring the miseries of war to half a world. No man lives to himself alone. There is a solidarity of well-being and of suffering. And there are those who, not from compulsion but from choice, help to bear as far as they are able the *karma* of others' sins. It is this that Christ bids us do. However refined the egoism, to seek a solitary salvation is egoism still. Christ bids us seek to save others, and this we can only do if we are willing to take upon us some of the *karma* of their misdeeds. Such a teaching should not sound strange in a land where Gautama the Buddha relinquished his abundant pleasures, not because of his own sorrow, but because of his overwhelming sense of the sorrow of the world.

So the 'selfless activity' of the *Gītā* may become instead unselfish service, not purposeless but redemptive. And for such service Christianity finds in Christ a motive, a compulsion. He, the Holy One, had no *karma* of evil deeds to work out. Yet he was the man of sorrows. The *karma* of others' sin He took upon Himself. He saved men, not by ignoring sin, but by identifying Himself with human need. And this Cross of Christ, as we have seen, is not only the measure of Christ's love. It is also the reflection of the love of God.[1] So we think no longer of each man working out alone the inexorable *karma* of his deeds with no real God to help. Christianity instead tells us of men linked to God and to each other, of God bearing men's burdens, and men inspired, through the thought of God's love, themselves to bear each

[1] See especially Chapter VIII, p. 175.

others' burdens. This is the Christian Gospel. This it is that gave to the writings of the first disciples their lilt, their joy.

In this the ideal of the *Gītā* finds its completion. Finely has the *Gītā* described the characteristics of the perfect man.[1] To them, Christianity can add the thought of active love which sums up all these virtues, and gives them a new meaning and motive. Only this love can deliver even virtues from their self-centredness. And love brings much insight. It enables men to see in the sorrows of martyrs and saints, not supreme instances of the world's injustice, but supreme instances of a love which can suffer gladly the *karma* of others' deeds. The Cross, which is the centre of Christian faith, is thus the centre also of Christian service. That Christian life is incomplete which does not know what it is to bear a cross itself. When St. Ignatius was on his way to martyrdom he wrote joyously, 'Now I am beginning to be a disciple'.[2] To Christian ears these words should not sound strange.

It is but natural that when Christ's law of love is spoken of, Indians should refer to the economic strife, the eager competition, which has marked our Western life. And if missionaries speak, as some before the war did speak, as if these accidents of Western civilization were Christian, then such an answer is justifiable and indeed unanswerable. It is the perpetual difficulty in attempting to expound the Christian Gospel that the preacher, if honest, has to do so with a confession of his own failure. The aspirations of the best in Hinduism stretch out far beyond the achievements of a conventional Christianity. They demand the Christian ideal itself. They are to be answered in the Beatitudes or in the life-service of men who have become entirely Christ's men, Christ's slaves. Yet for all failure, how many there are in the Christian Church who, in gratitude to Christ, are trying to share the *karma* of others' deeds. The realization of social injustice and the needs of the poor, which to many sensitive minds has become almost an obsession, the work of medical missions, the successful endeavour in India to

[1] See *B. G.* xii. 13-19, quoted on p. 113. [2] *To the Romans*, v.

raise the classes for whom Hinduism has no religion but devil-worship, and no message but of despair—these things are some illustration of that love which can regard the sorrows of others as its own. It is not in organized work that this love is most clear. It is shown best in the quiet lives of thousands of men and women who, in their ordinary spheres, are seeking to help others as far as they are able. We have seen, if a motive is adequate, how great a devotion can be. In the interests of their country, and their country's righteous cause, how many have shown a heroism and a consecration which a few years ago would have seemed incredible. And those who remember what they owe to Christ can find in Him the impulse to a love stronger even than the love of country. It is such a love alone which can be adequate for the desperate problems which in the West will be clamouring for solution. It is such a love which alone can in India make a nation of a congeries of warring castes. The source of this love is clear. We have it expressed for us in the familiar words of Paul and John: 'The love of Christ constraineth us.' 'Beloved, if God so loved us we ought also to love one another.'

The relation of Christianity to the Hindu way of loving faith is discussed in the next chapter. It is only necessary here to point out how congruous is the Christian answer, with that rapt devotion of Indian saints for which the doctrine of *karma* leaves no proper place. As we remember their passionate praises of the gods, how strange sounds the doctrine that these gods too are under *karma* and unreal; the only reality is the impersonal Brahman to whom no attribute of love or grace can be assigned. Emotion so heartfelt can be satisfied only with a God who is a Saviour, not a mere substrate of being. Around the crucified Jesus can gather the rich devotion which the Hindu saints have lavished on their gods. And such a worship need no longer be thought of as the worship of the transitory and unreal; for the love of Christ, who died to share the *karma* of men's deeds, is the love of the actual and eternal God.

CHAPTER X

CHRISTIANITY AND THE WAY OF DEVOTION

'LOVE to God', said Aristotle, 'does not exist; it is absurd to speak of such a thing, for God is an unknowable being.'[1] Such a view could never satisfy men so religious as are the Hindus. Even the Vedānta, which taught that the highest principle was indeed unknowable, had at the same time to admit the existence of gods, whom men, unillumined by knowledge, could worship, as if real, with prayers and sacrifices. And Śaṅkarāchārya, its great schoolman, is held in honour as the author of some of the most famous of the Śaivite hymns. It would appear that the distinction between a real and attributeless Brahman, and the personal, but illusory, gods, is to very many Hindus rather a tenet of their philosophy than a fact of their experience. The very Vedāntists include in their triple canon,[2] the *Bhagavadgītā*, which, to educated Hindus to-day, is the most prized of Hindu Scriptures. And in the *Bhagavadgītā*, as we have seen, Kṛishṇa claims men's adoration not as a lower or transitory god, but as a God ultimate and eternal. And by the masses of India, to whom the Vedānta is only a name, Śiva, or one of the *avatārs* of Vishṇu, is hailed as the greatest of the gods, and worshipped with a faith untroubled by the speculations of philosophy. As Tulsī Dās says, 'Why dost thou speak of the unknowable? Pray thou to Rāma and all is known.' Men feel that the gods grant their requests, deliver them from calamity, and, in

[1] *Magna Moralia*, II. xi. 5.

[2] The *prasthānatraya*, which, as we have seen, includes (*a*) the *Upanishads*, (*b*) the *Bhagavadgītā*, (*c*) the *Vedāntasūtras*.

response to their loving faith, save them even from the effects of their deeds.

In Christianity also faith is proclaimed as the means of salvation, and this 'loving faith', this *bhakti*, is directed towards Jesus Christ. To-day, as in Pliny's time, 'to sing a hymn to Christ as God' is one of the most obvious characteristics of Christian worship. In overwhelming sorrow, in peril on land, in shipwreck on sea, such words as

'Jesus, Lover of my soul'

come quickly to Christian lips. In such hymns as these, more than in formulated doctrines, Christian faith finds its most fresh and spontaneous expression. Christianity has thus a close affinity with the most influential phase of Hinduism in that it too is a religion of *bhakti*. In Chapters V and VI the attempt was made to illustrate the beautiful devotion which Hindus have shown towards their gods. It will be the endeavour now to indicate the nature of that loving faith to God in Christ which has been characteristic in Christianity. As this loving faith sees in Christ, not only the fit recipient of love, but also the perfect and final revealer of God, it has inevitably been condemned in India by those who hold that it is impossible for the highest knowledge of God to come to us through an historic person of the distant past, and who assert that it is arrogant, and indeed unseemly, to claim for any one form of the Divine, a universal worship and an exclusive devotion. After describing the nature of Christian *bhakti* it will be necessary therefore to deal with these two objections.

So different are men's temperaments and dispositions that, even within the same religion, the forms of religious expression may be very varied. Yet in spite of this diversity, in the case of a religion so defined by its history, it is not impossible to discover what is classic in the emotion and experience which Christianity engenders.

As we turn to the rich literature of Christian devotion, it is perhaps in the Middle Ages that we find the nearest approach to the rapturous *bhakti* of Indian saints. Thus St. Bernard's words, 'God is known only in so far as He is loved',[1] might serve as a motto for the whole *bhakti* movement. In the quiet of the forest, St. Bernard meditated on the Scriptures so that at last, after much discipline, he might be able, in an ecstasy which made him dead to the world, to ascend in spirit into the immediate presence of God, there with the angels to enjoy the beatific vision of the divine. So he could see in the luscious love-poetry of the *Song of Songs* a fit record of the commerce of the soul with its bridegroom Christ.[2] As a wife with her husband, the believer enjoys Christ's presence in a tender intimacy which has left all fear behind. Such love dalliance St. Bernard held to be the highest blessing of religion, vouchsafed only to those wholly consecrated unto God. And even for these, this rapt joy was only an occasional experience. Just as Māṇikka Vāśagar complains that after his moments of exaltation come times when he feels that Śiva has deserted him, so St. Bernard, and those like him, found that the ecstasy of love was followed by the weary sense of dryness and desolation. This type of devotion is in many ways beautiful and attractive, but, judged by the norm of Apostolic experience, it cannot be held classic.[3] St. Bernard himself tells us that in such intercourse of love the soul forgets Christ's majesty, and communes with Him as with lover or neighbour. Never do the Apostles speak as if their relation with Christ were with lover or friend. Always He is to them the holy Saviour whose grace they gratefully receive, whose will they humbly strive to obey.

Again, in the life of that sweet saint, St. Francis, we read that it was before a crucifix that he gave himself entirely to

[1] 'Tantum Deus cognoscitur quantum diligitur.'

[2] 'It has been said', says Miss Underhill, 'that the constant use of such imagery [of marriage] by Christian mystics of the mediaeval period is traceable to the popularity of the *Song of Solomon*. I think that the truth lies rather in the opposite statement; namely, that the mystic loved the *Song of Solomon* because he there saw, reflected, as in a mirror, the most secret experiences of his Soul.' *Mysticism*, 3rd edit., p. 163.

[3] Cp. A. Ritschl, *Justification and Reconciliation*, pp. 180, 594.

Christ. 'From that hour', says the chronicler in his quaint Latin, 'his heart was wounded and turned to water[1] at the memory of the suffering of his Lord.'[2] And innumerable men and woman since have, like St. Francis, melted in love at the thought of the bloody scourge, the agony, and the ignominy of the awful death. Gratitude for all that Christ endured, and the sense that it was for us He suffered, will always form part of the Christian's recollection of his Lord, and yet, as we turn to the New Testament, it is surprising how little the Apostles seek to arouse men's love by the detailed story of Christ's anguish. They had a more virile message; theirs it was to preach to men who needed pardon and moral power the gospel of an all-sufficient Saviour.

In truth, the records of Christ's life do not speak to us of a lover seeking from men their rapturous affection, nor of a sad sufferer, craving men's tenderness and pity. The disciples' attitude towards Christ is better called faith than love, for love may be between equals, whilst faith in the Christian sense is from the imperfect to the Perfect, from the sinner to the Saviour. Jesus was gentle to the children, gracious to the fallen woman who knew her sin, wonderfully patient with His disciples in their intractability. Yet there was in Him a strength and sternness which make 'tenderness' too weak a word to express His character. The evangelists write of Him as one whose body could be tired, as one who knew sorrow and disappointment. Yet His life, as they portray it, is not pathetic but majestic. Even when they speak of the sorrow of Gethsemane and the torture of the trial and crucifixion, they do so as men who are not so much harrowed by His agony as awed by His holiness. They present a Christ who moves us, not to pity but to worship. Hindu saints have thought to serve their gods by the frequent mention of their names. Christ would bid no man call Him Lord unless he does the things which He commands.

[1] *Liquefactum.*
[2] *Vie de S. François d'Assise*, par P. Sabatier, p. 64.

As we have seen, the Apostles preached Christ not as the poor sufferer upon the cross, but as the mighty Lord who, for our sakes, died and rose again. We have looked a little at the classic Christian relationship to Christ. Thus Paul's faith in Christ changed his whole life, and put at Christ's service the whole devotion of his intense and ardent nature. Christ lived, and Paul's union with Christ became so close that in his highest moments he could feel that Christ dwelt in him, that Christ's will informed his will, that he was in Christ. So he could say that for him life meant just Christ,[1] and he could even rejoice in his sorrows if by them his communion with the risen Lord was perfected. Yet he speaks but little of his love for Christ. It was Christ's love for him that filled his thoughts. Christ was his Redeemer. In Christ alone had come to him the certainty of forgiveness and strength for holiness. As the sinner whom Christ had saved, he adores the grace of Him who though rich had become poor. Through Christ he found the full revelation of God and God's purpose, and a redemption adequate for all his needs. So Paul shows his love, not in ecstatic praise, but in devoted service. He seeks to bring to others the good news, and in this work counts no sacrifice too great. And we find the same emphasis on service in the writings of John as in those of Paul. If we love God, says John, we must show it by our love to one another. Christ's love revealed itself in deeds. Our love must be energetic, showing itself in act. Men need our help, not God. If we are not showing love to the brother whose needs we see, what use is it to speak of our love to the invisible God ?[2]

So the characteristic attitude of the Christian to his Lord is not one of emotion, unmixed with thought, and unexpressed in deed. In some men feeling predominates; in others intellect, or will; yet it is as false in religion as it is in psychology to speak as if men could use these faculties in

[1] Phil. i. 21. [2] 1 John iv. 20.

isolation. Emphasis may differ, but a religion to be adequate must be as comprehensive as our personalities. The Christian's relationship to Christ concerns not a part but all his nature. Christ expects, from all His followers alike, a faith which is at once obedience, love, and knowledge. Each man may approach Christ from the standpoint of his need. As Clement of Alexandria says, 'The sick need a Saviour, the wanderers, one to guide them, the blind, one to lead them to the light, the thirsty, the living fountain; the dead need life, the sheep, the shepherd, the children, the tutor; but all mankind needs Jesus'. Some men find in Christ at first not so much the divine Saviour as the spiritual Hero, the incomparable Teacher. Later, as they seek to follow Him as their Master, they find in Him something more. They feel that He is speaking to them not as one who lived and died in the distant past, but as the ever-living Lord in whose hands is their eternal destiny. And their blithe admiration of the great teacher changes into a humble gratitude to their Redeemer. In others, as in Paul's case, it is with the experience of forgiveness through Christ that the Christian life begins. Such know themselves at once as 'Christ's men', Christ's slaves, bought with a price. And, as the years pass, men find in Christ not only power but knowledge. He is the revealer of the Father. In Him the world-old mysteries find an answer incomplete yet adequate. However men begin their Christian life, they go on to find in Christ all they need. He is nearer than a friend, yet we think of Him less as our Friend than as our Lord, for He is holy and we are not. He loves us. Ours it is to entrust our lives to Him in humility and obedience. His spirit dwells in men, but is manifest not in ecstasy, nor in a contemplation which makes them flee the world, but in 'Love, joy, peace, long-suffering, kindness, goodness, faithfulness, meekness, and self-control'.[1] As Dr. Dale so finely wrote, 'As the result of growing familiarity with our Lord, conscience becomes surer of

[1] Gal. v. 22, 23, R.V. marg.

Him than of itself, finds in His will the same awful obligation that it finds in the law of Duty; His will, because it is His, whenever we are certain that we know it, is supreme'.[1]

Faith in Christ thus involves the whole personality; and is it not in this that we have at once the strength of Christianity and the difficulty of its description? Christian experience is not sectional. Salvation does not come by knowledge to the wise and by emotion to the emotional. Neither knowledge nor emotion may remove a man from the sphere of activity and the effects of deeds. One phase of Christian experience carries with it all the rest. Our *bhakti* to Christ is at the same time a way of knowledge (*jñāna-mārga*) and of work (*karma-mārga*). It means redemption (*mukti*), but it is a redemption which involves not inactivity but deeds of love. Such an emphasis on duty does not exclude passionate emotion or grateful contemplation. Doubtless in the West, unlike our Master, while we have praised Martha's bustling activities, we have too often disdained Mary's quiet and reverent adoration. As St. Theresa said, 'To give to our Lord a perfect hospitality, Mary and Martha must combine'.[2] Work may be done as part of worship.

So faith in Christ sums up the whole of Christianity. Take Christ away and the Christian religion will have gone. And it is this which, to very many in India, seems at once the weakness of Christianity, and its offence.

This dependence of the Christian religion on its founder is regarded as its weakness. How can a religion, thus conditioned by time and space, be the revelation of the eternal and illimitable God? Religion does not need history. The soul of man can commune with the Highest without the mediation of historic fact. In the sphere of religion, history hinders and does not help, for what is history but the record

[1] *Christian Doctrine*, p. 110.
[2] Quoted by Miss Underhill, *op. cit.*, p. 514; see Luke x. 40–42.

of events which belong to the sphere of *māyā*, of illusion?[1] Even if the criticism of Western scholars had not shown that history was at best a science of probabilities, it would still be futile to turn to history. It is in the immediate vision of the eternal that spiritual truth is seen. And this intuition of the mystic[2] is more certain, it is argued, than the Christian's faith, for it is independent of historic fact and so not to be denied. It is strange how little educated Hindus seem interested in the historic truth of the stories told about Rāma and Kṛishṇa. With men of philosophic mind, a half-theistic faith in these gods seems to go quite well with Vedāntic idealism. And Vedāntists claim not unjustly that the Vedānta is the perfect mysticism, entirely removed from the sphere of history. And so Svāmī Vivekānanda's statement is often quoted and much approved, that Hinduism alone 'escapes shipwreck' on what he calls 'the rock of historicality'. To many educated Hindus this argument against the claims which Christianity makes seems not only incisive but conclusive. To answer this argument, more is needed than a documentary proof that Christ lived, and that the Christian attitude towards Him is in harmony with historic evidence, even if it cannot be deduced from it. The whole question of the relation of our life to history and of time to eternity is here in issue. In this brief

[1] Thus while in the West the emphasis is usually laid on the fact that history deals only with probabilities, and that therefore the religion based upon it must lack certainty, in India the emphasis is rather laid on the essential inability of historic facts to be the media of religious revelation: history belongs to the unreal and the eaternal; religion to the real and spiritual.

[2] No words are more variously used than 'mystic' and 'mysticism'. Thus if, as in a recent and brilliant book on Mysticism (*The Meaning and Value of Mysticism*, E. Herman), Mysticism is taken to denote the clear and purposed realization of communion with God, then Christianity is pre-eminently a mystical religion, and it is the main purpose of this book to show that it is this 'mystic' element that must be emphasized if the aspirations of Hinduism are to find their fulfilment in Christ. But it seems better to give the words a more definite meaning and the word 'mysticism' is used in this chapter to denote the attempt at a perception of the Divine which shall be immediate, i.e. unmediated by historic facts or revelation.

discussion—which is little more than a parenthesis—it is only possible to outline the following argument:

(*a*) We live in history.

(*b*) It is not the eternal we need but God, who is the God not only of eternity but of time.

(*c*) Such a God is revealed in historic facts.[1]

(*a*) *We live in history.*

However much men may despise the course of history, one thing is clear: they live in it and are moulded by it. It is easy to forget this and to speak of a man's sublime and innate power, without recognizing how insignificant he would be if unrelated to other men. There is in truth no such thing as an 'unrelated man'. The less individual a man's life is, the richer is likely to be his personality. No man could, even if he would, live to himself. A child is born into a family. He brings with him a temperament and capabilities inherited from his ancestors. Even before he learns to speak, he is influenced by those around him. The child grows up, and at first makes his own the ideals of his family. Later he may break away from these, but, before he reaches years of choice, he has already received thoughts and impressions which he wrongly imagines to be entirely his own. And he is the member, not only of a family, but of a section of society. He is born into a nation. No man then can cut himself off from his kind. We are not born 'man', but a particular man. We inherit a civilization, a language, a tradition, a religion. It is true that in our deepest spiritual experiences, we feel ourselves face to face with God alone. But even then it is presumptuous to forget that God is the God of the human race and that God has dealings with other men. We cannot approach God as if God had not spoken to any man before. What Bergson says in a slightly different connexion is applicable here. 'The great error of the doctrines on the spirit has been the idea

[1] The discussion owes much to W. Herrmann's pamphlet, *Warum bedarf unser Glaube geschichtlicher Thatsachen?*

that by isolating the spiritual life from all the rest, by suspending it in space as high as possible above the earth, they were placing it beyond attack as if they were not thereby simply exposing it to be taken as an effect of mirage.'[1]

Even in our prayers we have to remember that we are one of a race. To a far less extent than we imagine are we the creators of our own thoughts and ideals. We receive more than we create. Only in youth are men able to regard themselves as exceptional, unique. As riper manhood comes, men find their experiences strikingly like those of their kind. The aspirations and joys, the sorrows and disappointments, which in the crude vanity of adolescence we thought were so peculiarly our own, we find are much the same as other men's. Others have had the same sense of the burden of the trivial, the same longing after a larger life. They too have felt their home-sickness in the world and have craved for the permanent and the perfect. They too have been tempted, have fallen, and have achieved. In spite of all the differences of colour, caste, and race, humanity is essentially one. We are alike more than we differ, and humanity has had a history, long and arduous, full of failure, but full of glory. But if the souls of men are alike, they are unequal. We find in history men who transcend the limits of their time. Thus, in literature, there are writers whose works do more than belong to one age and place. We call them classic because we feel that the human mind will never leave them behind. Such plays of Shakespeare's as *Lear*, *Macbeth*, *Hamlet*, will be prized so long as men can feel the pathos, the tragedy, and the pity of human experience. And it is in religion as in literature. Here too there are the master minds. Here too there are records of spiritual striving and achievement of classic value. The present would be empty indeed if it did not take up into itself these memories of the past. We are members of a race and share its history. A man cannot rightly say 'My God' who does not feel that God is the God of the race. But if He be

[1] *Creative Evolution*, p. 283.

the God of the race, then the race's history cannot be without significance.

(*b*) *It is not the eternal we need but God, who is the God not only of eternity but of time.*

It has been said that 'the work of philosophy is to comprehend the world, not to make it better'. But quite different is the work of religion. Religion is connected with man's needs. And these needs are twofold, varying in degree in different men and races. There is the sense of the transitoriness of life and the desire for the eternal. There is the sense of moral weakness and the desire for moral power. The first of these needs has found admirable expression in the Vedānta, and if this need were solitary, we might be content to adopt the Vedāntic standpoint, deny to history any value, and seek the way to truth in the immediate perception of the divine. Certainly no religion can be adequate which does not answer the aspiration which mysticism expresses. Man has indeed yearnings for the untrammelled and the infinite, and it is part of the work of religion to redeem from the bondage of the present and the transient. But religion is more than the beatific vision of the eternal. Those glad moments of high emotion, when thought is lost in mystic vision, and men feel the infinite around them, are glad and beautiful and the purest pleasure, but this mystic joy in the eternal differs little in kind from the aesthetic delight with which an artist beholds a glorious sunset or the musician hears the greatest of oratorios. It is not enough to enjoy the sense of the ineffable and the infinite. We live in time, and in time have to face the trials and moral problems of our life. It is not so much the eternal as such that we need. We need to feel that even in time we belong to the eternal, and for the eternal we can live. For this great task of life the sense of identity with the infinite helps but little. It is power we require, not moments of breathless vision. To ignore the present is only possible for those who, with the Vedānta, say that this world's life is *māyā*, is illusion. But such a view evades, it does not solve life's problems; it empties life of all its contents; it regards as the highest phase of life that 'dreamless sleep' which resembles death. Our lives have to be lived; the world's work has to be done. There are difficulties to be met. There are loved ones to help and cherish. There are sufferers to succour, unjust to restrain, and weak to strengthen. The world's life, in its rich variety, is surely not without meaning; is not the sport of an illusion-making God. But if this be so, then the home-sickness for the infinite is not enough. There is a deeper home-sickness, a home-sickness after the God, who is a God of time as well of eternity, who enables us to live in time as those redeemed from its bondage, and to do life's work with joy, certain of the eternal world, and possessing already an eternal life.

(*c*) *Such a God is revealed in historic facts.*

History has a meaning. It is God we need and not the infinite, and God is the God of time as well as of eternity. Such a God reveals Himself in historic facts. It is through personality that there comes to us truth which is also power. A child believes in God's love if those around it are loving and testify that their love is learnt from God's. And for most men, God's grace becomes real and actual, not through meditation, nor through study, but through intercourse with men whose lives are strong and pure, and whose strength and purity are derived from God. Mathematics may be learnt to perfection from a man of brilliant intellect but repulsive character. Religion can be learnt only from religious men whose lives are devoted and sincere. Is not the whole *bhakti* movement of Hinduism an implicit criticism of the Vedāntic view that God is apprehended best by intuitive knowledge? If this attributeless abstraction could suffice, why should there be such eager adoration of the Gods? Tulsī Dās tells us that when Bhusuṇḍi asked the seer Lomas to tell him how to worship God, 'the great saint, being himself a philosopher, . . .

began a sermon on Brahman, the unbegotten, the indivisible, the immaterial, the sovereign of the heart, unchangeable, unwishful, nameless, formless, . . . identical with yourself, you and he being as absolutely one as wave and water; so the Vedas declare'. But Bhusuṇḍi complains, 'The worship of the impersonal laid no hold of my heart'.[1] The complaint is true. The worship of the impersonal does indeed lay no hold on the heart. It is the known, the personal, that the heart desires.

And God is made known as personal in Jesus Christ. By general consent, His is the most potent name in history. Spiritual experience is incommunicable, but innumerable men have testified that they have found, in Christ, God revealed in history as the God of eternity and of time. And this revelation of God in Christ awakens in men a faith which redeems from the temporal and enables men in time to live for the eternal. And this Jesus is not an accidental fact of the distant past. In Him history finds a meaning and an end. He is of the present as of the past. Men find in Him to-day redemption, power, and gladness. He speaks to us not as a dead Lord, but as a living Saviour. In him God is revealed in history, and this revelation is final and unique.

That Christianity should thus connect the revelation of God with one historic figure appears to Hindus not only the weakness of Christianity but its offence.

Some of this offence has certainly been due to the gratuitous intolerance with which in the past Christianity has been preached. Too often men have refused to recognize any good outside Christianity, and even when they have been compelled to acknowledge truth and beauty in other religions, they have done so, not gladly, but grudgingly, and have so qualified their words as to deprive them of any meaning. So far as

[1] *Rāmāyaṇa*, Book VII, *Dohā* 107, with *Chaupāi* following (Growse's translation).

missionaries themselves are concerned, such bigotry is for the most part restricted now to the narrowest of coteries, but in South India, at any rate, it is all too common in the Indian Church. Such is indeed natural, for the great mass-movements have been among the out-castes, and it is hard for such to see any nobility in the Hinduism which sanctioned their degradation and oppression, and denied them, not only the consolations of religion, but the elementary rights of manhood. Christian apologetic has been in so many cases unfair and wantonly destructive, that Hindus not unnaturally associate its claim with the arrogance of 'a ruling race'. Thus in a book of 'model addresses' to Hindus, even a book so admirable as the *Gītā* is disposed of by the retort: 'This Kṛishṇa, whom you say gave good teaching, was a murderer, an adulterer, a pander, a thief.'[1] Such an attitude is not only repellent, it is unchristian. The revelation given through the Son should enable us better to appreciate every word of God spoken by the prophets of India as of Judaea.[2] And yet when all is said, it must be admitted that Christianity does claim for itself a unique and supreme position. Apart from Christ men may believe in God but not in the full Christian sense. For the God in whom the Christian trusts is the holy Father revealed in Jesus Christ and 'faith' for the Christian means, not the mere recognition of God's existence, but the glad response to God's forgiving love which we know with certainty in Christ alone. So if we give to the words their Christian meaning, faith in God is only possible through Christ.

Such an attitude inevitably seems to the Hindu to be presumptuous. The doctrine of the descent (*avatār*) of the divine is as congenial to a large section of Hinduism as the doctrine of incarnation is to Christianity, but Hindus do not claim that any one *avatār* of God is comprehensive and final. Thus, in a very famous passage of the *Gītā*, Kṛishṇa declares

[1] This book was prescribed for the first examination in Tamil that the writer had to take.

[2] Cp. Hebrews i. 1, 2.

that 'Whensoever the law fails and lawlessness uprises, then do I bring myself to bodied birth. To guard the righteous, to destroy evil-doers, to establish the law, I come into birth age after age'.[1] So Hindus teach that the Buddha is one of the descents of Vishṇu,[2] and many would be quite willing to regard Christ in the same way. How often, for instance, will the Hindu chairman at a Christian lecture refer to 'the Lord of love, whom we call Kṛishṇa or Rāma, and you call Christ'. So even manuals of Christian piety are utilized in the worship of Hindu gods. Men to whom Kṛishṇa, not Christ, is the object of worship will yet prize Thomas à Kempis's *Imitation of Christ* as an aid to their devotion. And in a Tamil translation of this book made by a Hindu for Hindus, the reader is bidden to substitute for Christ whatever be the name of his favourite God, whether Kṛishṇa or Rāma or Śiva. To many Hindus who have been educated in a Christian school or college, the Gospels are more familiar than any Hindu scripture. Feeling the charm of Christ's character, yet unwilling to embrace an alien religion, such inevitably and almost unconsciously endow Kṛishṇa with the attributes of Christ, and learn to believe that this christianized Kṛishṇa is the Kṛishṇa of Hinduism. And all this is good. If, in the last century, Christianity had done nothing more in India than to cause men to substitute for the Purāṇic conception of Kṛishṇa this christianized idealization, its work could not be called a failure. Yet such an idealization cannot permanently suffice for the needs of religion.

In poetry we may be content with the beauty of a conception without inquiring into its truth, but in religion we need more than an ideal; we need an ideal which is certain and authoritative. Certainty in the objects of its devotion is just what Hindu *bhakti* is without. Increasingly men will have to face the question, 'What do we know of Kṛishṇa, Rāma, or of

[1] *B. G.* iv. 7, 8.

[2] Come to earth to teach atheism (i.e. Buddhism), in order that the enemies of the truth might be deceived and so destroyed.

Śiva? What assurance have we that our thought of them has any base in fact?'[1] Already the attitude of very many Hindus is really agnostic. Ultimately they say, there is no certainty in religion. God is unknowable. And such Agnosticism is not only theological; it is ethical. If it is hard to believe in God's perfection amid the actual experience of our sorrows, it is no easier to assent to a moral ideal which demands of us an uncompromising devotion to righteousness and love. Because an ideal unembodied in fact is uncertain, it is not authoritative. It depends for its nobility on the imagination which conceives it. And imagination may be degraded as well as exalted. From imagination has come not only the noble conception of the Kṛishṇa of the *Gītā,* but the debasing conception of the Kṛishṇa of the *Purāṇas.*

And thus in popular thought the lofty teacher of the *Gītā* is inseparably connected with the kiṇdly but lascivious ṣhepherd god.[2] Even in the *Rāmāyaṇa* of Tulsī Dās the warning has

[1] It is amazing how throughout the history of Hinduism this question has been evaded. So in Tulsī Dās's *Rāmāyaṇa* we read, 'Rāma is infinite, his perfections infinite, and his *legends of immeasurable expansion*; men of enlightened understanding will therefore wonder at nothing they hear' (Book I, *Dohā* 42; Growse's translation). As Mr. Benoy Kumar Sarkar truly says, 'The Hindu is fundamentally an agnostic . . . and therefore has ever felt at liberty to imagine and invent whatsoever God or Gods he chooses to adore. He has not feared to conceive the Divinity as He, She, It, or They. He has worshipped his Deity as father, mother, brother, sister, sweetheart, lover, friend, and what not. His polytheism or henotheism is based essentially on his agnosticism. . . . And the invention of deities has not yet ceased' (*The Folk-Element in Hindu Culture*, p. 260).

[2] Oman gives an interesting account of the Holī festival as he witnessed it in Lahore: 'There came another huge cart freighted with that incarnation of amorous passion, Kṛishṇa himself, and four or five of the gopīs who shared his wandering affections. The God and his favourites were personated by a handsome young man and some frail, if fair, women of the town' (*The Brāhmans, Theists, and Muslims of India*, p. 253). As the endeavour throughout has been to deal only with the higher aspects of Hinduism no mention has been made of that goddess-worship which has in it so little that is ennobling. Yet Oman estimates 'that the worship of Durgā and Kālī, attended in both cases with animal sacrifices on an extravagant scale, and with licentious songs and lewd dances of a highly unseemly character, is practically the religion of probably three-fourths of the Hindu population of Bengal, the remaining one-fourth being Vaishṇavas' (*op. cit.*, p. 24).

to be given, 'The fool, who in the pride of knowledge presumes to copy the gods, saying it is the same for a man as for a god, shall be cast into hell for as long as this world lasts'.[1] The appearances of Śiva to his saints are rightly called the sports of Śivā,[2] and in many of his temples are the *devadāsīs*, the consecrated prostitutes. We saw that in some of the most beautiful of his hymns, Māṇikka Vāśagar refers in words which would be intolerable in translation, to the charms of these servants of the God and his inability to resist their wiles. He confesses his weakness, because their attractions draw him away from thought of Śiva, yet nowhere does he condemn the association of these impure women with the temple worship.

To-day it is realized that only the highest is worthy to express God. No religion can be permanent which does not proclaim a holy God and demand of its worshippers holy lives. But only in the actual Christ have we an ideal which is certain and authoritative. He it is who is worthy to receive the worship which men can only rightly give to one who is the revelation of the perfect God. This is not to despise the beautiful emotion of so many of the Hindu saints. Who would laugh at the little girl for the love she lavishes upon her doll? But when in the joy of her motherhood the woman nestles her baby to her breast, will she desire any more the dolls which as a child she thought were real, and loved as if they lived? Her mother-instinct is satisfied; she is content. And he who knows Christ, not as the fair product of devout imaginings, but as the certain fact of past history and of his present experience, finds in Him all he needs, and strives to make Him known to men because he is confident that in Christ is what they seek. To do so is not superciliousness or arrogance. It is the spontaneous act of a love which would share with others its highest possession.

[1] Growse's translation, Book I, *Dohā* 79.

[2] His worshippers may expect from him partiality. So Sunthiramūrti Svāmī, one of the poets of the Tamil *Dēvāram*, in a hymn to Śiva, after naming some famous Śaivite saints, praises Śiva because 'even if these saints do wrong, thou dost account it right'.

CHAPTER XI

REDEMPTION: HINDU AND CHRISTIAN

THE deepest and most persistent aspiration of Higher Hinduism is for redemption, for deliverance from the seen and temporal. A world-view which failed to answer this quest for the eternal would be held unworthy to be called a religion. It is on this account that by many in India, Christianity is regarded as an alien and unsatisfying faith. The conflict of religions is ultimately one of spiritual values. If Christianity thus fails to meet the craving for redemption, it is inadequate to the world's religious needs. It is useless any longer to speak of its universality or finality.

I

For the most part in India redemption from the world has been sought by denying the reality of the world's activities. Thus the Vedāntist, who has become conscious of his unity with Brahman, sees in the phenomenal only illusion. Henceforth whatever deeds he does are unrelated to his self. So, in the Sāṅkhyan philosophy, redemption comes to the wise man when he realizes that his soul is changeless and inactive, untouched by the effect of deeds. Fearing the *karma* of deeds, he who would be redeemed, as far as possible abstains from them. It would seem that contemplation could not give the confidence of full redemption. Men sought to win this by psychophysical means. By Yoga, the mind is withdrawn from conscious thought until, in a cataleptic state, the soul becomes insentient and so free. Only the few could win redemption thus, but in the hearts of many is the same ideal. It is not the philanthropist who has been most praised, but the *sādhu* who, renouncing the world, is absorbed in things eternal. Men admit the lust and arrogance of many of these wandering 'saints', but whatever be the faults of some, the ascetic, or the contemplative recluse, has been the type of the religious man. And this fact, as it has been pointed out, 'speaks volumes for the condition and psychology of the Hindus, because, as Carlyle has well said, "The manner of men's hero-worship, verily it is the innermost fact of their existence and determines all the rest"'.[1]

This emphasis on the spiritual, forms India's supreme contribution to the history of religions. The naïve enjoyment of life's blessings, which, in times of peace, comes so easy to very many in the West, stands rebuked before the penetrative pessimism of the East. 'Asceticism', as Professor James says, 'goes with the profounder way of handling the gift of existence. Naturalistic optimism is mere syllabub and flattery and sponge-cake in comparison.'[2] Indians may strive for money and comfort as keenly as men of any other race, but they will not exalt this practice into a philosophy and assert that actually the blessings of this world are the supreme good. Against all secularism, articulate or implied, the spiritual philosophy of India is an unforgettable protest. It remains as a classic witness that

> 'Our destiny, our being's heart and home,
> Is with infinitude, and only there'.[3]

It is but natural that those who desire to be redeemed from the world should seek to flee from it. But to flee the world is not to solve, but to evade, life's problems. It is to create a solitude and call it peace. It is to make religion the monopoly of those so circumstanced that they can live unentangled in the world's affairs. These can never be more than a very few, and meanwhile the world is left more helplessly in the bondage of the material. It is not enough to seek to be

[1] J. C. Oman, *The Mystics, Ascetics, and Saints of India*, p. 271.
[2] W. James, *The Varieties of Religious Experience*, p. 364.
[3] Wordsworth's *Prelude*, vi. 604, 605.

redeemed. It is not the bondage we escape, but the liberty we gain that is the more important. Deliverance is not an end in itself. It is a means by which we win communion with God, eternal life.

In Hinduism the emphasis on the negative aspect of redemption is probably in large measure due to the doctrine of *karma*. So terrifying are the effects of past deeds that merely to escape from them seemed the highest good. At all costs and by any means, whether by meditation, by *yoga* or austerity, men crave deliverance that they may be no longer held, life after life, in the iron grip of cyclic recompense. To flee from this, men seek a life whose analogy is a dreamless sleep, a life not life, but death. Whether Indian thought can rightly be called Pantheistic is largely a question of definition, but John Caird's criticism of Pantheism may be applied to the solution of Hinduism: 'The infinite to which it would unite us is not an Infinite of larger, fuller life, but an Infinite in which all thought and life are lost. Its last result is not the conscious surrender of finite desire and will in order to conscious participation in the thought and will of God, but it is the passing away, as if by a suicidal act, of all consciousness and activity, all individuality into the moveless abyss of the unconditioned.'[1] What Eucken says of the mysticism of Plotinus might be used without alteration here: 'It is here first clearly seen what power the thought of union with the All is able to gain over the human soul. But it cannot be denied that there is no path leading from this inwardness back to the wide field of life.'[2]

And just here is the inadequacy of the solution to modern needs. It speaks of deliverance from the past, but has no word of hope for the future. It gives an opiate when men are seeking a tonic. It takes from history its meaning at a time when men are craving for their Motherland a greater place in

[1] John Caird, *The Fundamental Ideas of Christianity*, vol. i, pp. 108, 109. Caird's criticism is the more noteworthy as he judges Pantheism from the sympathetic standpoint of Hegelianism.

[2] R. Eucken, *The Life of the Spirit*, English trans., p. 353.

history. It leads to seclusion from the world when patriots feel that the times demand activity. Its analogy is, as we have seen, a dreamless sleep, and to-day educated India is awake and alert, looking forward to the future with proud confidence. There is a vivid sense of the country's present need and destined glory, and quietism seems less attractive than it did. In the renaissance of India, there is a new emphasis on duty and service; a message is wanted of life, not death; of hope and not despair. 'Who is there', says Rabindranath Tagore in great and eloquent words, 'that thinks the union with God and man is to be found in some secluded enjoyment of his own imaginings away from the sky-towering temple of the greatness of humanity, which the whole of mankind in sunshine and storm is toiling to erect through the ages? Who is there who thinks this secluded communion is the highest form of religion? O thou distraught wanderer, thou *sannyāsin*, drunk in the wine of self-intoxication, dost thou not already hear the progress of the human soul along the highway traversing the wide fields of humanity, the thunder of its progress in the car of its achievements which is destined to overpass the bounds that prevent its expansion into the universe? . . . He who thinks to reach God by running away from the world, when and where does he expect to meet him? How far can he fly—can he fly till he flies to nothingness itself? No, the coward who would fly can nowhere find him. We must be brave enough to be able to say: We are reaching him here in this very spot, now at this very moment.'[1]

A religion which inspires to action and may be experienced in activity—this is the expressed need to-day of India. Even men famous for their orthodoxy hailed Mr. Gandhi on his return from South Africa as the modern type of a true *sannyāsin*. What a change of ideal is here if the ascetic is no longer the man who flees from the world, but the man who suffers insult, imprisonment, and hardship, that by his untiring

[1] *Sādhanā*, pp. 129, 130.

labours he may deliver his countrymen from oppression.[1] But if ethics change and not religion, an unhappy cleft is made in the spiritual life. Men feel that activity is demanded of them and yet believe that inactivity is the higher life. Partly on this account is it that the *Bhagavadgītā* is so praised, for there side by side with the Vedāntic solution is the proclamation of the *karma yoga*, the way of the man active yet untrammelled by his activity. In devotion to Kṛishṇa, such a one fulfils the duty of his caste and yet is free in soul. So he may do his ordained work without attachment to the fruit of works. But if the fruit of work be thus so evil, what meaning and value has work itself? We hear much to-day of 'the Practical Vedānta'. It is Svāmī Vivekānanda's phrase. But what basis has our ethics, what motive has our service? 'This', he says, 'we must bear in mind always that in the Vedānta there is no attempt at reconciling the present life, the hypnotized life, this false life which we have assumed, with the ideal.' If this life is thus unreal, why struggle for the uplift of the race? Again, what meaning has the moral conflict of our own lives if, as he adds, 'no man becomes purer and purer: it is more or less of manifestation? The veil goes away and the native purity of the soul begins to manifest itself. Think you, that you are weak and miserable? Almighty, arise and awake and manifest your own nature. It is not fit that you think yourself a sinner, it is not fit that you think yourself weak.'[2] It is useless to call men to the Practical Vedānta of strenuous service for the Motherland if at the same time we proclaim that the present life is unreal, and the weaknesses and sins we combat are mere illusion.

It is not enough to provide an escape from the bondage of past deeds. It is a new life that is needed of moral content and present power. It is needed for the individual, it is

[1] And we may add, what an irony that the oppressors he withstood should have been Christians.

[2] *The Practical Vedānta*, Part I, reprinted in *Lectures on Jñāna Yoga* in the *Prabuddha Bhārata Vedānta Library Series*, Minerva Press, Madras.

needed for society. Earnest and enlightened Hindus complain that the initiative to social reform has come chiefly from the Christian Church, and that it is difficult, indeed almost impossible, to arouse among the larger number even of educated Hindus sufficient enthusiasm to secure the abolition of even the most flagrant abuses.[1] Religion, when it means escape from the world and not service in it, may be itself a hindrance. We find social reformers protesting 'against the excessive domination of religion', and asserting that 'some of our social evils are due to an excess of religiousness'.[2] How can it be otherwise, if religion is concerned only with deliverance from the bondage of past *karma*, if it has no message of hope and meaning for the future? It is not knowledge, as the Vedānta teaches, that is needed; it is power.

> 'Knowledge we ask not; knowledge Thou hast lent;
> But Lord, the will—there lies our bitter need,
> Give us to build above the deep intent,
> The deed, the deed.'[3]

If the traditional conception of redemption is proving inadequate to the demands of an active and progressive age, it cannot be said that Hindus are looking to Christianity for an answer at once to their craving for redemption and their moral need in daily life and duty. Much in Christianity is admired and imitated. To its influence many of the social activities of modern Hinduism are, as we have seen, avowedly due. But social reforms are not religion. They belong to the temporal, not the eternal. Most of all is Jesus Christ admired. Even when from Svadeshi motives Christ is not named, the Kṛishṇa

[1] Cp. *The Indian Social Reformer* (of Bombay) of Sept. 20, 1914, in an article on the Rescue Clauses of the Protection of Minor Girls' Bill. 'The fear of the Christian missionaries has been the beginning of much social wisdom amongst us. Our orphanages and boys' and girls' schools, and some other institutions, owe their origin to the fear of the missionary.'

[2] *The Social Reform Advocate* (of Madras), Oct. 16, 1915, p. 2.

[3] This stanza of Mr. John Drinkwater is used to conclude a very interesting series of short stories written by 'Kusika' in the *Hindu*, and afterwards republished (Madras *Hindu* Office, 1912). The stories deal with the problems of marriage—the status of the educated wife, the bestowal of dowries and the like—and the pitiable inability of enlightened men to turn their protestations into practice.

held up to our devotion is often a Kṛishṇa whose attributes are derived, not from the *Purāṇas*, nor even from the *Gītā*, but from the Christian Gospels. Very many Hindus cordially acknowledge that Christ is the greatest of the world's teachers. Yet these, too, often complain that Christianity fails to answer yearnings which Hinduism meets. Christianity is interested and efficacious only in the realm of the seen. Men assert, as if it were a commonplace requiring no proof, that the East is spiritual, and the West material. In India, religion is the commonest theme for fluent discussion, and the claim for the spiritual superiority of the East is often made by men from whose lips it is ludicrous in its incongruity. For such it is merely an assertion, convenient for the platform or the College debate, high-sounding, certain to win applause. But the claim cannot be thus lightly dismissed as the facile rhetoric of modern Athenians. It expresses the convinced belief of many sincere and high-minded men, who assert without fear of contradiction that in this one thing Christianity is inferior to the highest Hinduism. Wherever else Hinduism has failed, it has better impressed upon its followers the reality of the spiritual life. As a writer in the admirable *Indian Social Reformer* of Bombay put it [1]: 'Hinduism has instilled into the minds even of its most ignorant followers an unshakeable faith in the supremacy of the spiritual over the temporal, *an achievement which is as yet only an aspiration with Christianity*.' The statement is one that requires the most careful consideration. If 'an unshakeable faith in the supremacy of the spiritual over the temporal is as yet only an aspiration with Christianity', then so long as that is true, Christianity may hope to continue its work among the outcaste communities, but that is all. If it thus fails to meet the deepest aspirations of Hinduism we can never hope that the best and most spiritual in India will ever find in Christianity a gospel, and so far as caste Hindus are concerned it would be wise for the Churches to abandon what would then be the impertinence of their

[1] In a sympathetic review of Dr. Farquhar's *Primer of Hinduism*.

missionary labours. But if 'an unshakeable faith in the supremacy of the spiritual over the temporal' be indeed 'only an aspiration with Christianity', we are driven to ask whose fault is it, the Gospel or our interpretation of it?

II

Certainly such a charge could not be brought against the early Church. The Church opposed to idolatry on the one hand, and theosophic mysticism on the other, its proclamation of eternal life. Christians claim to be only sojourners here, their real home is in heaven.[1] Thus the *Didache* tells us that the prayer at the Communion service was, 'May grace come and this world pass away. *Marana tha*, Our Lord cometh'.[2] And with this same word '*Marana tha*, Our Lord cometh', Christians encouraged each other to face death gladly in the amphitheatre. So later we find Celsus, the arch-enemy of Christianity, blaming the Christians for their disregard of worldly prudence, and sneering at them 'because, however divided in other respects, they all use these words: the world is crucified to me and I to the world'.[3] Even one so flippant as Lucian could not help noticing their firm belief in the life that is eternal, and records with immense amusement 'that these miserable people have got it into their heads that they are perfectly immortal'.[4] Moral defects there were many in that early Church, but at least with them 'the assertion of the supremacy of the spiritual over the temporal' was not an 'aspiration' only but an 'achievement'. They claimed to be redeemed from the world and to live in the spirit. They believed in prayer and endured as seeing Him that is invisible. Their creed was unelaborated, but their religious experience was definite and positive, and to this reality and power of their spiritual life the progress of Christianity was chiefly due.

As we turn to the record of Christ's life and work, we see

[1] e.g. *The Shepherd of Hermas*, Book III, Similitude 1.
[2] The *Didache* (*The Teaching of the Apostles*), chap. x, 6.
[3] Origen, *Against Celsus*, v. 64.
[4] In his *Proteus Peregrinus*.

that in its assertion of the supremacy of the spiritual the early Church was but continuing the teaching of the Master. Liberal theologians have indeed attempted to describe Christ as a benign ethicist chiefly interested in details of conduct. His message concerning the unseen has been reduced to the proclamation of a loving God unable through natural law to manifest His power. The Kingdom of God has been interpreted as the realm of human kindness, and its extension regarded as coincident with the gradual evolution of a prosperous and benevolent world order.[1] But such an interpretation is inadequate. The Kingdom was not a society bound together by new ideals. It was the gift of God, and the very failure of His life only confirmed Christ's certainty of the Kingdom's final triumph. His death was the pledge of the victory of good over evil. The consummation of the Kingdom would not come by the gradual education of the race, nor even by the progressive influence of the Church. It would come by the power of God. The Kingdom was the heavenly realm in which men might share already the life which is eternal and triumphant. To be a member of the Kingdom is thus already to be redeemed from the world.

In Christ's teaching, redemption from the world is not flight from it. When St. Francis gathered around him his first followers, he read out to them as the rules of their order the words of Christ which seem to demand absolute poverty and complete self-renunciation.[2] But the Franciscan ideal does not represent in its fullness the ideal of Christ. As we have seen,[3] Christ's attitude to life was not ascetic. He speaks as one who loved flowers, birds, and the country-side. His kindly eyes

[1] One extreme corrects another and the writings of the recent 'eschatological' school (e.g. A. Schweitzer's *The Quest of the Historical Jesus*), perverse in their one-sidedness as they are, have thus been valuable in counteracting the 'liberal' view. For an incisive discussion of the whole problem see H. T. Andrews's *Eschatological Utterances of Jesus* in *London Theological Studies*, pp. 67–95.

[2] *Matt.* xix. 21, *Luke* ix. 1–6, *Matt.* xvi. 24-7. See P. Sabatier's *Vie de S. François d'Assise*, 28th ed., p. 85.

[3] See pp. 146–8.

notice every detail of the village life and He uses its homely facts to illustrate the deepest truths. Until the brief period of His ministry He was content quietly to earn for His family and Himself His daily bread. His first recorded miracle was at a wedding feast ; and marriage, which ascetics shun, and usually half scorn, He held in highest honour and laid down for it the strictest rules. Little children loved Him, and mothers freely brought to Him their babies to be blessed. He was no recluse, but one who mingled alike with saint and sinner, so that his enemies sneered at Him as a wine-bibber and a glutton. He was not one who spoke as if the needs of the body must be ignored. He bade men pray for daily bread. He was the good physician whose joy it was to heal the suffering. So there was no 'otherworldliness' in His attitude to life. How could there be when all life's blessings are the good gifts of a loving Father who delights to bestow upon all men His bounty. To be 'otherworldly' would be ingratitude to the gracious God whom Christ proclaimed. The otherworldly despair of this world and look forward to a distant heaven to enjoy. Christ, on the contrary, brought heaven down to earth. The Kingdom of God was already in their midst. The natural joys were not bled white that men might better prize the heavenly. Instead they gained new strength and beauty through the knowledge that the present life may partake already of the eternal. Though He bade men follow Him even to the Cross, He yet could speak of His message as glad tidings, as a gospel. It was a feast, and not a fast, that He instituted on the eve of His betrayal as the memorial of His death. In His farewell words to His disciples, though He speaks of tribulation, He promises them His joy and peace.

With Him 'the supremacy of the spiritual over the temporal' was not an 'aspiration' only, but an 'achievement'. He did not evade life's duties. Instead He gave to things temporal an eternal meaning. His communion with the Father was perfect and uninterrupted. His faith was unperturbed by His incomparable trials and seeming failure. He speaks of a

Kingdom of God, not future only, but present. Already the powers of the supernal world were His and were meant to be His followers. Not to 'see the Kingdom', not to enjoy 'eternal life', was the greatest loss that men could know. Pitiable to Christ seemed the folly of those shrewd folk who think only of worldly gains. No man can serve at the same time God and Mammon. There can be no truce between worldliness and the spirit of Christ. Worldliness sees only the things of this world, and, because it cannot see the realm of God's mercy, thinks that these earthly goods are the only prizes worth seeking. And with this limitation of horizon, there goes always the spirit of anxiety. Men fear to lose the only things they think of value. Such are forgetful of a higher good; they are forgetting the Father's love which may permit sorrow, but will not permit evil to befall His children.[1]

It is from this point of view that we can understand those commands of Christ which St. Francis took to be the rules of every perfect life. Renunciation in itself has no moral value. On the contrary, wantonly to refuse the good things of life is to deny that they are God's gifts. But the gift of all the world would be worse than useless if it cost the life of the soul. Greater than any earthly good is the Kingdom of God. This first we must seek; for it no sacrifice, if necessary, can be too great. In time of war men gladly offer up for their country their treasure and their lives, and speak of their offering not as a sacrifice but a privilege. The Kingdom of God has come and is yet to come. In Christ men may already share in a communion with God which means joy and power. But the kingdom is yet to be perfected. None on earth have known its blessings to the full. Many know them not at all. For the sake of the greater, Christians must be ready to sacrifice the less. Yet they can do so with joy. They are God's children. They can be confident that with them all is well. Christianity does not mean flight from the world, but it does involve

[1] For a profound discussion of the whole subject see A. G. Hogg's *Christ's Message of the Kingdom*.

detachment from it. 'Except ye fast to the world ye shall in no wise find the Kingdom of God.' [1]

If the Christian records ended with the death of Christ, we could scarcely speak of Christianity as a Gospel. In Christ's lifetime His disciples could not understand His teaching. Expectant of an earthly kingdom, they could not make their own the blessings of that spiritual Kingdom which was already present. Only after Christ's death and resurrection did men appropriate the Christian salvation. Christ had died for them, but that was not all. Christ had risen again from the dead, and after His resurrection they found already theirs the power and joy of the heavenly Kingdom. We have seen how Paul interprets his great experience.[2] For him too there were times when temptation was hard to meet and disappointment very great, yet he could write, 'I have been crucified with Christ, and it is no longer I who live, but Christ who lives in me.' 'No doubt', as Professor Mackintosh well says, 'the verse was written at a white heat, and the apostle, had he been cross-examined, would have admitted that he did not after all mean that Christ and Paul were so absolutely one as to be indistinguishable; but this only indicates that language has broken down under an intolerable strain, and that words, which at their best must always be general, are unequal to expressing a fact that is totally unparalleled. What St. Paul asserts is at least infinitely nearer to truth than its negation would be. He stands for a truly spiritual union; a reciprocal appropriation and interpenetration of spirit by spirit. The bond between them is sufficiently powerful to support the assignation of the same predicates to both. Our solidarity with Christ is such that in His death we also die; in His grace we are buried; with the Risen Lord and in Him, we too rise to newness of life.' [3] Already Paul shared in the bliss of

[1] One of the *Logia* of Jesus discovered at Oxyrhynchus and first published in 1897.

[2] Chap. VIII, pp. 166–9.

[3] H. R. Mackintosh, *The Person of Jesus Christ*, p. 335.

that eternal realm where Christ was. His mysticism did not mean abstraction from the world into an insentient identity with an attributeless principle. It meant a communion with the living God from which came the strength he needed for his tireless labours and an indomitable courage. In strange contrast to the hardness of his lot, he can speak of his joy and triumph. Already he lived in the eternal as in the present. The eternal was his home, for there Christ dwelt.

What was the central fact in Paul's experience has been but little emphasized in the modern Church.[1] To many the simple truth that Christianity means, not only redemption from sin, but redemption from the world, comes now with an unfamiliar sound. When the Church through its prosperity became first secularized, one extreme led to another. For worldliness, otherworldliness seemed the natural cure. Monasticism arose with its flight from the world order. With the repristination of Christianity at the Reformation, the Protestant Church rejected everything which pertained to monasticism and the monastic ideal; and rightly, for Christianity 'does not praise a fugitive and cloistered virtue'.[2] But the reformers did not realize that asceticism was the inevitable reaction to worldliness. Monasticism was condemned, but the Protestant Church found nothing to put in its place to meet the need it sought to answer. Christianity was proclaimed as redemption from sin. Too little in the Protestant Church has it been proclaimed as redemption from the world. Even its preachers have often been shy and uncertain of the unseen. Science has seemed to deal with realities more actual than the data of religion. As Eucken used so impressively to point out, the amazing development of the material resources of life has left the soul still more uncertain of itself and without confidence and joy. 'The very contrast of the external wealth with the

[1] I owe much here to Julius Kaftan, *Zur Dogmatik*, pp. 296, 297.

[2] Cp. the famous passage in Milton's *Areopagitica*: 'I cannot praise a fugitive and cloistered virtue, unexercised and unbreathed, that never sallies out and seeks her adversary, but slinks out of the race, where that immortal garland is to be run for, not without dust and heat.'

inward poverty allows the emptiness to be better seen, and causes a growing feeling of dissatisfaction.'[1] Whatever we may think of his remedy, Eucken's diagnosis of the prosperous days of peace is surely true. Physical well-being cannot provide happiness nor content. Life as it gains in speed may lose in meaning. Men get the desire of their hearts only to find leanness in their souls.

For the most part the adaptation of Christianity to the 'spirit of the age' is implicit. Sometimes it is explicit. Thus Bousset, as a historian of insight, recognizes how large a place in the Christian Gospel is filled with the thought of redemption from this world. But he complains that Christianity so preached does not allow for 'such representatives of modern culture as Bismarck, who aroused from sleep as with a magician's wand the German idealist dreams, so that on every hand we hear of the duty of self-preservation, self-assertion, and strife for world-dominion'.[2] The events of recent years provide a horrible commentary of what it means to subordinate the Christian to the Bismarckian ideal. But it would be Pharisaism and hypocrisy to speak as if only in Germany did Christian teachers thus try to force the Christian Gospel into the mould of modern culture. Elsewhere, if the Christian doctrine of redemption has not been thus candidly rejected, it has too often been implicitly ignored. We have remembered Christ's command that we should be in the world more often than His assumption that we should not be of it, and so have largely failed to influence the world in which we have been too much at home. We have forgotten Christ's teaching that anxiety is sin, and just because of this the Church, which would have protested effectively against men being coerced into drunkenness or vice, has been acquiescent in regard to social conditions which make the freedom and joy of the kingdom almost impossible for many. We have too often forgotten

[1] *Können wir noch Christen sein?* p. 174.
[2] *Das Wesen der Religion*, p. 208.

that the Christian Gospel means liberation from the bondage of the temporal.

The immense emphasis in the New Testament on the risen life of Christ and our share in it has been missing in modern preaching. Eternal life has been too often regarded as a vague and merely future thing instead of as a present possession, actual if incomplete.

Christianity has been preached in India by Westerners, and inevitably the one-sidedness of Western Christianity has been reflected in their preaching. It is only among the non-caste population that the Church has won conspicuous success, and this too has tended to call attention to the social rather than the spiritual aspect of the Gospel. This work among the outcaste communities is a magnificent piece of Christian philanthropy. Men degraded by centuries of oppression and ignorance have proved themselves capable of a fine Christian manhood. We may well make our own the words of an early Christian writer and say 'these things do not look like human works; they are the power of God; they are the evidences of His manifestation.'[1] Yet we have to confess that to many Hindus the 'divine power' is less obvious than the 'human works'. They admire the efficacy of the organization and the energy and devotion of its directors, but they fail to see in it a religion answering to their needs. Partly the fault is theirs. Denying that good deeds belong to reality, men may miss the meaning of transformed lives. But inevitably the material advance is, even to sympathetic observers, far more apparent than the spiritual.[2] In the mass-movement Churches, many Christians have advanced socially with such celerity that

[1] *Ep. to Diognetus*, vii.

[2] To speak of 'rice Christians' is absurd. As a matter of fact, in the mass movements pecuniary help is rarely given; in those of which I myself have knowledge, not at all. But Christianity brings with it education and a better mode of life. In the case of those from the most degraded communities, there is an ignorance, dirt, and poverty which simply have to go when they become Christians, and even from such communities there are to-day many Christians of whom the Church may well be proud and whom it is a pleasure and an honour to know.

there is among others a feverish eagerness to emulate their successes, and Christians thus often impress their neighbours more by their power of getting on in the world than by the reality of their inner life. Many a missionary finds to his bitter disappointment that he is regarded not as the humble servant of Christ, come to bring the Good News of His salvation, but as the influential sahib, looked up to more as a competent organizer than as a spiritual guide.[1] Some have indeed tried to show in their lives such self-sacrifice that Indians will see in them true *sannyāsins*, but such attempts have been pathetic in their failure.[2] No missionary in India has a right to live other than with extreme simplicity, but however simply a European lives, there are still many in India to whom his privations will seem luxuries. Most missionaries win the respect, and many also the affection, of their neighbours, but the missionary does not, and cannot, live according to the Indian ideal of a religious man. Proverbs express better than philosphemes the life of the people, and many of the Indian proverbs speak of that avidity for money which is at least as common in India as in the West.[3] But though

[1] Thus in an interesting tale of modern Indian life there is this characteristic reference to missionaries. 'Their temporal influence is as high as their spiritual influence is low.' 'When I reflect on their thousand and one unchristian cares, I cease to wonder that they have made so little progress in their evangelistical mission ; that they have yet made so faint an impression on intelligent India with a keen reason and an ancient philosophy which regards the *killing out of all desires and the completest self-abnegation as the only paths to salvation*. . . . I am not ignorant of the immense material good which even these missionaries have done to the country and are still doing. I know that they have played and still play a very important part in spreading broadcast western education and culture over the land at a most opportune moment. India's best thanks are due to them for this as also for their serving as an object lesson of worldly prosperity. But I have no patience with them as spiritual teachers and evangelists of the great and gentle heart that perished on the cross.' *Thillai Govindan*, by 'Pamba', Madras, 1903.

[2] Cp. Benjamin Robinson's *The Brāhman's Holy Land*, the record of such an attempt. After seven years Mr. Robinson returned home in shattered health and, in spite of all his asceticism, he found that *Jāti* is birth and an Englishman must always be an alien to Hindus.

[3] Thus in Tamil one of the commonest proverbs runs, 'Say money (*paṇam*) and even a corpse (*piṇam*) will open its mouth.'

Indians may be as intent on money-making as it is possible for men to be, they know that not here is reality, and they feel that no religion can be adequate which does not mean redemption from the world. The activities of the Christian Church may be admired and imitated, yet men do not feel that we bring the message of this redemption. We are not able to meet the deepest aspirations of Hinduism unless we learn to speak as men do to whom the eternal is the present, and the spiritual the supremely real.

How much more Christian than much of our Christian preaching is this criticism of the centennial report of one of the most honoured of the Missionary Societies working in India. The report had recommended Christianity on the ground that Japan's position as a world-power was connected with the spread of Christianity there. Besides, business men approved of foreign missions because Christianity helped to create wants which increased business. A writer in the *Indian Social Reformer* thus comments on these arguments: 'How does this argument fit in with the memorable declaration of the Master that His Kingdom was not of this world?' And 'that He who made Himself a scourge of small cords to drive out of the temple the traders and money-changers who made His Father's house a house of merchandise, should be held up to the acceptance of the world on the ground that His teachings have been found by experience to help business men, surely borders on the grotesque. India will never accept any religion on the ground that it will bring her political power or commercial eminence. All appeals that rest on that ground are bound to be worse than ineffective.' 'If we were pleading for the acceptance of Christianity', adds this Hindu writer, 'we would lay stress rather on any larger, vaster opportunities of self-sacrifice and self-surrender in the pursuit of the Divine purpose, which it may open up to mankind. The appeal of Calvary, even from the tactical point of view, is worth immensely more to a religion than that of all the kingdoms and principalities of the world.'[1]

The rebuke is just, but it ought not to have been deserved. It would be a tragic irony if in a land where men, even when they have not sought, have prized the eternal, Christian missionaries should need to be reminded that the power of the Gospel is in its spiritual and not its temporal benefits. The missionary enterprise has suffered much in the past from the rigidity of its phrases and the harshness of its doctrines, but we have lost, not gained, if our reduced and more genial theology represents a religion uncertain of the unseen and hesitant even as to its own finality. It is not enough that we should serve, we must also see. We are not doing our God-given work if, like those lighthouse-keepers of whom Maeterlinck somewhere speaks, we cannot keep our light burning because we have given away our oil to the poor. If men have not seen in Christianity the supremacy of the spiritual, that is our fault, not the Gospel's. We need to enter more fully into our Christian inheritance. We must do so or admit that Christianity cannot satisfy those deep needs which Hinduism for all its failure has striven to express.

The greatness of the demand made upon our Christian resources is the opportunity which reveals their vastness. Christianity, like Hinduism, is a religion of redemption, but of a redemption adequate to our world-task. The Christian message does not bid us flee the world. If it did, Christianity would have nothing new to give to India. Asceticism has been practised in India with incomparable rigour. To imitate the Hindu doctrine of redemption would be to fail. So far as it goes, the Hindu doctrine is unsurpassable. But it is one-sided and so inadequate. By its breach between the seen and the unseen, the Hindu doctrine has emptied life of its meaning.

[1] With the protest of this Hindu it is interesting to compare Eucken's words: 'The atheist in his denial of religion thinks more religiously than the utilitarian who turns the Divine into a mere means of human welfare.' *The Truth of Religion*, p. 465.

For Christian preaching to ignore the value of life's ordinary tasks would be simply to repeat, and without excuse, the Hindu error and be involved in the same inadequacy. The educated classes of India are intent on the activities of this life; the best of them are interested in social reform and national regeneration. It is the tragedy of the present situation that their religion does not provide motives and power for such activity. Here lies the need and the opportunity of the Gospel. As Christianity rejects the idea of a *karma* order in almost entire independence of the Supreme Being, Christian thought is not compelled, as Hindu has been, in the quest for unity, to deny the reality of life in the world. Instead, Christianity proclaims a truer unity, and one which does not take from life its meaning. This world is God's creation, and exists, not as an end, but as a means, to serve the purpose of God's Kingdom. So its blessings may be enjoyed and yet subordinated throughout to the supreme end of faith in God and service to men. Redemption is to life, not death. God is our Father; we are meant to be His sons. God made the world. We may enjoy its blessings as gifts of His Fatherly love, and its sorrows we may have strength to endure. Joy is no longer an emotion only: it is a duty and a possibility. As children of God we are given freedom to enjoy and a task to perform. History finds in Christianity meaning, and a goal. In history Christ came. The end of history is the Kingdom of God. We may do our work for the world as those who see in that work a service for the eternal. We look forward to perfect life after death, not because this life is empty, but because, in spite of sorrow and imperfection, life is already so good and full of meaning. We may live in time as those who know that their life already partakes of the eternal.[1] The Gospel means redemption, but it is a redemp-

[1] So time and eternity are related. As F. von Hügel says: 'A life lived within the more or less successiveness of our own mode of Existence' may be 'in willed touch and deliberate union with God, the Simultaneous and the Eternal'. *Eternal Life*, p. 66.

tion not of world-weariness but of gladness. The perfection of our redemption is not insentience, but life more abundant.

Christianity is a religion of joy, yet an asceticism of spirit has formed, from the first, part of the Christian character. They misrepresent the Gospel who so emphasize the sacredness of the secular as to secularize the sacred, who are so at home in the world as to have lost their home-sickness for God. There is what has been called 'the brokenness of Christ'. In a world of sin and sorrow we may not live as if these things were not. We are combatants, not spectators, in the conflict between good and evil, and soldiering is a costly calling. God's revelation of Himself in Christ was completed in the context of sin and sorrow.[1] The New Testament everywhere assumes that the religion of the Cross means for every Christian the bearing a Cross. Renunciation is not sought and prized as in itself a good. The material is only evil as it becomes the vehicle of the anti-spiritual. But the temporal must be subordinated to the eternal. The supreme good and duty is to do God's will, and in such service renunciation is inevitably involved. It is the Cross of Christ which gives to the Christian redemption its moral content. Redemption is not absorption into the Undifferentiated, the Infinite. It is communion with a holy God, impossible without the realization of forgiveness. And in classic Christian experience, as we have seen, this forgiveness is most closely connected with Christ's death. Here best we know that love which condemns our sin while it pardons us and saves. A redemption so conceived is ethical through and through. It comes, not through intuition, but through self-surrender. It is a redemption which of necessity shows itself in love. Yet this love is not the restless activity of those who seek to find in action the peace their faith has lost. It is the inevitable expression of communion with God, the outward

[1] Cp. Dora Greenwell's lines:

> 'I sought Thee 'mid the leaves,
> I found Thee on the dry and blasted tree,
> I saw Thee not, until I saw the thieves,
> There crucified with Thee.'

manifestation of a life which already is eternal. The Christ who died rose again. The Christian message is not one only of pardon, but of life in Him. And this eternal life is not a future abstraction; it is a present experience. So in Christianity spiritual certainty and loving service are inevitably connected. 'If we refuse to be in Christ the brothers of men, we cannot be in Christ the sons of God.'[1]

It is thus our fault and not the Gospel's if 'the supremacy of the spiritual over the temporal' seems in Christianity an 'aspiration only' and not an 'achievement'. The Christian Gospel does not need new accretions, but our understanding of it needs much to be enlarged, and is at all times incomplete. Each age interprets the Gospel for its own circumstances, and it is through large demands that the amplitude of our resources is discovered. No one race can ever enter into the fullness of Christ. The Christian Church sends its missionaries to India to give, not to receive; but in seeking to preach Christ in India we not only give, we receive. In trying to present Christ from the standpoint of new needs, we find how much greater than we imagined are the riches of Christ. In Christ is a gospel adequate to West and East. The success of Christianity in India will not depend on our energy and organization alone. It will depend very much on the Church's understanding of the Gospel it proclaims. Blind to the good, and eagle-eyed to the bad in Hinduism, the harshness of missionary preaching in the past has left us an evil heritage, and caused many in India to associate the missionary enterprise with arrogance and racial pride. We need to be among men as those who serve, but our service alone will not suffice. It is a Christian Church certain of its faith and sure of the eternal, which can alone proclaim Christ adequately to India. It is the Indian Church, not European missionaries, which alone can be in India the effective messenger of the Christian Gospel; but the

[1] J. Macleod Campbell, *The Nature of the Atonement*, p. 318.

Indian Church is as yet much influenced by the West, and has not been unaffected by that implicit secularism which saw in the gradual growth of comfort the supreme good. The deepest religious experience in the Church of the West is reticent and unobtrusive, and is often unknown not only to Hindus but to Indian Christians. And this is but natural. When our Lord came He found the truest piety, not among the professional theologians and the accredited religious leaders, but among 'the people of the earth', the quiet ones who in meekness and faith were looking for the redemption of Israel. And in every age and Church there have been those who, often in obscure and humble circumstances, have lived as 'more than conquerors', who are redeemed from the world. With them the eternal has been more than the temporal. Losses may come to them, failure and bereavement, yet without bitterness or defeat they hope on and love. Though they desire for their children life's natural blessings, yet they desire for them far more, Christian character and faith. The missionary enterprise is itself a witness to the Christianity of such. If Indians knew better the devotion and self-sacrifice which lie behind so many of the gifts from those so situated that every gift means sacrifice, they might think differently of the Church's missionary work. And in the mission-field as in the Church at home there are many whose lives already partake of the power of the eternal life. In ill-health it may be, in loneliness and disappointment, they yet witness to the joy and triumph of the Christian life. The experience is there: we need to express it better in the message we proclaim.

The events of recent years have shown with apocalyptic terror the awful inadequacy of a material civilization. But they have done more than this. They have shown how very many in the Christian Church were far more Christian than they knew. Their secularity was only a veneer. When the testing came it was seen that duty was more to them than comfort, more than life itself. The shallow and obtuse optimism of the days of peaceful security has become indeed an anachronism and an absurdity. But instead, thanks to the 'rich dead', there is great ground for hope.

> 'There's none of these so lonely and poor of old
> But, dying, has made us rarer gifts than gold.
> These laid the world away; poured out the rich,
> Sweet wine of youth.'

And this spirit of sacrifice, of which Rupert Brooke's war sonnets are thus the unforgettable expression, has not been without avail. We understand better what Christ meant when He asked what profit was there if a man gained the whole world of things, at the cost of his own soul. Our old complacency has been shattered and our home-sickness for God reawakened through tribulation. We are realizing that in God is our only hope; that education cannot save us, nor improved social conditions, but only faith and love. It has become impossible for us to construe our religion only for this world. Into the unseen world have gone so many of our best and dearest, too young and vigorous for us to think of them as merely dead.

The Church in the West in its sore trial is thus learning to utter a larger message. Christianity is not only a gospel of pardon for the past. It is a religion of complete deliverance. We are called to do our tasks in the world, and they are arduous, irksome often, and sometimes very stern. Yet we are meant to live as those who live in, and for the eternal, whose lives are lived with Christ in God. The Gospel is so great as to save, not from guilt only, but from anxiety. It enables weak men in otherwise intolerable trials to be strong. It makes men the masters, instead of the victims, of their circumstances, and gives them the confidence that, though sorrow and death come, their Father in Heaven will deliver them from evil. Thus the faith which has sustained so many in every age is becoming more articulate. We need to express it in our Christian message. We need to proclaim that redemption is not from sin only but from the world. And it is just this message which alone is adequate to the deep and searching demands expressed in the Hindu doctrine of redemption.

Our task is done. It remains to epitomize the argument. We have seen in the *Ṛigveda* the sublime figure of Varuṇa fading in the background, whilst Indra, the genial soldier-god, became predominant. The moral order had no holy God to give it sanction.

Religion became more and more a theurgy, and priestly speculators, discontented with the multiplicity of deities, seek the Infinite, and not the Holy, the One behind the many. So Brahman, the priestly speech, is exalted until at length it becomes the cosmic soul, and with this the Ātman, the individual soul, is identified, and Brahman-Ātman is proclaimed as the sole reality. Side by side with this development is the growing acceptance of the doctrine of *karma* as the presupposition of all religion and speculation. But if deeds thus bind in inexorable bonds, where can deliverance be obtained? Men found the deliverance they sought in the great equation already reached. The Ātman is the Brahman; the individual soul may realize its identity with the cosmic soul and so be redeemed from the flux of time and the cycle of rebirth. In the *Gītā* a new and better way is given. The Supreme was one who could love and be loved, who could be reached not by meditation and asceticism only, but by worship and service. Yet the theism reached is unstable, and the development of the thought of the *Upanishads* proceeds until it reaches its logical consummation in Śaṅkarāchārya's great system. Brahman is the sole reality. He is real because, being without motive or action, he is free from the effect of deeds. All the world of gods and men, all the operations of *karma*, the practices of religion, and the sanctions of ethics, belong to *māyā*, to illusion, and appear real only because of our ignorance. But this conclusion could not satisfy, and endeavours were made, by such as Rāmānuja, to continue the thought of the *Gītā* and give the Supreme some character and meaning. Yet always the difficulty remains unsolved; if God has motives, if He loves, if He acts, will not He too fall under the karmic law? Briefly we glanced at the more popular religion, the heartfelt devotion to the gods. Here worship is given to gods conceived as living and sentient, but the moral sublimity of Varuṇa is unrecovered. The gods are not the guardians of the moral law. The moral order is the inexorable law of *karma*, and with this order Hindu thought finds it hard to relate the activities of the gods.

In contrast, the attempt was made to describe in a few meagre pages the Gospel of Jesus Christ and the classic Christian experience. Christ proclaimed a Father of love to whom every soul of man was of infinite value. He spoke of a kingdom all must enter. He called men to break with their past, to substitute for anxiety trust, for self-will obedience to God, for selfishness service to men. He bade men follow Him, confident that, even when discipleship meant persecution and death, it was yet the greatest of all blessings and the truest of all joys. Though Christ's earthly career ended in failure, yet He died, as if death were a victory, witnessing to the end of God's love, certain that the work He had begun would never be superseded. And we saw how men so different as Peter, Paul and John, found in Him the answer to their deepest needs, and a redemption, not from sin only, but from anxiety and feebleness.

The attempt was made to relate the Gospel to the aspirations of Higher Hinduism. Christianity recognizes no system of *karma*. The world, it teaches, was created by God's love and exists to fulfil the purposes of His love. So the world of nature is a means and not an end. There is no karmic system, operating of itself, without the control of God. And this belief in God's love relieves that intolerable burden of suffering which makes men seek at any cost its explanation. The Christian Gospel recognizes retribution, but not a retribution external and mechanical. Because the world exists for the purposes of love, retribution too must serve love's end. And Christianity can bring into a man's life recreative powers so great that it is natural to speak of a new birth, a life compared with which the old life was death. Yet there is no failure to recognize the truth for which punishment stands; for our forgiveness comes to us through the Christ who died upon the Cross. And the devotion which we give to Christ is not rapt feeling only, but a solemn faith and obedience fitly given to one who is the revelation of a holy God. He is one with God, and our communion with Him is communion with God.

Christianity does not presuppose the existence of the karmic order; redemption does not mean world-flight, for the world was created by God and serves God's ends. Yet, as we in the West so readily forget, the Christian redemption is a redemption from bondage to the temporal. We are redeemed into the present possession of an eternal life. We need a new emphasis on this in our Christian teaching. We need a new realization of it in our Christian practice. A Church whose faith is but a wan aspiration cannot be the effective missionary of Christ. How can we go with the message of deliverance to those who feel their bondage to the karmic law, if we ourselves are shy of the spiritual, and hesitant as to the recreative energies of the new birth; how proclaim Christ as the worthy object of India's devotion if our faith in Him seems to the warm-hearted devotee of Hindu gods but a chilly indifference; how meet the age-long craving for the infinite, if we speak as those whose interests are all in time, to whom the Eternal is but a great surmise?

Thus the attempt to relate the Christian Gospel to the needs of Higher Hinduism compels us to a new realization of the greatness of our Christian resources and the inadequacy of our appropriation of them. For the Church's task in East and West we need, not so much a new theology, as a deeper and more adequate religion. Christianity is not only an ethical religion, but an ethical religion of redemption. We need to find in the Christian Gospel what we were meant to find, joy and confidence, the present possession of eternal life.

In the Christian Gospel the truths which the doctrines of Hinduism seek to answer are realized. The problem of retribution is completely faced. The intense devotion of the *bhakta* can gather round the perfect, holy figure of Jesus Christ. The age-long craving for redemption can find its satisfaction, but the Christianity we preach must be adequate to Christ's Gospel and India's needs. Christianity is a religion of redemption, not from sin only, but from the world.

APPENDIX

Passages in the *Bhagavadgītā* assigned by Dr. Garbe to its Vedāntic redaction.

(I. 1-19 connecting with the narrative of the *Mahābhārata.*)

II. 17, 72.

III. 9-18, 23.

IV. 24, 31, 32, 34, 35.

V. 6, 7, 10, 16-22, 24-6.

VI. 27-32.

VII. 7-11, 14, 15, 19, 25, 26, 29, 30.

VIII. 1-4, 20-8.

IX. 1-6, 16-19, 29.

X. 12-42.

XI. 7, 13, 15, 16, 18, 19, 37-40.

XIII. 2, 4, 12-18, 27, 28, 30-3.

XIV. 26, 27.

XV. 12-15.

XVII. 23-28.

XVIII. 45, 46, 50-4.

(74-8 connecting with the narrative of the *Mahābhārata.*)

LIST OF EDITIONS QUOTED

Āchārya, Śrī Ānanda. *Brahmadarśanam, or Intuition of the Absolute.* London. 1917.

Anavarathavināyagam Piḷḷai, S. The *Tiruvāśagam* of Māṇikka Vāśagar, with introduction and life. (In Tamil.) Madras. 1907.

Barnett, L. D. *The Heart of India.* London. 1908.

Bergson, H. *Creative Evolution.* Eng. trans. London. 1911.

Bertholet, A. *Seelenwanderung.* Tübingen. 1906.

Buddhismus und Christentum. 2nd edit. Tübingen. 1909.

Besant, Annie. *Karma.* London. 1910.

Bhandarkar, Sir R. G. *Vaishṇavism, Śaivism, and Minor Religious Systems.* Strassburg. 1913.

Bornemann, W. *Unterricht im Christentum.* 3rd edit. Göttingen. 1893.

Bousset, W. *Das Wesen der Religion.* 3rd edit. Tübingen. 1906.

Bruce, A. B. *St. Paul's Conception of Christianity.* Edinburgh. 1896.

Caird, J. *The Fundamental Ideas of Christianity.* 1904 reprint. Glasgow.

Campbell, J. Macleod. *The Nature of the Atonement.* 6th edit. London. 1906.

Dale, R. W. *Christian Doctrine.* London. 1902 edit.

Davids, T. W. Rhys. *Buddhist India.* 2nd imp. London. 1903.

Deissmann, G. A. *Die neutestamentliche Formel, 'in Christo Jesu'.* Marburg. 1892.

Denney, J. *The Death of Christ.* London. 1902.

Jesus and the Gospel. 2nd edit. London. 1906.

Deussen, P. *Allgemeine Geschichte der Philosophie, I. I. Allgemeine Einleitung und Philosophie des Veda bis auf die Upanishads.* 2nd edit. Leipzig 1906.

The Philosophy of the Upanishads. Eng. trans. Edinburgh. 1906.

Das System des Vedānta. 2nd edit. Leipzig. 1906.

Dowson, J. *A Classical Dictionary of Hindu Mythology*. 4th edit. London. 1903.
Dubois, Abbé J. A. *Hindu Manners, Customs, and Ceremonies*. 3rd edit. Oxford. 1906.
Du Bose, W. P. *The Gospel in the Gospels*. London. 1906.

Eucken, R. *The Truth of Religion*. Eng. trans. London. 1911.
Können wir noch Christen sein? Leipzig. 1911.
The Life of the Spirit. Eng. trans. 2nd edit. London. 1913.

Fairbairn, A. M. *The Philosophy of the Christian Religion*. 4th edit. London. 1905.
Farquhar, J. N. *Gītā and Gospel*. 2nd edit. Madras. 1906.
The Crown of Hinduism. Oxford. 1913.
Modern Religious Movements in India. New York. 1915.
Forsyth, P. T. *The Person and Place of Jesus Christ*. London. 1911 edit.
Frazer, R. W. *Indian Thought, Past and Present*. London. 1911.

Garbe, R. *Sāṅkhya und Yoga* (*Grundriss der Indo-arischen Philologie und Alterskunde*, III. 4). Strassburg. 1896.
Die Bhagavadgītā. Leipzig. 1905.
Garvie, A. E. *Studies in the Inner Life of Jesus*. London. 1907.
Gennrich, P. *Die Lehre von der Wiedergeburt*. Leipzig. 1907.
Glover, T. R. *The Conflict of Religions in the Early Roman Empire*. 4th edit. London. 1910.
Gough, A. E. *The Philosophy of the Upanishads*. 3rd edit. London. 1903.
Griswold, H. D. *Brahman*. A Study in Indian Philosophy. New York. 1900.
Gwatkin, H. M. *The Knowledge of God*. 2 vols. 2nd edit. Edinburgh. 1907.

Haering, T. *The Christian Faith*. Eng. trans. 2 vols. London. 1913.
Harnack, A. *Das Wesen des Christentums*. Leipzig. 1906 edit.
The Expansion of Christianity. Eng. trans. 1st edit. London.
Reden und Aufsätze. Giessen. 1904.
Herman, E. *The Meaning and Value of Mysticism*. 2nd edit. London. 1916.
Herrmann, W. *Warum bedarf unser Glaube geschichtlicher Thatsachen?* 2nd edit. Halle. 1891.
Der Verkehr des Christen mit Gott. 4th edit. Stuttgart. 1903.

Hogg, A. G. *Karma and Redemption.* Madras. 1909.
Christ's Message of the Kingdom. Edinburgh. 1911.
Hopkins, E. W. *The Religions of India.* Boston. 1895.
Howells, G. *The Soul of India.* London. 1913.
Hügel, F. von. *Eternal Life.* 2nd edit. London. 1913.

Ihmels, L. *Centralfragen der Dogmatik in der Gegenwart.* Leipzig. 1911.

Jacob, G. A. *The Vedantasāra.* A Manual of Hindu Pantheism. 4th imp. London. 1904.
James, W. *The Varieties of Religious Experience.* 7th imp. London. 1905.

Kaegi, A. *The Ṛigveda.* Authorized translation by R. Arrowsmith. Boston. 1886.
Kaftan, J. *Die Wahrheit der Religion.* Basel. 1888.
Dogmatik. 5th and 6th edit. Tübingen. 1909.
Zur Dogmatik. Tübingen. 1904.
Jesus und Paulus. Tübingen. 1906.
Keith, A. Berriedale. *The Sāṁkhya System* (*The Heritage of India Series*). Calcutta and London. 1918.
Kṛishṇasvāmī Aiyar, C. N. *Śrī Śaṅkarāchārya.* 3rd edit. Madras.

Law, R. *The Tests of Life.* 2nd edit. Edinburgh. 1909.
Lightfoot, J. B. *The Epistles to Colossians and Philemon.* London. 1900 edit.
Loisy, A. *A propos d'histoire des religions.* Paris. 1911.

Macdonell, A. A. *Sanskrit Literature.* 2nd imp. London. 1905.
Vedic Mythology. (*Grundriss der Indo-arischen Philologie und Alterskunde*, III. i. a.) Strassburg. 1897.
Mackintosh, H. R. *The Person of Jesus Christ.* Edinburgh. 1912.
Macnicol, Nicol. *Indian Theism from the Vedic to the Muhammaḍan Period.* Oxford. 1915.
Moberly, R. C. *Atonement and Personality.* London. 1907 edit.
Monier-Williams, M. *Buddhism.* London. 1889.
Morgan, W. *The Religion and Theology of Paul.* Edinburgh. 1917.
Mozoomdar, Pratāp Chandra. *The Oriental Christ.* Boston. 1883.
Müller, F. M. *India: What can it teach us?* London. 1899 edit.
The Six Systems of Indian Philosophy. London. 1903 edit.

Nallasvāmī Piḷḷai, J. M. *Studies in Śaiva Siddhānta.* Madras. 1911.

Oldenberg, Herrmann. *Die Lehre der Upanishaden und die Anfänge des Buddhismus.* Göttingen. 1915.

Oman, J. C. *The Mystics, Ascetics, and Saints of India.* 2nd imp. London. 1905.

The Brāhmans, Theists, and Muslims of India. 1907 edit. London.

Paterson, W. B. *The Rule of Faith.* London. 1912.

Poussin, Louis de la Vallée. *Le Védisme.* Paris. 1909.

Le Brahmanisme. Paris. 1910.

Pratt, J. Bissett. *India and its Faiths.* London. 1916.

Pringle-Pattison, A. Seth. *The Idea of God in the Light of Recent Philosophy.* Oxford. 1917.

Ragozin, Z. A. *Vedic India.* 3rd edit. London.

Ramsay, Sir W. M. *St. Paul the Traveller and the Roman Citizen.* 10th edit. London. 1908.

Reischle, M. *Theologie und Religionsgeschichte.* Tübingen. 1904.

Ritschl, A. *The Christian Doctrine of Justification and Reconciliation.* Eng. trans. Edinburgh. 1900.

Robinson, J. A. *St. Paul's Epistle to the Ephesians.* 2nd edit. London. 1904.

Sabatier, P. *Vie de S. François d'Assise.* 28th edit. Paris.

Sarkar, Benoy Kumar. *The Folk-Element in Hindu Culture.* London. 1917.

Schaeder, E. *Zur Trinitätsfrage.* Leipzig. 1912.

Schomerus, H. W. *Der Śaiva Siddhānta, eine Mystik Indiens.* Leipzig. 1912.

Seeberg, A. *Der Tod Christi.* Leipzig. 1895.

Stevens, C. B. *The Theology of the New Testament.* Edinburgh. 1901.

Sukhtankar, A. V. *The Teachings of Vedānta according to Rāmānuja.* Vienna. 1908.

Tagore, Rabindranath. *Sādhanā.* London. 1913.

Telang, K. T. *The Bhagavadgītā.* S. B. E. viii. 2nd edit. Oxford. 1898.

Titius, A. *Jesu Lehre vom Reiche Gottes.* Leipzig. 1895.

Der Paulinismus unter dem Gesichtspunkt der Seligkeit. Tübingen. 1900.

Troeltsch, E. *Die Absolutheit des Christentums und die Religionsgeschichte.* Tübingen. 1902.

Underhill, E. *Mysticism.* 3rd edit. London. 1912.

Ward, James. *The Realm of Ends, or Pluralism and Theism.* 2nd edit. Cambridge. 1912.

Weinel, H. *Paulus.* Tübingen. 1904.

Wendt, H. H. *The Teaching of Jesus.* Eng. trans. Edinburgh. 1909.

Westcott, B. F. *The Epistles of St. John.* London. 1883.

An Advanced Text-book of Hindu Religion and Ethics. 2nd edit. Benares. 1904.

Aspects of the Vedānta. 3rd edit. Madras.

Encyclopaedia of Religion and Ethics. Edited by J. Hastings. From 1908.

Foundations. London. 1914 imp.

London Theological Studies. London. 1911.

The Cambridge Mediaeval History. From 1911.

The Imperial Gazetteer of India. Vol. 2. Oxford. 1909.

INDEX

Achārya, Śrī Ānanda, 35.
Ādityas, 26–8.
advaita, 77.
Aeschylus, 6.
Agni, 25, 26, 28, 33, 47, 61.
ahaṁkāra, 105, 106.
ākāra, 84.
ākāśa, 86.
Ānanda, 153, 154.
ānanda, 71, 83.
ānandin, 71.
āṇavam, 136.
Andrews, H. T., 231.
aparā vidyā, 81.
apurva, 93, 94.
Āraṇyakas, 23, 52.
Aratus, 7.
Aristotle, 206.
Arjuna, 98, 102, 104, 107, 108, 109, 182.
Arnold, T., 177.
Arrowsmith, R., 26.
Ārtabhāga, 59.
Artemis, 7.
aruḷ, 137.
Ārya Samāj, 4, 20.
asat, 33, 45, 83.
āśramas, 42.
asuras, 45.
Atharvaveda, 23, 28, 35, 39–41; date of, 24; magic of, 40; speculation of, 48–50.
Ātman, 246; development of idea of, 48–51; description of, 65–75.
avatār, 121, 133, 206, 219.
avidyā, 81.
Audulomi, 97.
Ayan, 132.

Bādarāyaṇa, 21, 56, 76, 77.
Bāhva, 84.
Bālāki, 56.
Barnett, L. D., 101, 117.
Barth, A., 43.
Bergson, H., 214.
Bernard, St., 208.
Bertholet, A., 58.
Besant, A., 182, 185.
Bhagavadgītā, 21, 74, 78, 173, 219, 227, 246, 247; not mentioned by Abbé Dubois, 3; its importance to-day, 98; its probable influence on Bādarāyaṇa, 77; quoted by Śaṅkara, 81; its date and structure, 98–102; the more Theistic teaching of, 102–11; its modification of Sāṅkhya-Yoga, 107–11; the Vedāntic element of, 111–12; its spiritual influence marred by (1) its unethical Sāṅkhyan Philosophy, 113–14; (2) the association of its ideal Kṛishṇa with the Kṛishṇa of the *Purāṇas*, 114, 115; its 'selfless' activity and the unselfish love of Christianity, 202–4; passages assigned by Garbe to a Vedāntic redaction, 250.
Bhagavān, 102.
Bhagavān Dās, 20.
Bhāgavat religion, 104, 111.
Bhāgavata Purāṇa, 3.
Bhagīratha, 131.
bhakti, 22; meaning of, 110; illustrations of Hindu, 116–40; the nature of Christian, 207–12.
Bhandarkar, Sir R. G., 99, 101, 116, 117, 130.
Bharata, 122.
Bhusuṇḍi, 217, 218.
bhūta āśraya, 93.
Boehme, Jacob, 70.
Bornemann, W., 149.
Bousset, W., 236.
Brahmā, 71, 121, 132.
brahma-ātma-aikyam, 57.
brahmachārin, 42.

Brahman, 17, 37, 38, 189, 246; original meaning of, 46; development of the idea of, 47, 48; unity with, 59, 65–75; nature of, 66–8; Śaṅkara's teaching on, 82–4; Rāmānuja's teaching on, 183, 184.
Brāhmaṇas, 23, 35, 55, 57; date of, 24; account of, 41–4; speculation of, 44–8, 50, 51.
Brahmaṇaspati, 37, 38.
Brāhma Samāj, 143, 144, 187.
Brahmavādin, 21.
Bṛihadāraṇyaka Upanishad, 56, 59, 60–2, 66, 69, 71, 73, 74, 91, 94.
Bṛihadratha, 64.
Bṛihaspati, 37.
Brooke, Rupert, 245.
Bruce, A. B., 163, 166.
Buddha, Gautama the, 43, 72, 153, 154, 187, 220.
buddhi, 89, 105.
Buddhism, 15.
Butler, Bishop, 180.

Caird, J., 225.
Campbell, J. Macleod, 243.
Carlyle, 224.
Cerinthus, 174.
Chaitanya, 9.
Chaṇḍāla, 63, 96.
Chhāndogya Upanishad, 50, 56, 60, 61, 63, 66, 67, 73, 74, 92.
Chidambaram, 78.
chit, 83.
Christ, legend of, 7; equated with Hindu leaders, 9; pagan witnesses to, 142; 'Westernization' of, 143, 144; teaching of, 145–9, 231–4; His place in His Gospel, 149–53; character of, 154–8; death of, 153, 154; its relation to the doctrine of *karma*, 200–2; its significance to Peter, 160–2, to Paul, 165–70, to John, 172–7; His resurrection, 159, 160; its significance to Paul, 166, 167, 234, 235; the nature of the *bhakti* rendered to, 207–12.
Christianity, its claim to be the absolute religion, 2, 10; the attempted proofs of this, 11; the congruity of this claim with the history of religions, 14–19; its dependence on the historic Christ, 212, regarded as its weakness, 212–18, and its offence, 218–22; an ethical religion of redemption, 19; not regarded by Hindus as a religion of redemption, 228–30; its emphasis on the supremacy of the spiritual over the temporal, 146–8, 231–5; the need to recover this emphasis in our teaching and practice, 236–46.
Chrysostom, 7.
Clement of Alexandria, 6, 142, 211.
Colebrooke, 69.

Daksha, 37.
Dale, R. W., 211.
Daśaratha, 121.
Davids, T. W. Rhys, 28, 55.
Dayānanda Sarasvatī, 20.
Deissmann, G. A., 167.
Denney, J., 152, 166.
Deussen, P., 23, 31, 33, 38, 46, 53, 60, 73, 81, 83, 96, 181.
Devas, 59, 62.
devayāna, 60–2.
dhāraṇā, 105.
dhyāna, 105.
Didache, 230.
Dowson, J., 131.
Drinkwater, J., 228.
Dubois, J. A., 3.
Du Bose, W. P., 148, 157.
Duperron, Anquetil, 53.
Durgā, 221.
Dyaus Pitar, 145.

Eggeling, J., 41.
Eucken, R., 225, 236, 240.

Fairbairn, A. M., 145.
Farquhar, J. N., 4, 9, 98, 144, 184, 187, 229.
Fioretti, 118.
Five Fires, The, 61, 94.
Forsyth, P. T., 155.
Francis, St., 118, 208, 209, 231, 233.

Fraser, J. N., 117.
Frazer, R. W., 116.

Gandharvas, 59.
Gandhi, M. K., 226.
Ganges, 131.
Garbe, R., 99, 100, 101, 106, 250.
Garvie, A. E., 150.
Garutmān, 33.
Gāyatrī, 47.
Gennrich, P., 64, 164, 188.
Glover, T. R., 1, 8.
gopī, 3.
Gough, A. E., 58, 63, 69.
Govinda, 79.
grace (in Śaiva Siddhānta), 137.
Greenwell, Dora, 242.
Grierson, Sir G. A., 116, 119.
gṛihastha, 42.
Griswold, H. D., 65.
Growse, F. S., 119.
guṇas, 84, 103, 105, 106.
Gwatkin, H. M., 72.

Haering, T., 198.
Hari, 121, 122.
Harnack, A. von, 1, 10, 54, 153, 159, 200.
Henotheism, 30.
Herder, 188.
Herman, E., 213.
Hermas, 230.
Herrmann, W., 158, 214.
Hesiod, 6.
Hinduism, its definition, 19, 20; its three great doctrines, 20; its independence of history, 213; a religion of redemption, 16, 17, 223–30.
Hiraṇyagarbha, 35.
Hogg, A. G., 196, 233.
Holī, 221.
Homer, 7.
Hopkins, E. W., 101, 183.
Howells, G., 112.
Hügel, F. von, 241.

Idolatry, condoned by Theosophy, 3; attacked by Ārya Samāj, 4; Tukārām's, 117–19.
Ignatius, St., 204.
Ihmels, L., 13.
Imitation of Christ, 220.
indh, 45.
indha, 45.
Indian Social Reformer, 228, 229, 239.
Indra, 25, 26, 28, 29, 33, 45, 74.
indriya, 45.
Indu, 29.
Irenaeus, 174.
Īśā Upanishad, 69.
Islām, 15.
Īśvara, 71, 72, 94, 189.

Jacob, G. A., 69, 72, 83.
Jaimini, 93.
James, W., 224.
Janaka, 56, 59, 65, 66.
Japan, 4, 239.
jñāna-mārga, 212.
John, St., 171–7.
Judaism, 15, 16.

Kaegi, A., 26.
Kaftan, J., 11, 147, 151, 166, 235.
Kaikeyī, 122, 123.
Kailāśa, 131, 132.
Kālī, 9, 221.
Kālidāsa, 99.
kali yuga, 188.
kalpa, 86.
kāma, 34.
Kamban, 119.
Kaṇṇappan, 135, 136.
Kant, 11, 49.
karma, an essential doctrine of Hinduism, 20, 22; as oldest god, 48; origin of belief in, 57, 58; the doctrine in the *Upanishads*, 58–65, in Śaṅkara, 92–5, in the Śaiva Siddhānta, 136; ignored by Brāhma and Prārthanā Samājes, 20; its twofold importance: (1) it provides a theodicy easily understood and generally accepted, (2) it secures recognition of the principle of retribution, 180; but (1) as a theodicy it leaves little room for God, and has increased the sense of misery, 184–8, (2) by over-emphasizing retribution, it has led to an endeavour to escape

entirely from the effects of deeds, 188–190; the answer of Christianity to the problems the doctrine of *karma* seeks to solve, 190–202; congruity of this answer with aspirations which the doctrine of *karma* fails to meet, 202–5, 247.
karma mīmāṁsā, 79, 93.
karma yoga, 227.
karma mārga, 222.
Kāṭhaka Upanishad, 67, 74, 75.
Kathenotheism, 30.
Kauśalyā, 121, 122.
Kaushītaki Upanishad, 56, 63, 74.
Keith, A. B., 99, 100, 101.
Keshab Chandra Sen, 143.
Kingdom of God, as 'the highest good', 11; Christ's teaching on, 147–9; His place in, 151–3; the 'liberal' misinterpretation of, 231.
kramamukti, 94.
Kṛishṇa, 9, 142, 206; of the *B. G.*, 3, 98, 100, 101–15, 220, 221; of the *Purāṇas*, 3, 114, 115, 124, 221; of Tukārām, 116–19.
Kṛishnasvāmī Aiyar, C. N., 20, 78.
Kumārila Bhaṭṭa, 79.
Kurukshetra, 98, 109.
Kurus, 98.
'Kusika', 228.

Lakshmaṇa, 122.
Law, R., 174.
Lévi, M. S., 25.
Lightfoot, J. B., 170.
Lindsay, T. M., 10.
liṅga, 3, 130.
Loisy, A., 14.
Lomas, 217.
Lucian, 230.
Luther, 130, 155.

Macdonell, A. A., 35, 38, 181.
Mackintosh, H. R., 151, 234.
Macnicol, N., 70.
Madura, 126, 127, 130.
Maeterlinck, 240.
magic, 25, 28, 39, 40, 46.
Mahābhārata, 81, 181.
Mahā Parinibbāna Sutta, 154.
Maitrāyaṇa Upanishad, 64, 65, 75.
Maitreyī, 69.
manas, 106.
Maṇḍana, 79.
Māṇikka Vāśagar, 21, 208, 222; life of, 125–8; poems of, 128–40.
Manu, 81, 188.
Mass movements, 5, 186, 237, 238.
Mātariśvan, 33.
māyā, 69, 70, 85, 87, 107, 112, 136, 216.
māyin, 70, 88.
Mill, J. S., 190.
Milton, 235.
Mīmāṁsā, 100, 101, 131.
Missionary enterprise, 5, 10, 13, 229, 243; Hindu criticism of, 238; unworthy arguments for, 239.
Mitra, 26, 28, 33.
Moberly, R. C., 199.
Monier-Williams, M., 72.
Morgan, W., 164.
Mozoomdar, P. C., 143, 144.
Müller, F. M., 3, 25, 30, 53, 61.
Muṇḍaka Upanishad, 68.
Mysticism, definition of, 213; criticism of, 214–17, 225.

nāma, 48.
Nallasvāmī Piḷḷai, J. M., 124, 130, 133, 134, 136.
Nambūtiri, 80.
Neo-Platonism, 10, 15.
Neo-Kṛishṇa movement, 98.
nirīśvara-vāda, 182.

Oldenberg, H., 71.
Oman, J. C., 221, 224.
Origen, 142, 230.

Pālapādam, 63.
Pāṇḍavas, 98.
Paṇḍharpur, 117.
Pantheism, 10, 225.
parā vidyā, 81.
Parmenides, 34.
pāśam, 136.
Pascal, 179.
Patañjali, 100.

Paterson, W. B., 19.
Paul, St., his attitude to Paganism, 7; his experience of the Gospel and his interpretation of it, 162–71, 210, 234, 235.
Pavamāna, 29.
Periya Purāṇa, 128.
Pessimism, ascribed to *Upanishads*, 64, 65; Hindu and Hebraic, 65; its superiority to optimism, 179.
Peter, St., 160–2.
pitṛiyāna, 60–2, 94.
Plato, 49.
Pliny, 142, 207.
Plotinus, 225.
Plutarch, 8.
Pope, A., 179.
Pope, G. U., 124, 125, 137.
Porphyry, 10.
Poussin, L. de la Vallée, 25, 42, 43.
Practical Vedānta, 227.
Prajāpati, 36, 43, 44, 45, 47, 50, 59.
prakṛiti, 70, 105.
Prāṇa, 49.
Prārthanā Samāj, 20, 187.
Prasthānatraya, 21, 206.
Pratt, J. B., 180.
Pringle-Pattison, A. Seth, 194.
Pṛithivī, 145.
Purusha, 38, 39, 48, 49, 50, 51, 105, 106.

Qu'rān, 16.

Rādhā, 9, 117.
Raghu, 124.
Raghubīr, 124.
Ragozin, Z. A., 40.
Rāma, 21, 119–24, 206, 213, 220, 221.
Rāmakṛishṇa, 8, 9.
Rāmānuja, 21, 77, 78, 183, 184.
Rāmāyaṇa, versions of, 119; Tulsī Dās's, 119–24, 218, 221.
Rām Mohan Rai, 20, 143.
Ramsay, Sir W. M., 7.
Raṅgāchāriar, M., 97.
Redemption, religions of, 15–18; teaching of *Upanishads* on, 65–8, 72–4; teaching of Śaṅkara on, 95–7; Christianity an ethical religion of, 18, 19; deepest aspiration of Hinduism, 223; too negatively taught for modern needs, 225–7; Christianity not regarded as a religion of, 228–30; Christ and the Early Church emphasized the redemptive aspect of Christianity, 230–5; our need to recover this emphasis to-day, 235–46.
Reischle, M., 10.
Religions, types of, 15–17; history of, 14.
'Rice Christians', 237.
Ṛigveda, 16, 21, 23, 42, 49, 57, 145, 246; date of, 24; interpretation of, 24, 25; religion of, 24–32; philosophical hymns of, 32–9.
Ṛishi, 38, 45.
Ritschl, A., 156, 208.
Robinson, Benjamin, 238.
Robinson, J. A., 170.
Rossetti, Christina, 194.
Rudra, 28, 43, 71, 130.
Rukmiṇī, 117.
rūpa, 48.

Sabatier, P., 209, 231.
sachchidānanda, 83.
Sādhanā, 54, 226.
Sādhyas, 38.
Śaiva Siddhānta, 124, 133, 134.
śakti, 80, 139.
samādhi, 75, 105, 167.
Sāmaveda, 23.
saṁsāra, 16, 43, 57.
Śāṇḍilya, 51.
Śaṅkarāchārya, 21, 56, 72, 173, 206, 246; life of, 78–80; relation of his teaching to Bādarāyaṇa's, 77; his teaching on theology, 82–4, cosmology, 84–92, psychology, 88–92, transmigration, 92–5, 181, 182, redemption, 95–7.
Sāṅkhya, 69, 70, 75, 81, 83, 99, 100, 173, 182, 223; described, 103, 105, 106; unethical, 113, 114.
sannyāsa, 103, 109.
sannyāsin, 42, 79, 109, 110, 128, 238; Mr. Gandhi as modern, 226.
Sarkar, Benoy Kumar, 221.
sat, 33, 83.

Śatapatha Brāhmaṇa, 42–5, 47, 48, 51, 55, 65.
Satrughna, 122.
Savitar, 47.
Schaeder, E., 153.
Schomerus, H. W., 124, 127, 136.
Schopenhauer, 53, 64, 178, 193.
Schwartz, 3.
Schweitzer, A., 231.
Seeberg, A., 161, 162.
Śīlas, 55.
Śiva, 21, 71, 78, 80, 206, 221, 222; in Tulsī Dās, 120–4; in Māṇikka Vāśagar, 124–140.
Skambha, 49, 50.
smṛiti, 81, 110.
Social Reform Advocate, 109, 228.
Social reform, religion as a hindrance to, 228.
Soma, 25, 26, 28, 29, 61, 62.
Sophocles, 7.
Spinoza, 70.
śraddhā, 61, 93.
Śrīnivāsa Iyeṅgar, P. T., 19.
Śrīraṅgam, 3.
śruti, 81, 110.
Stevens, C. B., 161, 172.
Sukhtankar, V. A., 78.
Sumitrā, 122.
Sunthiramūrti Svāmī, 222.
Sūrya, 47.
Svarga, 63.
Śvetaketu, 60.
Śvetāśvatara Upanishad, 69–71, 75, 101.

Tacitus, 142.
Tagore, Rabindranath, 1, 54, 226.
Taittirīya Upanishad, 86.
Tanjore, 3.
tapas, 33, 34, 43, 48.
Tāyumānavar, 134.
Telang, K. T., 99.
Temple, W., 13.
Tennyson, 1, 156.
Tertullian, 6, 142.
Tevijja Sutta, 72.
Theodicy of Śaṅkara, 85, 86; doctrine of *karma* as, 181–9; of Christianity, 192–5.
Theosophy, 3, 182.
Theresa, St., 212.
Thibaut, G., 70, 76, 77, 81.
Thillai Govindan, 238.
Tirumanthiram, 133.
Tirumūlar, 133.
Tiruvāśagam, 124–40.
Tiruvāthavūrar Purāṇa, 126.
Tiruvilaiyādal Purāṇa, 126.
Titius, A., 146, 148, 169.
Torāh, 16.
Trajan, 142.
Transmigration, see *karma*.
Trichinopoly, 3.
Troeltsch, E., 14.
Tukārām, 21, 116–19.
Tulsī Dās, 21, 119–24, 217, 221.

Umā, 120, 121, 139.
Underhill, E., 208, 212.
upādhi, 84.
upanayana ceremony, 97.
Upanishads, 16, 17, 21, 24, 246; not philosophic sources, 56, 76; praise by Western scholars of, 53; Brāhmanically edited, 55; Kshatriya influence in, 56; sombreness of, 64; their doctrine of *karma*, 58–65, of redemption, 65–75; theistic tendencies in, 71; lack of ethical interest, 73, 74; basis of Śaṅkara's teaching, 81; referred to in *B. G.*, 112; their permanent place in the history of thought, 75.

Vāch, 33, 46.
Vaishṇavism of *B. G.*, 102; of Marātha country, 117.
Vālmīki, 119.
vānaprastha, 42.
Varuṇa, 26–8, 30, 32, 33, 40, 41, 246, 247.
Vasishṭha, 27.
Vāsudeva, 101, 104.
Vāyu, 47.
Veda, 23, 24.
Vedānta, 4, 24, 50, 107, 112, 223, 228; systems of, 77; Śaṅkara's exposition of, 81–97; its alleged universality, 96, 97.
Vedāntasāra, 72, 83.

Vedānta-sūtras, 21, 76.
vidyā, 81.
Virāj, 38.
viśesha, 84.
Vishṇu, 80, 101, 102, 131, 132, 206.
Vishṇu Purāṇa, 115.
Viśishṭādvaita, 77.
Viśvakarman, 36, 78.
Viśvedevas, 31.
Viṭhobā, 117.
Vivekānanda, Svāmī, 54, 213, 227.
Vṛitra, 25.

Ward, J., 179.
Ways, the two, 60, 92.
Weinel, H., 162.
Wendt, H. H., 146.
Westcott, B. F., 171.
Wordsworth, 224.

Yādava, 104.
Yājñavalkya, 56, 58, 59, 65, 66, 69, 70.
Yajurveda, 23.
Yama, 29, 33, 60, 67, 92, 94.
Yoga, 75, 81, 100, 103, 108, 109, 223, 225.
Yogin, 80, 110, 113.

Zoroastrianism, 15.